BITTEN BY THE BLUES

CHICAGO VISIONS AND REVISIONS

Edited by Carlo Rotella, Bill Savage, Carl Smith, and Robert B. Stepto

BITTEN

★ BY THE ★

BLUES

★ THE ALLIGATOR
RECORDS STORY ★

BRUCE IGLAUER
AND
PATRICK A. ROBERTS

THE UNIVERSITY OF CHICAGO PRESS

Chicago and London

The University of Chicago Press, Chicago 60637
The University of Chicago Press, Ltd., London
Published 2018
Printed in the United States of America

27 26 25 24 23 22 21 20 19 18   1 2 3 4 5

ISBN-13: 978-0-226-12990-7 (cloth)
ISBN-13: 978-0-226-58187-3 (e-book)
DOI: https://doi.org/10.7208/chicago/9780226581873.001.0001

"Give Me Back My Wig," from *Hound Dog Taylor and the HouseRockers*. Words and music by
Theodore Roosevelt "Hound Dog" Taylor. © 1971 by Eyeball Music. All rights reserved. Used
by permission.

"Now That I'm Down" and "Cotton Picking Blues," from *The Son Seals Blues Band*. Words
and music by Frank "Son" Seals. © 1973 by Eyeball Music. All rights reserved. Used by
permission.

"That's Why I'm Crying," from Koko Taylor, *I Got What It Takes*. Words and music by Samuel
Maghett. Copyright © 2010 Conrad Music, a division of Arc Music Corp. and Leric Music Inc.
All rights administered by BMG Rights Management (US) LLC. All rights reserved. Used by
permission. Reprinted by permission of Hal Leonard LLC.

"Two Headed Man," from *Living Chicago Blues, Volume 2*. Words and music by Lee Baker Jr.
kpa Lonnie Brooks. © 1978 by Eyeball Music. All rights reserved. Used by permission.

"Oreo Cookie Blues," from *Strike Like Lightning*. Words and music by Lonnie Mack. © 1985
by Mack's Flying V Music. All rights reserved. Used by permission.

"My Woman Has a Black Cat Bone." Words and music by Harding "Hop" Wilson. © by
Cicadelic Music. All rights reserved. Used by permission.

"Richest Man," from C. J. Chenier and the Red Hot Louisiana Band, *Too Much Fun*. Courtesy
of Blame Music/Little Brother Music.

"Old School," from Elvin Bishop, *Can't Even Do Wrong Right*. Words and music by Elvin
Bishop, Willy Jordan, and Jojo Russo. © by Jojo Russo Music and Crabshaw Music. All rights
reserved. Used by permission.

"Lochloosa," from JJ Grey & Mofro, *Brighter Days*. Words and music by JJ Grey. © JJ Grey
Music. All rights reserved. Used by permission.

Library of Congress Cataloging-in-Publication Data

Names: Iglauer, Bruce, 1947– author. | Roberts, Patrick A., author.
Title: Bitten by the blues : the Alligator Records story / Bruce Iglauer and Patrick A. Roberts.
Other titles: Chicago visions + revisions.
Description: Chicago ; London : The University of Chicago Press, 2018. | Series: Chicago
  visions and revisions | Includes index.
Identifiers: LCCN 2018015312 | ISBN 9780226129907 (cloth : alk. paper) | ISBN
  9780226581873 (e-book)
Subjects: LCSH: Alligator Records (Firm)—History. | Blues (Music)—History and criticism. |
  Sound recording industry—Illinois—Chicago—History.
Classification: LCC ML3792.A55 I45 2018 | DDC 781.643/149—dc23
LC record available at https://lccn.loc.gov/2018015312

♾ This paper meets the requirements of ANSI/NISO Z39.48-1992 (Permanence of Paper).

CONTENTS

Photographs follow page 118.

ACKNOWLEDGMENTS

There are so many people who inspired me and helped me in the birth and growth of Alligator that it's impossible to list them all. But it's essential to name four—my mother, Harriett Iglauer, who taught me that being a little (or more than a little) obsessive-compulsive isn't such a bad thing, and that all important decisions in life are ethical decisions; my mentor, Bob Koester of Delmark Records, who taught me by example that you have to let your gut lead your head and record the music that touches your soul, or none of this is worth it; Lillian Shedd McMurry of Trumpet Records, who showed me that you can be a tough businessperson and be totally honest at the same time, and that there are more important qualities than tact and diplomacy; and my wife, Jo Kolanda, who has cheered on my craziness for so many years and taught me the meaning of true love.

I also give my most heartfelt thanks to the terrific men and women who have worked at Alligator, often for decades, giving heart and soul to the label while the musicians and I get all the glory: Peter Amft, Derek Ault, Joann Auster, Eric Charles Babcock, Ted Bonar, Craig Bonnell, Henry Carpenter, Lynn Coleman, Marco Delgado, Bob DePugh, Jill Dollinger, Roy Filson, David Forte, Sam Genna-wey, Mickey Gentile, Andy Gerking, Bill Giardini, Mindy Giles, Mike Grill, Blake Gumprecht, Lee Gutowski, Bill Haas, Pam Hall, Rich Hay, Chantal Huynh, Rosaly Huynh, Chris Young Kierig, Nora Kinnally, Tim Kolleth, Matt LaFollette, Chris Levick, Joel Leviton, Marc Lipkin, Eli Martinez, Julie McGill, Richard McLeese, Matt

Minde, Chris Moncada, Ken Morton, Kevin Niemiec, Diane Otey, Kerry Peace, Lolita Ratchford, Zanelle Robey, Anthony Roger, Luisa Rosales, Carl Schultz, Sharron Scott, Robbin Sebastiani, Ira Selkowitz, Jay Septoski, Rick Septoski, Lisa Shively, Quintin Simutus, Katie Smith, Mark Steffen, Steve Symonanis, Otis Taylor, Erik Veldt, Hilton Weinberg, Cindy Wells, Jay Whitehouse, and Bill Wokersin.

I have received invaluable counsel and help from Hans Andréasson, Peter Aschoff, Linda Cain, Rick Estrin, Suzanne Foschino, Terrance Godbolt, Andre Hobus, Scott Kravetz, Michael Kurgansky, Tom Leavens, Erik Lindahl, Marc Lipkin, Tommy Lofgren, Irv Michaels, Jim O'Neal, Clay Pasternak, Marc PoKempner, Lucasz Raz, Bob Riesman, Beau Sample, Ben Sandmel, Hans Schweitz, and the essential Dick Shurman. Thank you all.

—Bruce

I wish to thank Jennifer Berne, Ally Ginsberg, Ivy Hettinger-Roberts, Justin Ginsberg, and Eva Lettiere-Roberts for their support. I also thank David Steiner for his encouragement and wisdom. And of course, many thanks to Bruce.

—Patrick

We both wish to thank the staff at the University of Chicago Press, particularly executive editor Tim Mennel and Chicago Visions and Revisions series editor Carlo Rotella, for their hard work and patience.

For further information, please visit www.bittenbytheblues.com.

INTRODUCTION

It's a pleasant summer evening in 2014 in Evanston, an upscale suburb of Chicago, and the music room at SPACE, a sort of mini-concert hall located a block away from luxurious hundred-year-old homes, is beginning to fill up. The casually dressed patrons, mostly middle aged and overwhelmingly white, are being escorted to their reserved tables, many having dined at the fancy pizzeria next door. The stage crew is testing the state-of-the-art sound and lighting system, confident that the musicians will sound and look good in the bare-brick-walled, hardwood-floored room. The bands' management is setting up a display of CDs and T-shirts at the merchandise table in the back. Almost the entire staff of Alligator Records—a group of fifteen men and women ranging in age from thirty to sixty-six—has come out for this special night.

Everyone has come to see two blues musicians whose recent releases on Alligator have been declared as heralding the future of the blues—Jarekus Singleton of Clinton, Mississippi, and Selwyn Birchwood of Tampa, Florida. Jarekus has just turned thirty and Selwyn is twenty-nine. Both are college graduates who won their recording contracts as a result of their performances at the International Blues Challenge, presented annually in Memphis by the Blues Foundation. During the competition, 125 bands and 100 solo-duo blues artists, chosen through contests sponsored by local blues societies, compete for recognition from the small but fervent international blues community. Tonight's audience has been lured here by a media barrage—an article in the *Chicago Tribune*; the label's advertising on the Monday night blues show on WXRT, Chicago's venerable FM rock station; on-air sponsorship of WDCB, a noncommercial jazz station in the city's suburbs; and blasts sent by Alligator to more than two thousand area fans who are on the label's email lists.

This is the first time that Selwyn and Jarekus have performed on the same stage, and there is a palpable sense of anticipation. Will these young bluesmen deliver the same energy, charisma, sense of tradition, emotional gravitas, and just plain entertainment that their revered forebears did? How will these new kids hold up in comparison to blues giants like B. B. King and Buddy Guy? Will they be the saviors of a music venerated by loyal but aging fans but often declared by others to be dead or dying? And for me, the question is more personal: will these two men, more than thirty-five years younger than I am, carry forward the legacy of Alligator Records so that it continues to be a home for a living genre of music long after I'm gone?

Now flip the calendar back to 1970 and travel with me just twenty miles south. On a Sunday afternoon in late winter, Florence's Lounge is beginning to fill up. It's a small brick building with glass block windows on a potholed side street in a ramshackle neighborhood on Chicago's South Side. Outside the club, half a dozen men are crouched over a game of dice, while others drink from half-pint bottles in brown paper bags. Inside, the patrons, mostly middle aged and overwhelmingly black, are finding seats in the vinyl-upholstered booths held together with duct tape, ordering drinks from the bar, and filling up the few tables toward the back. Some are wearing the fancy dresses and polyester suits that they wore to church that morning, and some are in work clothes. Some are carrying the pig ear sandwiches they've bought at the food truck parked outside.

Florence, who lives upstairs, is behind the bar. At one table is 100-year-old Mr. Hill, a former Buffalo Soldier with thick hair who boards with Florence. Another regular patron, who calls himself Mordesz, has brought a large journal to document every song and every musician who performs, as he does each Sunday. Mordesz writes in a strange language that he declares to be Korean, although he himself is not Korean. Other regulars are well-known local musicians—Left Hand Frank, a rough-edged, down-home guitar player who does fabulous Donald Duck impressions; Lefty Dizz, a flamboyant guitar showman wearing a double-breasted sharkskin suit and a hat with a plume; and Magic Slim, a hulking man with a rough complexion whose size makes his guitar look like a matchstick. A few tables have been pushed aside to make room for the band; there is no stage. For a PA system, a microphone has been plugged into one of the guitar amplifiers. There is no merchandise table because the band's only recordings, two 45s cut for local labels, are no longer available.

Everyone has come to see Hound Dog Taylor & The HouseRockers, three local musicians who play the rawest of electric blues at Florence's every Sunday. Each week they play for an audience of southern-born, working-class people who grew up with the blues. It's music for black people who may be living in the city but whose roots are in the country, people who came north during the Great Migration to find decent jobs and leave southern segregation and oppression behind. The sense of anticipation is palpable here too, but the fans are anticipating dancing, drinking, socializing, and temporarily forgetting the burdens of hard, low-paying jobs and life in the ghetto.[1] The blues is an essential part of their world; it is their

---

1. Some people may find the word *ghetto* offensive. I don't mean it to be. Chicago is widely regarded as one of America's most segregated cities, and just about everyone in the Chicago blues world whom I have known over the decades—black, white, and otherwise—uses the word to refer to huge swaths of the city, primarily the South and West Sides, where black people have historically been forced to live because of de facto segregation and redlining and because poverty forced them into the cheap housing available there. Although these areas contain some pleasant homes and well-maintained buildings, most residents have to deal with substandard housing conditions, oppressive policing, irregular city services, poorly funded schools, few jobs, lack of grocery stores and other retailers, more crime and violence than in other parts of the city, and, of course, concentrated poverty. One way that African Americans have historically responded to these conditions has been to create a richly distinctive black American culture that fosters a sense of pride even in the face of dehumanizing racist practices. This culture encompasses social interactions and institutions, language, music, food, religion, and much more. All this social and cultural meaning is compressed into a common phrase such as *ghetto blues club* (as opposed to *North Side blues club*). It begins to describe the parallel universe that I felt I was entering when I first went to see Hound Dog Taylor at Florence's.

heritage, part of the glue that holds together their community of expatriates in the tough and turbulent city. No newspaper or radio station publicity has drawn patrons to Florence's Lounge; they come here every week or heard about the gig from their friends or neighbors. These are lifelong blues fans. No one here is worried about the future of the blues, and no one belongs to a blues society or foundation because none exists yet.

In this crowd there are only a few white faces, including one framed by a mop of unruly black hair and a thick beard. Although this twenty-three-year-old has a full-time job and doesn't do drugs, the crowd at Florence's would call him a hippie. He may seem out of place, but he's clearly not a cop, and more important, he obviously loves Hound Dog Taylor & The HouseRockers. He shows up almost every Sunday, usually with a few other white blues fans.

It was here at Florence's Lounge in 1970 that the dream of Alligator Records was born and my lifelong adventure began. At first, it was simply a dream to record Hound Dog Taylor & The House-Rockers. Then it became a dream to record many of Chicago's other great blues artists. As Alligator grew, the dream expanded to include musicians from other cities and even other countries, including some who challenged traditional definitions of the blues. Over the decades, I've had the opportunity to work with some of the giants of blues and roots rock music. I've been thrilled to play a part in the creative process, producing or coproducing more than 120 albums. I've been on the road and in the recording studio with some of the legends of the blues, gotten to know these larger-than-life musicians personally, and had some of them call me their friend.

I've also built a business based on the music I love. I've learned how to survive in the ridiculously competitive and ever-changing world of the record business. I've delivered music on LP, 45, eight-track, cassette, CD, digital download, and through streaming on the internet. Alligator has placed songs in hit movies and flops, on good TV shows and terrible ones, in advertisements for deodorant, sea-food restaurants, beer, macaroni and cheese, and sports drinks—all with the goal of earning enough money to record the music I love and pay the musicians, songwriters, and Alligator's staff. I never, ever wanted to be a businessman. I viewed businessmen as money hungry and sometimes ruthless. But I had to learn to be one, and a good one, to survive. I learned that a business can be run with goals beyond profit, and that money can be an effective tool to reward creativity and build a bridge between cultures.

Since Alligator began recording more than four decades ago, the blues scene has changed dramatically. The forty-plus Chicago ghetto clubs that featured blues every weekend in 1970 have almost all disappeared. The remaining black blues audience has embraced a lightweight hybrid of blues, Memphis-style soul music,[2] and dance music called Southern Soul, more of a party music than the hard-edged blues that African Americans were listening to in the 1950s, 1960s, and 1970s. Younger African Americans have long since turned from blues to soul and hip-hop. Meanwhile, white musicians and fans have embraced the blues. When I founded Alligator, I had no intention of recording anyone except African Americans. But as white blues musicians stopped imitating their black inspirations and started making their own statements, their music spoke to me. Over the years, Alligator has become a home for some of the most creative and exciting white blues and roots rock musicians, but the label's bedrock has always been black blues artists.

For Alligator's first release, *Hound Dog Taylor and the HouseRock-ers*, the promotional flyer carried the headline "Genuine House-

---

2. It's hard to draw distinctions between blues, rhythm and blues, and soul music, particularly because the term *rhythm and blues* (R&B) is used in two different ways. It is often used to describe any popular secular recording or song created by African American musicians, such as blues, vocal group music, ballads, and dance songs. The term also refers to a specific genre of music created in the early 1940s by trained musicians who incorporated blues elements in more structurally sophisticated songs, sometimes blending in the instrumental harmonies of pop music and jazz and the rhythms of popular dance music of the time. Early R&B artists include Louis Jordan, Roy Brown, the Orioles, and Dinah Washington. Soul music developed in the late 1950s and early 1960s, as black musicians began creating nonreligious songs using the vocal stylings, rhythms, and song structures of gospel music paired with secular lyrics. Examples of early soul music artists are Ray Charles, Jackie Wilson, James Brown, and Sam Cooke. Blues is the rawest, oldest, and structurally simplest of these genres. At its essence, blues is a folk music; in general, its traditional instrumental structures and lyric forms were created by unschooled musicians who learned from watching one another.

rockin' Music." That headline became our slogan, and we wear it proudly today. *Genuine*, because the music we record is deeply rooted in the blues tradition even when it reaches beyond the purists' definition of the blues. It's created by musicians who have honed their art not on synthesizers in their bedrooms but in front of live audiences, in response to the emotional needs of their listeners. *House*, instead of *theater* or *arena* or *stadium*, because our music is ultimately intimate, even when it's big and loud. It's not meant to be *presented* by the artist but to be *shared* between the musicians and the audience, just like what happened every Sunday at Florence's. And *Rockin'*, because it's designed to move you. Most of Alligator's records move your feet or your body, but we also try to make records that move that other part of you: your soul. It's music that can cleanse your inner pain by pulling that pain right out of you—the "hurts so good" feeling that is so special to the blues. And sometimes it embodies the pure pleasure generated by musicians pouring their energy into a timeless groove.

My initial mission, the mission of Alligator, was to carry Chicago's South and West Side blues to a worldwide audience of young adults like me. Now it has become a mission to find and record the musicians who will bring the essence of the blues—its catharsis, its sense of tradition, its raw emotional power, and its healing feeling—to a new audience, the blues audience of the future. I hope that some of you who read this book will become part of that audience. But if you do, be careful—listening to this music is addictive, and the habit may be lifelong.

PART I

The house was rocking to a raw boogie groove. From the moment I walked in, sheets of distorted electric guitar filled the room. I could hear the unmistakable sound of steel on steel as a slide tore up and down the strings. Drums pounded out a shuffle beat so infectious and elemental that even I could dance to it. And through it all pushed a rough-edged voice barking the blues. This wasn't the kind of blues that made you cry in your beer; this was the blues that made you forget everything you'd want to cry in your beer about. I knew immediately that there could be no listening to this music with only half an ear. I had discovered Florence's Lounge, in the heart of Chicago's South Side, the closest place in the city to a Mississippi juke joint. It was exactly what I had come to Chicago to find.

I threaded my way through the crowd toward the rear of the bar, the source of all that rhythmic chaos. Everyone there seemed to know everyone else, and they were all having a wonderful time. Some people glanced at me as I squeezed past, no doubt wondering what a young, bearded, long-haired white guy was doing in that neighborhood, in that bar, on that particular Sunday in the late winter of 1970. But nobody gave me any trouble. The music and atmosphere were simply too much fun.

On my left was a bar that ran most of the length of the smoky room. On my right was a row of eight or nine booths with patched leatherette seats and chipped Formica tables. People filled the barstools, crowded into the booths, and crammed the aisle. Some women wore elaborate wigs, with hair piled up into flowing curls. Many of the men had their hair straightened in the stiff, shiny style called a process; others sported Afros. Some wore fedoras, cowboy hats, or floppy denim caps. These were working-class people out to have a great time with their friends and neighbors, doing their best to forget that tomorrow was another workday.

When I finally reached the back of the club, I found the origin of all that glorious racket — Hound Dog Taylor & The HouseRockers. Perched on the edge of a metal folding chair was Hound Dog, a tall, skinny man wearing a white shirt, narrow silver tie, and beige suit shiny from wear and cleaning. His thin hair was glossy across the top of his head, and the sweat running down his face framed an expression of pure, music-making joy. On his left hand, the fifth finger (out of six!) was sheathed in a shiny steel tube that careened up and down the neck of his cheap guitar. Stomping the beat with first one foot and then the other and grinning broadly, Hound Dog leaned in to the microphone and sang the blues in a high, cracking voice. Whenever he hit the high notes on his guitar, he threw his head back and squeezed his eyes shut. With his stomping feet, flying slide, and comic facial expressions, you couldn't take your eyes off him. Whenever someone requested a song, he'd respond with a grin, hollering, "I'm wit' you, baby, I'm wit' you!"

To his left was Brewer Phillips, a thin, light-skinned black man with high cheekbones and a crooked, broken-toothed smile. He hammered out bass lines on a battered Fender Telecaster as he danced to the music, sometimes kicking his left leg high into the air. His shirttail hung out, and his pomaded hair stood up in little clumps. He played with all the energy and joy of a young boy pretending his broom was a guitar. Every now and then he encouraged Hound Dog by shouting, "Well, all right!"

Sitting just behind Hound Dog and Brewer was Ted Harvey, a round-faced man with tightly cropped hair. Chewing on a wad of gum, he banged on a drum kit consisting of only a snare drum, two cymbals, and a bass drum, with one tom-tom mounted on top that he never seemed to hit. Playing with his eyes closed, he drove the band with un-stoppable, swinging grooves that were impossible to resist.

I don't remember how long Hound Dog and his band played. The music just kept going, and the energy never dissipated, even when Hound Dog slowed the beat down and tore into an intense slow blues. I don't think anybody in the audience enjoyed the music as much as the three men who were creating it. They were clearly meant to play together. That afternoon I fell in love with Florence's and with Hound Dog Taylor & The HouseRockers. The nights that I had spent in the Chicago blues clubs had given me a glimpse of a parallel universe — another America, a black America with its own culture and its own wonderful music. It was an America hidden in big-city ghettos and small southern towns unknown to my friends and me. At Florence's, the door to that parallel universe swung open, and I eagerly stepped through.

1

Virtually nothing in my early life equipped me to start an independent record label devoted to the blues. I was a lonely, nerdy kid with few social skills. Although I could play a few chords on a guitar, I couldn't sing in tune or read music. I had no interest in business. I had almost no exposure to African American culture, and I didn't know a thing about the blues. I had no knowledge of its history, no understanding of its cultural significance, no familiarity with its rhythms and textures, and no clue about its creators. Yet something in my life prepared me to fall in love with the blues and find within it a source of inspiration, emotional healing, and a sense of belonging. A lot of older black blues DJs would say on the air, "If you don't like the blues, you've got a hole in your soul." The blues filled a big hole in my soul.

Just before my sixth birthday, my father, John Iglauer, died as a result of a medical mistake made during routine surgery to have a kidney stone removed. He was thirty-five. Although I have few memories of him, he was always present in my life because my mother and paternal grandmother raised me to be the same kind of ethical, outspoken, driven man that he had been. He had grown up in a prominent, secular Jewish family in Cincinnati, Ohio, and as a young man he rebelled against his insular, well-to-do upbringing. He was a liberal idealist with a passion for fighting against corruption. He chose a career as a city manager committed to cleaning up city government at a time when most big cities were still run by strong mayors and political machines doling out city services, jobs, and contracts based on political connections.

His first job after graduating from Syracuse University was at the International City Manager's Association in Chicago, an organization battling corrupt city governments. It was in Chicago that he met my mother, Harriett Salinger, who came from a well-established Jewish family in South Bend, Indiana. After her family lost almost everything in the Depression, she won a scholarship to the University of Chicago, where she was studying for a master's degree in social work at a time when few women attended college. She was immediately taken with my father; he was energetic and talkative and seemed to have a boundless passion for everything from world affairs to baseball.

In the spring of 1941, they married and moved to Montclair, New Jersey, where my father took a job as the Montclair assistant city manager. When World War II began, he tried to enlist but was turned down for health reasons. He and my mother moved to Ann Arbor, Michigan, in 1944, where he took a job with the Michigan Municipal League writing charters for newly incorporated towns. My mother gave birth to my sister, Carol, in 1944, and I came along in 1947.

I later learned that not only was my father passionate about clean government, he was also publicly outspoken about racial issues and civil rights. During my childhood he wrote to the local newspaper to complain about their policy of describing African Americans (but no one else) by race. He also took flying lessons from two black pilots, who may well have been Tuskegee Airmen, at a time when many white people would have assumed that no black people were competent to teach them anything as technically complex as flying.

During the summer of 1951, when I turned four, we moved to Grand Rapids, Michigan. My father had taken a job there as deputy city manager. We settled into a comfortable home and I began attending nursery school. Our friendly neighborhood was full of families raising large broods of postwar children. Life was good: there were lots of kids to play with, school was fun, and my parents loved each other. Then two years later, my father died.

Shortly after his death, my mother, sister, and I flew to Cincinnati to stay with my paternal grandmother, Clara Senior Iglauer. When we arrived at my grandmother's big house, my mother, devastated by my father's death, went to bed and stayed there through most of the summer. We hardly saw her. It was then that my grandmother began nurturing me. Like my mother, she was a college-educated woman, which was unusual for someone of her generation. Every morning she and I sat on her porch and read the newspaper aloud to each other. I loved being with her; we spent most summers at her house from then on. In 1958, when I was eleven, we settled permanently in Wyoming, Ohio, a suburb of Cincinnati a few miles away from my grandmother's home.

My grandmother employed an African American cook and housekeeper named Mittie Evans. I became devoted to her. Mittie was a heavyset, down-to-earth woman who often tied her hair up in a bandana and thought nothing of removing her dentures while she worked. My mother and grandmother loved me, but they both had a hard time showing physical affection. Mittie always had a hug for me. I spent hours in the kitchen (often sitting on the floor, under the table) while she prepared meals, talking with her and listening to soap operas, adventure serials, and gospel music that played on the radio. Besides Mittie, I had almost no contact with African Americans. There were no black kids in my neighborhood, and only a handful attended Wyoming High School.

When we moved to Ohio, I entered seventh grade, but I found it hard to adapt. There seemed to be unspoken rules about how to be a teenage boy, and I knew none of them. Raised by women, I was in every sense a mama's boy. Imagination games in which I acted out being a cowboy, spaceman, or soldier had always been much more interesting to me than baseball or football. I became an easy target for bullies.

Despite the lack of male role models, I have no doubt that my mother and grandmother were raising me to be like my father. My mother frequently spoke about how ethical he was and showed me the scrapbooks he had kept throughout his life. Both my mother and grandmother taught me by example to have an inquiring mind and to be unafraid to question authority. As my grandmother grew older and more forgetful, she sometimes called me John, my father's name. It was the greatest compliment she could have given me.

From early on, music became a way for me to soothe the loneliness I often felt. My mother loved music. She would often sing Broadway show tunes or 1930s and 1940s pop songs around the house. We would sometimes sing them together, although not very tunefully. Recognizing that I had almost no friends after we moved to Ohio, my mother bought an acoustic guitar for me in the hope that it would provide some consolation. (I never learned more than a few basic chords and licks.) The folk music revival was in full swing, and folk music had captured my interest much more than rock and roll. I began trying to sing and play polished popular folk songs by commercial groups like the Kingston Trio and Peter, Paul and Mary without knowing the unvarnished folk traditions from which their music sprang.

I was also intrigued by edgy, experimental jazz. I saw John Coltrane perform at the 1965 Ohio Valley Jazz Festival at Cincinnati's Crosley Field and was amazed by the intensity and angst of his playing. It seemed as though he was searching for the perfect note, and after conventional notes failed him, he wrenched different sounds out of his saxophone, ones that had never before been attempted. Looking back, I realize his performance had all the raw passion that I later discovered in the blues.

I eventually gave up my own aspirations of being a musician. I had the guitar and I had a harmonica, but if my guitar playing was bad, my harmonica playing was worse. Nonetheless, I liked being *around* music. If I couldn't succeed as a performer, perhaps I could make things happen for musicians who had talent but lacked promotional skills. I took my first stab at helping a musician when I talked a coffeehouse owner into booking Barry Chern, a teenage folksinger and friend from Columbus. I even pitched Barry to Fraternity Records, which was distributed by the Cincinnati-based King/Federal label, whose roster included Freddie King and James Brown. (Fraternity's biggest hits were by Lonnie Mack, perhaps the first blues-rock guitar hero. Lonnie later recorded three albums for Alligator.) Harry Carlson, who ran Fraternity from an office in a seedy building downtown, turned me down, but he took the time to meet with me and listen to the reel-to-reel demo tape I had brought.

In the fall of 1965, I headed to Lawrence University, a liberal arts college in Appleton, Wisconsin, with my acoustic guitar, my commercial folk records, and my awkward social skills. There were fraternities at my college, but nobody wanted to pledge me. I tried to learn how to live in a dorm with a bunch of guys. Although I had a difficult time blending in, I enjoyed academics and studied hard in the classes that interested me—English, history, and theater.

In late January 1966, I rode a bus two hundred miles south to attend the University of Chicago's annual folk festival. It was a trip that changed my life. On the bill was Mississippi Fred McDowell, a traditional blues guitarist who performed Mississippi hill country blues. I had never heard of McDowell, but when he began to play and sing, it felt as though he reached out to me over twenty rows of seats, grabbed me by the collar, slapped me, and yelled, "Wake up, boy! This is for *you*." His music seemed more honest, more direct, and more authentic than anything I had ever heard. Here was an illiterate southern black man, forty years older than I was, playing guitar with a slide on his finger. It seemed we had almost nothing in common. Yet somehow I felt he was speaking directly to me. Back in Appleton, I went to the town's only music store and ordered *Mississippi Delta Blues*, released on the tiny Arhoolie label and the only McDowell record the store could find in a catalog. It took more than six months for the store to locate a copy. I listened to it almost every day.

Two other records were crucial in pointing me and many others of my generation toward blues music. Toward the end of 1965, Elektra Records issued a budget-priced sampler LP called *Folksong '65*. Although the record featured established folk musicians like Judy Collins, Tom Rush, and Tom Paxton, the album's hard-edged lead track, "Born in Chicago," was by an unknown group called the Paul

Butterfield Blues Band. Led by Butterfield, a good singer and electrifying harmonica (or, as most blues musicians call it, harp) player, the band understood how to play electric blues Chicago style, having learned not from records (like the Rolling Stones did) but from playing with black blues musicians in the city's South Side clubs. In fact, Butterfield hired the group's bass player and drummer, Jerome Arnold and Sam Lay, away from Howlin' Wolf. Just as the music of Mississippi Fred McDowell had seemed so direct and honest, the music of the Paul Butterfield Blues Band seemed gritty, powerful, and more grown up than any of the rock and roll music I was hearing on the radio or the folk music on the rest of that sampler.[1]

Then in 1966, Vanguard Records released the groundbreaking three-LP series *Chicago/The Blues/Today!* This set was my awakening to real Chicago blues. It introduced a young rock and folk audience (including me) to the music of Buddy Guy, Junior Wells, James Cotton, Otis Spann, J. B. Hutto, Johnny Shines, Johnny Young, Big Walter Horton, Charlie Musselwhite, and more. The liner notes described the tough blues clubs on Chicago's South and West Sides, and the music sounded as tough as the clubs. I began searching for every blues record I could find, although there weren't many available in Appleton, Wisconsin. I volunteered to do a blues show on the college radio station, WLFM. I was given a slot one evening a week to play music from the station's tiny library of blues albums and my own small but growing personal collection. Although my blues knowledge was next to zero, I knew more than most of my listeners did. What I learned came primarily from LP liner notes and articles in folk music magazines.

I wasn't spending every moment listening to blues. I also stayed busy going to class, chasing girls, protesting the Vietnam War, marching for civil rights, and carrying on late-night conversations with the

1. Although I wasn't a big fan of the British blues bands that sprang up in the 1960s, many white blues fans were first exposed to the blues through the early recordings of the Rolling Stones, John Mayall and the Bluesbreakers, Fleetwood Mac, Ten Years After, and, later on, Cream and Led Zeppelin. I never found the British blues artists to be very convincing singers, but they were a huge factor in creating the blues fans of my generation.

friends I was finally making. I was becoming a sociable young adult with a scruffy beard who liked to wear corduroy bell-bottoms and cowboy boots. I studied almost anything that didn't involve math or science. I finally majored in theater. I wasn't a good actor, but I was fascinated by how theater and society had interacted over the centuries. I envisioned myself as a career academic. Teaching theater history in college seemed like a good, safe, fun way to spend my life. The blues was a passionate hobby. But a career? The thought hadn't yet entered my mind.

2

As I entered my final year at Lawrence in 1968, I was scared. Like many young men of my generation, I desperately wanted to avoid being drafted into the war in Vietnam. With the date of my draft eligibility approaching, I signed up for a series of education courses and decided to delay my graduation until December 1969 so that I could become a student teacher and eventually earn my teaching certificate. Teachers weren't being drafted, and teaching high school seemed a better fate than getting my head shot off in a war I didn't believe in.

In the spring of 1969, I talked the college into letting me book a blues band for the fall homecoming concert, which gave me an opportunity to make my first blues pilgrimage to Chicago, the center of the blues world. I knew only one way to enter this world—through the door of the Jazz Record Mart. I had read about this mysterious place in the pages of the Canadian folk magazine *Hoot*, which I had picked up at the Mariposa Folk Festival outside of Toronto a few years earlier. In that issue, writer Richard Flohil capped his review of a number of blues albums with this life-changing advice: If you want to hear live blues in Chicago, find your way to the Jazz Record Mart at 7 West Grand Avenue and ask the owner, Bob Koester (who is also the head of the Delmark Records label), to take you to the clubs on the South and West Sides of the city. On a Monday morning, armed only with this information, I boarded a Greyhound bus for Chicago.

The Jazz Record Mart didn't look like much. Located in a seedy area north of downtown, it was housed in an old storefront building with dirty windows. The floors inside bore the scuffs and gouges of years of use, and the dusty wooden bins of LPs and old 78s had seen better days. The wall behind the counter was covered with cheaply printed handbills and handwritten scraps of paper. Stuck to the peeling paint with curling pieces of tape, they announced shows like, "Junior Wells Every Sunday at Peyton Place" and "Earl Hooker, Pepper's Lounge, Tuesday Nights." I knew I had come to the right place.

Holding forth behind the counter was a stocky, square-faced man in his midthirties with black hair and black-rimmed glasses. It was Bob Koester, the near-mythical figure I had read about in *Hoot*. He had started the Delmark label in his dorm room at Saint Louis University, and over the years he had recorded Deep South bluesmen like Big Joe Williams and Sleepy John Estes and seminal Chicago artists like Junior Wells, Magic Sam, and J. B. Hutto. My first impression of him was that he was always "on." He talked nonstop, leaping assuredly from topic to topic. While lecturing on why 1930s jazz and blues producer Lester Melrose was an underappreciated hero of American music, Koester interrupted himself to berate one of his long-haired employees for sweeping the floor improperly, then resumed with a sharp left turn into a critique of US foreign policy followed by an overview of Chicago blues in the 1940s as a prelude to a review of the bands he had seen perform in the South Side clubs the previous weekend, then interrupted himself again to instruct a customer as to which Gene Ammons record to buy—a decision requiring a summary of who the key musicians in jazz history were—only to be sidetracked by the need to yell at one of his employees again, leading to a complaint about hippies and their deadbeat ways, and then a return to the subject of jazz history with an explanation of why Frank Teschemacher and the Austin High Gang of the early 1920s were the first white musicians who actually understood traditional jazz and played it with real feeling (because they were hanging out on the South Side, sneaking into clubs to listen to Louis Armstrong). Koester seemed to have an opinion about nearly everything. Dazzled, I thought, "I'd like to grow up and be *that* guy."

When I managed to get a word in edgewise, I explained that I had come in search of a blues band to play for my university's homecoming in Wisconsin. Having read that Koester acted as a guide for out-of-town blues fans, I was hoping he would take me out to a real blues club. But judging by his reaction, he seemed to view me as another deadbeat college student who wasn't worth his time. He turned to one of his long-haired employees and said, "Fishel, are you going out to hear blues tonight? Can you take this kid with you?" The employee he spoke to was John Fishel, a University of Michigan student and cochair of the first Ann Arbor Blues Festival, which was to take place that summer.[1] Fishel became my first guide into the world of Chicago blues.

That evening, the two of us rode a city bus west, traveling from the high-rise buildings and stores of the Loop past the grimy tenements, boarded-up buildings, and burned-out lots of the West Side, still scarred from the 1968 riots following the assassination of Martin Luther King Jr. We arrived at my first Chicago blues bar—a small storefront club on West Madison Street called Eddie Shaw's. I noticed immediately that we were the only white people in the place, which both excited and scared me. What little I thought I knew about blues bars—that they were tough, dangerous joints in run-down buildings—I had picked up from liner notes and pictures on albums like *Chicago/The Blues/Today!* But Fishel seemed comfortable there, and it quickly became apparent that the other patrons were going to be either friendly or uninterested in us.[2]

1. The Ann Arbor Blues Festival, held the first weekend in August 1969, was the first national blues festival, and perhaps the first real blues festival ever. It was an all-star event that featured B. B. King, Muddy Waters, and Howlin' Wolf among others, and it set the standard for future blues festivals.

2. I've often been asked if I, as a white man, ever ran into trouble in any of the South or West Side blues clubs. On the contrary, in almost every club the patrons went out of their way to make me feel welcome. I was twice threatened in the clubs, once with a knife and once with a broken bottle. I don't think either aggressor had the intention of hurting me; they just wanted to see if they could scare me, and they quickly saw that indeed they could. In both cases, other patrons quickly came to my rescue. The streets outside the clubs could sometimes be dangerous; my car was broken into and vandalized a few times. Even before I started Alligator and was just a fan, it was not unusual for a musician to volunteer to walk me to my car when I was leaving a club.

In the corner of the bar, a drum set and guitar and bass amplifiers stood ready for the band. The jukebox played a stream of current R&B hits. We found a table, and I nursed a beer while taking in the scene of moving and dancing bodies, wobbly pedestal tables, burgundy red walls, and dim, shadowy lighting. Loud talk, laughter, and music filled the club. Eddie Shaw, a popular blues sax player and occasional bandleader, tended bar, with his big, friendly voice booming over the music. The house band casually plugged in and began playing some standard tunes. They were led by a singing drummer named Little Addison, with Boston Blackie on guitar.[3] As we nursed our drinks, Fishel explained the tradition of Blue Monday jams in Chicago. The most popular blues musicians played five or six nights a week, but not Mondays. The Monday jam sessions gave both established stars and aspiring artists the opportunity to play in clubs where they didn't normally perform as a way to build their reputations or score a future paying gig. Usually a house band played while musicians sat in and tried to "cut the heads" of whoever else was there.[4]

Waiting to sit in at Eddie Shaw's that night were the famous Otis Rush (one of the artists on the *Chicago/The Blues/Today!* series) with his trademark pompadour and Jimmy "Fast Fingers" Dawkins, a young West Side guitar player who had just cut his debut album for Delmark.[5] There was also a tall, gangly man with a strange, doglike face and an odd line cutting across his chin that formed a horizontal cleft. It was Hound Dog Taylor. I had heard of him and knew that he played slide guitar and that he had done a little recording.[6] When

3. In 1993, during an argument over money, Boston Blackie was shot to death by Tail Dragger, a blues singer strongly influenced by the vocal style of Howlin' Wolf.

4. The original Muddy Waters band earned the nickname "The Headhunters" because they went from club to club more or less trying to steal gigs from other bands and to impress women. Supposedly, Buddy Guy established his reputation in Chicago by winning a bottle of whiskey at a Blue Monday guitar competition with Otis Rush and Magic Sam at the Blue Flame on the South Side. Whether for whiskey, money, or pride, those head-cutting contests were a rite of passage in the blues community, an important part of proving that you were a real bluesman.

5. I was familiar with Dawkins's guitar playing on *Chicago Blues*, an Arhoolie record I liked that featured Johnny Young, a singing guitar and mandolin player, and harmonica genius Big Walter Horton.

6. He had cut only two 45s, both for tiny local labels—one for Firma and the other for Bea & Baby. Firma was owned by Carl Jones, a part-time bartender at Theresa's Lounge and the brother of Richard Jones, a producer and writer for Bessie Smith. Although I met Carl a few the band started their next set, Hound Dog was called on to play. He pulled up a chair in front of the band, sat down, lowered the mike stand, and lit a Pall Mall. He took a drag and began telling a joke that lacked any structure whatsoever. It was a story about something funny that had happened to him, but it was impossible to follow because of his thick Mississippi accent and because he kept laughing as he told it. His toothy smile was infectious, and when he laughed, or rather cackled, he buried his mouth in his hand. He also stammered when he talked (though not when he sang) in a voice that seemed always on the verge of cracking.

Hound Dog finished his tangled story and took another drag or two from the cigarette before placing it on the heavy base of the mike stand. Then he started a song. Almost immediately it fell apart. None of the other musicians could find his beat. They struggled for a minute or two before Hound Dog waved at them to stop. Then he tried it again. This happened two or three times; I don't believe he ever completed an entire song. He did, however, tell more jokes. Much laughter ensued, although for me there was mostly incomprehension. I thought to myself, "Here's a guy everybody likes but who can't really play. They're letting him sit in because it's a jam session and he's having fun." I wrote him off as a clown and didn't think much more about him. The next day I rode the bus back to Appleton, exhilarated by what I had experienced in Chicago.

I returned to Chicago often that spring and fall as I finished my last semesters at Lawrence. Each time, I hung out at the Jazz Record Mart or in the Delmark Records "office," which was housed in the Jazz Record Mart's filthy basement. I got to know Bob Koester, his employees, and the other hard-core blues fans who congregated there. The Jazz Record Mart was a mecca for pilgrims like me, young people fascinated by blues music and the musicians who lived and breathed it. It was the only place we could find out who was playing in the South and West Side ghetto blues clubs, because these bars were never mentioned in Chicago newspapers or on radio stations.

times, I never knew him well. I never met Cadillac Baby, who operated Bea & Baby, nor did I have the opportunity to visit the club he ran, which no longer existed by 1969.

Sometimes, Bob deigned to take me out to the clubs himself, which I considered quite an honor.

For the Lawrence University homecoming, I ended up booking the famous Chess Records artist Howlin' Wolf, who came to Appleton in September 1969 and put on a tremendous show.[7] The student organizers, however, did a mediocre job of promoting the concert, and attendance was poor. I was upset; I had delivered a world-class blues band to my college; the concert should have been a success and should have turned on more students to the music I loved. I thought I knew how it should have been promoted, so I decided to prove it by promoting another blues concert myself. I convinced the Student Activities Committee to lend their names to the event. I told them I'd guarantee the cost of the band, so they had nothing to lose.

I scraped up six hundred dollars and called Dick Waterman, a booking agent famous in the blues world, who represented a young blues guitarist named Luther Allison. John Fishel had told me about Luther, who had just cut (but not yet released) his first album for Delmark and who, along with Magic Sam, had been one of the breakout artists at the 1969 Ann Arbor Blues Festival. Brash and energetic, Luther wasn't of the Muddy Waters–Howlin' Wolf generation. At thirty years old, he looked more like Jimi Hendrix than B. B. King. Once I had Luther booked, I began promoting the concert on my radio show, repeatedly playing Luther's two available recordings, "My Luck Don't Ever Change" and "Gotta Move On Up," from Delmark's anthology *Sweet Home Chicago*. As the November 22 concert date approached, I printed three posters of differing sizes. My friend Peter Aschoff and I drove from Green Bay to Oshkosh to Fond du

7. After their sound check, Wolf and the band were hanging out behind the hall where the concert was to take place; they were going to drive back to Chicago after the concert and thus had no hotel rooms. I went up to meet them, very much in awe of their leader, a blues giant. When I asked Wolf if there was anything I could do for him, he complained of an upset stomach and wished he had a Bromo-Seltzer. I ran four blocks to the drug store, bought a package of the antacid, and ran four blocks back to give it to him. Only a few months later I moved to Chicago and saw Wolf on the West Side. He remembered me as "the hippie who brought me the Bromo-Seltzer." Wolf generally projected an intimidating, "don't mess with me" persona, but he always had a friendly word for me whenever I saw him.

Lac to Madison, putting up posters in every dorm, record store, and kiosk we could find—a small poster three weeks before the show, a larger one ten days before the show, and, on the day before the concert, an even larger one featuring Luther's Delmark publicity photo.

The promotion worked. We sold out the four-hundred-seat theater (at two dollars per ticket) and had a hundred more people waiting in the lobby hoping to get in. Luther was a revelation. Dressed in a robin's-egg-blue velveteen suit, he played his guitar and sang with amazing energy, roaming the stage and out into the audience with a long guitar cord and, backed only by bass and drums, playing for two and a half hours nonstop. With the lobby still filled, we decided to offer Luther a hundred dollars more to play another set for the people who couldn't get in to the first show. As the night went on, Luther broke one guitar string after another, at the end playing on only three strings while three broken ones dangled from his guitar. The show was a triumph for me and for the visibility of blues in Appleton. Afterward, Luther and the band crashed at my apartment. I felt that he and I had bonded, that he had somehow adopted me into the blues family. It was one of the most thrilling nights of my life.

I began to dream about spending a year "living dangerously" in Chicago and working for Bob Koester before heading off to graduate school. I headed to Chicago, trying to impress Koester with my posters and the story of my concert in the hope that he might hire me for some kind of job at the Jazz Record Mart or Delmark. But that would be possible only if I didn't have to worry about the draft. A lottery by birth date had been announced for the following Monday, December 1, 1969. My future and that of millions of other young men depended on the results. It had been announced that only those with the first one hundred dates could be drafted. When my birthday came up number 284, I knew I was safe from the military. Breathing a sigh of relief, I returned to Chicago to plead my case for employment to Koester. He offered me a part-time job as the Delmark shipping clerk for the princely salary of thirty dollars a week. I was to start right after the upcoming holidays. My dream was becoming a reality.

I moved to Chicago on January 1, 1970, and found a shabby efficiency apartment on Dakin Street at the edge of the Uptown neighborhood on the city's North Side. For seventy dollars a month I rented one room with a tiny kitchenette and walk-in closet. I furnished it with a mattress on the floor, my grandmother's ancient TV set, and a single chair and lamp that I had pulled out of a dumpster. I lined my LP collection up against the baseboards. The neighborhood was seedy; I later learned that the corner of Broadway and Irving Park, only a block away, was the biggest heroin-dealing corner on the North Side. The building was a hundred yards from a curve on the elevated train tracks, and at night, until I adapted to the noise, I was awakened every twenty minutes by the steel-on-steel screaming of the train wheels against the track. This was quite a change from the comfortable, quiet suburb where I had grown up.

I began the New Year working at Delmark Records in the basement of the Jazz Record Mart. Although Bob was only paying me for twenty hours of work a week, I showed up first thing every morning and worked until the store closed at 9 p.m. My job included unloading trucks, packing boxes, picking up LPs from the pressing plant, walking the daily deposit to the bank, and sweeping the store. The store's manager always arrived late, so for the first hour of each day I worked behind the counter, playing any record I wanted and educating myself about blues and jazz.

Bob ran an amazing store, with a huge selection of blues and jazz records that were available in only a few other shops around the country. He knew his music, but he wasn't so good with his staff. He had a short fuse and wasn't easy to please. He berated his clerks, including me, in front of his customers and occasionally fired them publicly. (He fired me more than once, but I ignored the dismissals and showed up the next day as if nothing had happened.) He enjoyed shattering old 78s over the heads of his employees. He was constantly critical of my work. Sometimes he tested the quality of my packing by throwing my sealed boxes against the concrete basement wall to see if they would split open. But he could also be a warm, hilarious, smart, and generous man. He had a level of self-confidence and comfort in his own skin that I admired, as well as an unmatched depth of musical knowledge and the vision and drive to make a business out of recording and marketing the noncommercial music that he loved.

Almost everyone in my generation who founded a blues, folk, or jazz label in Chicago spent time at the Jazz Record Mart and sought Bob's counsel. He was the only experienced record man we knew. Former Delmark and Jazz Record Mart employees included Pete Welding, who started Testament Records[8] and was an important producer and blues writer; Pete Wingfield, a British musician who later had a hit record called "I'm Eighteen with a Bullet"; and Chuck Nessa, who started the cutting-edge Nessa jazz label. Another of Bob's protégés, Jim O'Neal, founded the Rooster Blues label. Bruce Kaplan's Flying Fish label was also created under Bob's tutelage. The famed harmonica player Charlie Musselwhite also worked for Bob but left after the two of them had a fistfight.

I don't know whether Bob saw potential in me or not. Despite a tumultuous working relationship, I idolized him, never wanted to disappoint him, and constantly felt the need to prove myself worthy of his trust. Maybe my desire to please him had something to do with my never having had the opportunity to make my own father proud. I took my job seriously and I took my failures hard.

The worst of these failures was my mishandling of Delmark's option for the recording of Luther Allison's second album. I had only worked at the Jazz Record Mart for a few months when Luther stopped by while in town from Peoria, where he lived with his family. I still felt a strong bond with Luther; his scintillating concert at my college had been my entree into the blues world. Luther was "my guy" and, I thought, my friend. Over lunch at a restaurant down

---

8. Testament released blues records by J. B. Hutto, Johnny Shines, Eddie Taylor, Floyd Jones, Robert Nighthawk, Otis Spann, and Houston Stackhouse. Pete also recorded musicians from Bentonia, Mississippi, the hometown of Skip James. My friend Bruce Bromberg, who owned the HighTone label, later bought the Testament catalog.

the street, he shared with me his vision for his second Delmark album. Among other things, he wanted to know what I thought about recording an album that mixed blues with more modern R&B using a big horn section. Knowing that Bob liked to keep his albums simple, raw, and spontaneous, and not wanting to say anything that might contradict Bob's vision of Luther's next album, I avoided responding. I thought Luther's production ideas might pit my boss and hero Bob against my friend and hero Luther.

Luther and I had agreed that we would go out that night and hit some clubs. I met him at his motel and delivered a letter from Bob that said Delmark was officially exercising its option to record Luther's next album. "I was told to give this to you," I said, "and you're supposed to sign it to acknowledge the agreement and give it back to me for Bob." Luther took a look at the letter and said, "I don't know if I'm going to sign this." My heart sank. I didn't know what to do. Torn between my loyalty to Luther and my loyalty to Bob, I decided to wait it out. "He didn't say he wouldn't sign it," I thought to myself with crossed fingers. "He said he wants to think about it. We'll go out to some clubs, and at the end of the night, I'm sure he'll sign." We ended up at Theresa's, where Luther sat in with the house band and was spectacular.

Returning to the motel, we sat in his car in the parking garage, and Luther told me that he wasn't willing to sign the contract extension. He promised that he would call Bob first thing the next morning and explain why. We shook hands. The next day, Luther never called. He left me on the hook to tell Bob that he had rejected the agreement. I felt terrible. Bob had sent me with a specific task and I had let him down. I should have called Bob the moment Luther balked at signing and let him handle it. Because of my affection for Luther, I hadn't been loyal to my boss. Bob had every reason to fire me, and I assumed he would. But he didn't. I was amazed that a man who could be so unforgiving forgave me.

But I was unable to forgive Luther. So overwhelming was my sense of betrayal that I didn't speak to him for twenty-five years. I had been his ally and friend, even to the point of endangering my job and alienating my boss. Years later, I bumped into Luther back-stage at a festival in Europe. "I don't know what I did to you to make you so mad at me," he said, "but I'm sorry. I did a lot of things in my drinking days that I wouldn't have done once I got sober." Then he stuck out his hand, and with mixed feelings, I shook it. That reconciled us. Luther went on to record four albums that we released on Alligator. It took me a long time to accept that people I liked and respected could do things that I didn't like or respect. It also took me a long time to admit to myself that sometimes I could do things I didn't like or respect.

During my first few months in Chicago, I developed friendships with a small group of young blues fans who hung out at the Jazz Record Mart. We called ourselves Blues Amalgamated. Our membership included Jim O'Neal, Amy Van Singel, Rick Kreher, Paul Garon, Tim Zorn, Steve Tomashefsky, and Rebecca Sive-Tomashefsky, along with the self-declared "Kansas hillbilly" Wesley Race, who was beloved by us all. We were a band of like-minded blues geeks who spent most of our nights and weekends hitting the blues clubs on Chicago's South and West Sides. On Fridays, we often started the evening by squeezing into the basement of the Jazz Record Mart to watch selections from Bob's collection of sixteen-millimeter films, shorts, and cartoons. He sometimes showed soundies, short films of live performances by well-known black musicians from the 1940s, like Louis Jordan, Duke Ellington, and Wynonie Harris.

I quickly discovered that, contrary to my naive view that blues clubs were dangerous places, they were not much different from any working-class bar in any big-city neighborhood. Many of the patrons knew one another; they had grown up together down south or lived on the same streets in Chicago. The blues bars were a place to see old friends, pursue members of the opposite sex, drink, dance, and unwind.

The South and West Sides were distinct areas of the city, each with hundreds of thousands of residents. The blues musicians in each part of the city had their own musical styles. On the South

Side, which had an older and more established African American community, you tended to see guitar players who focused more on Delta-based chord patterns or slide guitar. Muddy Waters is a good example. His regular gig for years was at Smitty's Corner at 35th and Indiana, in the heart of the Bronzeville neighborhood. The South Side had also fostered more harmonica players than the West Side, players like Little Walter, Junior Wells, and James Cotton. The South Side clubs I visited regularly included Theresa's Lounge, Pepper's Lounge, Expressway Lounge, Florence's, Louise's South Park Liquors, Josephine's, the Blue Flame, Queen Bee's Lounge, the Stardust Lounge, Peyton Place, Turner's Blue Lounge, Porter's Lounge, the Cinderella Lounge, the 1125 Club, Rose and Kelly's, and, starting in the early 1970s, the famous Checkerboard Lounge operated by Buddy Guy and L. C. Thurman. Two large "show lounges," the Burning Spear and the High Chaparral, booked national acts ranging from blues musicians to vocal groups to balladeers to funk bands.

Among my favorite South Side clubs were Theresa's, Pepper's, and Rose and Kelly's. Theresa's was a cozy club at 48th and Indiana owned by Theresa Needham, a large, outgoing woman who had opened the club in the late 1940s. She often tended bar and acted as a tough-mama figure to the musicians. It was well known that Theresa had a gun in the drawer behind the bar, and she kept a big dog in the back room for extra security. The club was in a partial basement, a few steps down from the street, with windows at sidewalk level. The low-ceilinged room was long and narrow, and the walls were lined with wood paneling. Typical of many blues bars, the room's exposed pipes were wrapped in Christmas tinsel year-round. Eight or nine booths lined one wall, and small tables occupied the front of the band area (the ceiling was too low to have a raised stage). The place would be jam packed at eighty people. The doorman, who suffered from narcolepsy, predictably was called Sleepy. Theresa's was one of the few blues clubs that regularly had some white patrons because it was not far from the University of Chicago, but the vast majority of the crowd was African American. Theresa's had bands performing every night of the week; weekends featured Junior Wells when he was in town. Before Buddy Guy opened the Checkerboard, he often led the house band.

Besides Theresa's, Pepper's was probably the best-known blues club on the South Side. Owned by Johnny Pepper, this larger club occupied a double storefront on 43rd Street at Vincennes.[9] Painted on the outside of the building was a large mural depicting Muddy Waters in white robes, surrounded by Howlin' Wolf, Little Walter, and Sonny Boy Williamson II ("Rice" Miller). Because Pepper's had a special license allowing it to stay open late, fans and musicians often went there after the other clubs had closed. You could feel sure that if you went into Pepper's, you would find somebody worth hearing, from Lefty Dizz to Scotty and the Rib Tips. In late 1970, Johnny Pepper opened another location on South Michigan Avenue just south of downtown in a space that had been jazz pianist Ahmad Jamal's Club Alhambra and was still decorated with a fantastic Moorish motif. This new location was called Pepper's Blues in the Loop, although it wasn't actually in the Loop. Johnny eventually closed both the 43rd Street and South Michigan Avenue locations and opened Pepper's Hideout, another club with a late license, at 2335 South Cottage Grove. It survived for many years.

Rose and Kelly's was a simple neighborhood bar on 39th Street. Rose and Kelly were a married couple from Louisiana. On the nights they had music, they served bowls of homemade gumbo to the patrons. J. B. Hutto, one of Chicago's most underrated blues musicians, could be found at Rose and Kelly's when he wasn't playing at Turner's Blue Lounge. He was a marvelous singer with a huge voice who could bend notes in a way that sounded like he was singing work songs in a cotton field. A raw guitar player, J.B. usually couldn't afford to pay for good band members, but sometimes in their lack of sophistication, the musicians he could afford were able to create some startling grooves and infectious, off-kilter rhythms.[10]

9. Half a block down the street at 423 East 43rd Street was a club called the Psychedelic Shack. When Buddy Guy and his partner L. C. Thurman took over the operation in 1972, they renamed it the Checkerboard Lounge. It became the most famous blues club on the South Side, closing in 2003. The address is now an unmarked vacant lot.

10. J.B. inspired his nephews Ed Williams and James Young to become blues players, and they later formed future Alligator artists Lil' Ed & The Blues Imperials.

The West Side started just west of downtown and ran to the western city limit. It was a strip about a mile wide bounded roughly by North Avenue on the north and 16th Street on the south. It had become a predominantly African American community after World War II, and the residents who lived there were likely to have migrated from the South more recently than those on the city's South Side. Both the musicians and audiences on the West Side seemed younger than those on the South Side. As members of the post–B. B. King string-bending generation, the key West Side bluesmen were primarily guitar players who had grown up playing modern, urban electric blues rather than electrified acoustic blues. The West Side was famous for powerful guitarists like Magic Sam, Otis Rush, Freddie King, Luther Allison, Eddy Clearwater, Jimmy Dawkins, and Mighty Joe Young. West Side clubs included the Majestic M (formerly the L&A), the Riviera, Tom's Musicians' Lounge, Big Duke's Flamingo and Big Duke's Blue Flame Lounge, Ross and Ma Bea's, the Sportsman's Lounge, the Key Largo, Lovia's Lounge, the Upstairs Lounge, the Rat Trap, Necktie Nate's, the Del Morocco, and the 1815 Club (previously Club Alex). Also, there were weekend jams on the stage in the parking lot of guitarist Oliver Davis's Delta Fish Market, at the corner of Lake Street and Kedzie Avenue.

Like the South Side clubs, the West Side clubs had their own crowds and favorite bands. I went regularly to Big Duke's Flamingo to hear Carey Bell.[11] Otis Rush often played the 1815 Club, a former bowling alley, which was owned by the same Eddie Shaw whose previous club I had visited in the spring of 1969. Howlin' Wolf appeared at the Riviera and later at Big Duke's Blue Flame. He finally

11. Big Duke had two clubs: Big Duke's Blue Flame at Madison and California and Big Duke's Flamingo at Roosevelt and Washtenaw. I preferred the Flamingo for its house band, which featured my friend Carey Bell, a terrific harmonica player, and the gang of musicians who hung out with him—guitarists Eddie Taylor and Royal Johnson, bassist Joe Harper, and drummers Willie "Winehead" Williams and Art "Dogman" Jackson. It was a loose gig, with musicians rotating on and off stage, each playing various instruments. There almost never was an intermission. The Flamingo had the ambience of a shabby funeral home. Big Duke's Blue Flame was a barnlike concrete-block building where the audience sat at picnic tables. Howlin' Wolf played there regularly in the early 1970s. It was also the first club where Lil' Ed & The Blues Imperials played.

took up residency at the 1815 Club. Mighty Joe Young played at the intimate Ma Bea's, along with Sugar Bear and the Beehives, a band led by bassist Willie Kent. I saw Luther Allison and Eddy Clearwater at the Majestic M (where Magic Sam had played regularly when it was known as the L&A). The Rat Trap was a down-and-out place where a guitarist named Big Red and a harp player named Easy Baby usually performed. Tom's Musicians' Lounge (formerly Walton's Corner) had a late license and, like Pepper's on the South Side, everyone would congregate there when the other clubs closed.[12]

Because we were spending so much time in the clubs discovering just how alive and exciting the blues scene was in the early 1970s, it seemed almost inevitable that the members of Blues Amalgamated would create a blues magazine. While traveling across Europe in the summer of 1969, I had dropped into the famous Dobell's record shop in London. I picked up two British blues magazines, *Blues Unlimited* and *Blues World*, which were full of blues information and clearly produced by passionate fans. I read them from cover to cover multiple times, surprised by the idea of magazines devoted entirely to blues. The members of Blues Amalgamated often lamented the lack of an American blues magazine, particularly in a city where so many blues musicians lived and performed.

In February 1970, just six weeks after I moved to Chicago, I announced to the gang of blues fans at the Jazz Record Mart that it was time to stop bemoaning the lack of an American blues magazine and start one ourselves. Half a dozen people showed up at my tiny apartment for the first meeting; we became the core staff of the magazine. We decided to call it *Living Blues* because we wanted to write about

12. Walton's Corner had been the home base for Freddie King before he burst onto the national scene in 1961 with his hit "Hide Away" (named after another blues club, Mel's Hideaway). By the time I moved to Chicago, Freddie had become one of the few blues musicians adopted by the rock audience. In 1971, Freddie opened for Leon Russell at the huge Auditorium Theatre in downtown Chicago, then played a midnight show at Tom's Musicians' Lounge. A huge man who made his Gibson guitar look tiny, Freddie delivered one of the most exciting, physical sets of music I have ever experienced, ending by grabbing the microphone stand and sliding it up his guitar to the high E for the final note of "Hide Away." I was sitting so close to the stage that some of the sweat flying off his head landed on my arm. I remember thinking, "I'll never wash again."

the tradition of blues, not as history or a series of recordings but as a living form of black music being performed by black musicians for black audiences in the present day. None of us was black, but we knew of no way to find or solicit black blues fans who might be interested in writing for the magazine.

At that meeting, we began planning the first issue. An interview with Howlin' Wolf would be our first cover story. I offered to compile a series of interviews with musicians and call it "Remembering Magic Sam," to honor the West Side blues giant who had recently died at the age of thirty-two. We talked about records to review and gathered news about who was in the clubs and in the recording studio. As the first issue came together, I reached out to potential advertisers to raise money to print it, and Bob Koester loaned us three hundred dollars in seed money. We typed the first issue on an electric typewriter at one of the staff members' apartments.

The first issue came out just before the second Ann Arbor Blues Festival in the summer of 1970. We loaded hundreds of copies into the back of my old Rambler sedan (inherited from my mother) and drove to the festival. John Fishel, the festival's cochairman, who had taken me to the West Side the year before, let us park in the middle of the field and sell *Living Blues* out of the trunk. We optimistically assumed everyone at the festival would want a copy, but we were disappointed in the sales. Nevertheless, we were determined to continue.

It quickly became clear that Jim O'Neal, a journalism student who was much more knowledgeable about blues than I, was the obvious choice to serve as editor. Amy Van Singel, who would eventually marry Jim, was also very knowledgeable. She wrote articles and did most of the layout. I stayed involved with printing, production, advertising, and distribution. Creating each issue was a struggle. We eventually started doing more professional typesetting using a Vari-Typer, a crude mechanical typesetting keyboard that had belonged to the *Chicago Seed*, an underground newspaper.

After the birth of Alligator in 1971, I had less time to devote to the magazine, which was published quarterly. I was technically the owner of *Living Blues* (someone had to be named when we opened the bank account), but Jim and Amy were doing the hard work of creating each issue. I sold it to Jim in the late 1970s for a dollar. Considering that the magazine was barely paying for itself, I may have overcharged him. After years of struggling to make a profit, Jim sold *Living Blues* to the University of Mississippi in 1983, and it became a bimonthly publication. *Living Blues* still doesn't make money, but the university is proud of it and the magazine has had a series of excellent editors, including Jim himself. The fact that *Living Blues* still exists after almost fifty years is quite amazing. I'm proud to be one of its founders.

Although most of the staff of *Living Blues* knew much more about blues than I did, I was learning fast. When I came to Chicago, I knew so little about guitar players that I couldn't tell the difference between B. B. King's and Albert King's styles, which for hard-core blues fans is like saying, "I can't tell a baseball from a rock." As I learned more, my musical tastes were evolving. I went to see Mississippi Fred McDowell at the Quiet Knight, a large North Side folk music club. While he was still his wonderful self, his solo Mississippi blues didn't move me the way it had when I first saw him at the University of Chicago. Though I still loved country blues, it no longer excited me the way urban electric blues did.

3

For me, part of the allure of blues has always been the larger-than-life personalities of the musicians themselves. The macho side of many bluesmen spoke to me as a young man. A friend of mine once said, "When I was a teenager and first heard Muddy Waters sing, 'I'm a man,' I thought, 'That's what *I* want to be.'" I could relate. My friends and I loved the spontaneity of the music, the joyful party atmosphere of the clubs, and the self-assured charisma of the musicians who created that joy. We were lucky outsiders who had entered a community that not many other white people had discovered.

As I found my place on the blues scene, I finally felt at home. Luther Allison, a charismatic, real bluesman, had been the first blues musician who seemed to accept me as a member of the blues community. My promotion of his concert had been a triumph. First he had thrilled an audience of four hundred people, and then he had gone to my apartment and crashed on my bed while I slept on the couch. I felt that he saw me as more than just another fan.

Junior Wells was another bluesman with whom I developed a bond. Like Luther, Junior carried himself with a confident, macho swagger that I admired. Bob Koester introduced me to Junior at the Blue Flame, at 39th and Drexel, in the late spring of 1969, when I was traveling to Chicago from Appleton at every opportunity. A small, slender man who liked to wear flashy jewelry, colorful polyester suits, and expensive shoes, Junior was among the most popular of the South Side bluesmen. He started his career in the late 1940s with guitarists Louis and Dave Myers, forming a group known as the Four Aces with the addition of drummer Fred Below. In 1952, Junior switched places with Walter and joined Muddy Waters's band. Little Walter, who had a hit record with the instrumental "Juke," hired the Aces as his band. Walter had pioneered a revolutionary harmonica sound that was copied by almost every harp player who followed him. Playing with heavy amplification, he created a thick wall of sound by cupping a cheap microphone and harmonica together. By varying the pressure within his hands, he created distortion from overloading the microphone, making the harmonica sound almost like a tenor saxophone. Junior was originally a devotee of Little Walter's style and became a master of amplified harmonica while still a teenager. Following his brief stint with Muddy, Junior went on to record singles for the States label, owned by black entrepreneur Leonard Allen, and the Chief, Profile, Bright Star, and Mel-Lon labels, all owned by another black businessman, songwriter and producer Mel London. During the 1960s, some of Junior's 45s, like "Messin' with the Kid," "Little by Little," and "Come On in This House," were local and regional black radio hits.

Junior's first exposure to white audiences was with the classic *Hoodoo Man Blues* album on Delmark, with Buddy Guy on guitar recording under the pseudonym "Friendly Chap" because he was under contract to Chess Records. Produced by Bob Koester in 1965, *Hoodoo Man Blues* is a crucial Chicago blues record. At a time when blues albums were generally collections of one artist's singles, *Hoodoo Man Blues* was the first LP recorded by a working Chicago blues club band. Its release was followed almost immediately by Junior's cutting five tracks for the groundbreaking *Chicago/The Blues/Today!* series on Vanguard Records. These two recordings had made Junior one of the blues artists best known by the new white audience. By the late 1960s, Junior had fallen under the musical influence of James Brown, developing a percussive harp style that emphasized phrasing over melody. Using a clean-sounding vocal microphone rather than

the more distorted sound popularized by Little Walter, Junior punctuated his playing with grunts and tongue clicks. The actual harp
notes were often less important than how he organized and shaped
them rhythmically to fit the song.

Junior's home club was Theresa's, and he usually performed there
with the house band on weekends when he wasn't on the road. Theresa's was always full of musicians. Buddy Guy had led the house
band through much of the 1960s before beginning to make his own
name at a national level. By the 1970s, the house band's lead guitarist was usually Sammy Lawhorn, a wonderful, lyrical player who
made subtle use of the tremolo bar to frame his notes in shimmer-
ing vibrato. Occasionally Phil Guy, Buddy's brother, was a second
guitar player. Typically the house band at Theresa's warmed up the
crowd with guest vocalists like Andrew "Big Voice" Odom, a strong,
gospel-inflected singer who was also known as "Little B.B." Sometimes the vocalist was a muscular singer who called himself Muddy
Waters Junior but who, strangely, didn't sound at all like the actual
Muddy Waters and didn't even perform Muddy Waters songs.

After the band's first set, it was star time. Junior Wells would leave
his barstool and unhurriedly stroll up to the cramped stage area. In
addition to being an excellent harmonica player, Junior was a brilliant singer. Like the best blues and gospel vocalists, he could bend
vocal notes from being slightly flat up to the correct pitch, creating
tension and release. He could also swoop from low to high notes
with ease. As he performed, he would squeeze his way through the
crowded bar, singing to various women, getting up close and personal. It seemed as though he might have had sexual encounters with
all the women in the club (except Theresa, of course). Junior had a
reputation as a lover.

Because *Hoodoo Man Blues* had helped make Junior one of the
few bluesmen performing regularly for white audiences, Junior was
intensely loyal to Bob Koester. And because I was introduced to
Junior as Bob's friend, Junior was going to look out for me. People
treated Junior with a certain amount of deference and caution; he
was known to be a dangerous man who would never back down from

a fight.[1] During intermissions at Theresa's, he often took me outside to drink gin out of a bottle in a brown paper bag and chase it with orange juice while he told stories and philosophized about what it meant to be a man.

On one of the nights when Junior and I stood drinking outside of Theresa's, an acquaintance approached him and asked for a ten-dollar loan until the following week. Junior politely pointed out that the man already owed him twenty dollars, which suggested that perhaps the man's credit wasn't so good. The would-be borrower was persistent, and eventually Junior pulled out a crisp, new hundred-dollar bill, folded it lengthwise, and dropped it between his feet. "There it is," Junior said to the man. "Pick it up, motherfucker. Pick it up. It's yours." The man looked at Junior, looked at the hundred-dollar bill, and looked back at Junior. He knew that Junior usually carried a gun in his belt and a knife or a razor in his pocket. He also knew that, if he bent down to pick up that hundred-dollar bill, he was likely to be on the receiving end of one or the other. "There it is," Junior said again. "Pick it up, motherfucker." Finally the man raised his hands and backed down the street. Junior Wells was a badass, but if you were his friend, you were his friend for life.

Only ten days after I moved to Chicago, Bob asked me to come to a Junior Wells recording session. I was to act as gopher (the person who would go for whatever was needed—food, drink, guitar strings, and so on). It was the second of two sessions for an album titled *Southside Blues Jam*. The session took place at Sound Studios, in a downtown office building at 222 North Michigan Avenue. I arrived at the studio wide-eyed. I had never seen a studio or a recording console. I had never seen such fancy, delicate microphones. Soon

---

1. Pepper's Lounge on 43rd Street usually had a few members of the Disciples street gang hanging around outside the door. I think Johnny Pepper paid them for protection from other gangs. One night one of them got into an argument with Lefty Dizz on the street and followed him inside the club. The Disciple jumped onstage to take a swing at Dizz. Junior was sitting at the bar. Without leaving his seat, Junior pulled out a pistol and shot the gangbanger. The Disciples were said to have then taken out a hit on Junior. According to Junior, he shot six of them before they decided it wasn't worth it to continue attempting to kill him. I know people who saw the shooting at Pepper's. I don't know for sure that Junior shot six Disciples, but I find it entirely believable.

the musicians Junior had picked for the recording began to arrive. There was Otis Spann, one of the best blues piano players of all time and *the* iconic figure of Chicago blues piano. Junior's touring partner, the famous guitarist Buddy Guy, appeared, as did Louis Myers, who had been a member of Junior's first band.

But the rhythm section had failed to show up. Fred Below, a former bandmate of Junior's and one of the most influential Chicago blues drummers, and Earnest Johnson, the solid house bass player from Theresa's, were both missing. Below finally called the studio from the police station at 51st and Wentworth, where he and Johnson were locked up. The person driving them to the session had been stopped for a traffic violation and had no driver's license. The police arrested everyone in the car. Bob gave me a wad of cash and sent me to bail them out. By the time I got back to the studio with Fred and Earnest, it was close to 11 p.m. and Junior was pretty buzzed. Remarkably, Bob wasn't angry or fuming or discouraged. He simply took it in stride. There was a lesson in that: when working with blues musicians, the unexpected happens way too often.

I soon learned another valuable lesson. Producing a record wasn't just about mastering the technical elements of recording; it was also about managing personalities. As the session finally got under way, I sensed developing tension between Buddy and Louis, each of whom had years of history playing with Junior. Both wanted to take the lead guitar parts, and neither seemed prepared to play behind the other. Realizing he had an impossible problem, Bob took Louis aside and, after a brief conversation, handed him some cash. Louis left.

Finally, at around midnight, the recording began in earnest. I began to realize that Junior had come without a song list of any kind. While sitting at the piano bench with Spann, he had been remembering some old songs and asking Spann to sing and play them. He used these as a starting point to improvise new lyrics. Some of the lyrics sprang from Junior's wandering streams of consciousness, and some from current events. It was magical and marvelous. Inspired by each other, Junior and Buddy were having a wonderful time riffing and improvising. Finally, Buddy stepped to the microphone and they traded lyrics on a song that included verses from Guitar Slim's "The Story of My Life" and John Lee "Sonny Boy" Williamson's "Good Morning Little Schoolgirl."

I could hardly believe what was happening to me. It seemed like I had moved from Wisconsin to heaven. I couldn't imagine anything in life being more thrilling than to sit four or five feet from Junior Wells and Buddy Guy while they made a record right in front of me. And I had helped! It was at that point I knew this was what I wanted to do with my life. Thoughts of graduate school and teaching theater history were replaced with a desire to spend many more nights like this. Just as I had imagined myself as a cowboy or spaceman, I now imagined myself as a record producer. And all that time I was watching Bob Koester to see how he handled this odd situation of Junior's pulling together a group of musicians who had no idea what they were going to record.

Throughout 1970 and 1971 I attended every Delmark recording session. With each one, I gained some new insights and made mental notes about what worked and didn't work in the studio. At the recording sessions for Mighty Joe Young's *Blues with a Touch of Soul* in early 1971, I was again surprised that Bob didn't seem to do any advance planning. For example, Joe came to the session wanting to record a version of "Sweet Home Chicago." Recording an overdone standard was a bad idea, and Bob nixed the song. But Bob didn't know that Joe had planned to cut it. Showing respect for the bandleader by letting him direct the session was a fine idea in principle, but the results were unpredictable.

Another lesson I learned at Mighty Joe Young's sessions was that sometimes a producer should overrule the bandleader and insist on better musicians as well as fresher songs before everyone heads into the studio. Joe brought in Jimmy "Fast Fingers" Dawkins to play rhythm guitar. Joe himself was an outstanding rhythm guitar player. But rhythm guitar was not Jimmy's strength; he was a soloist, not a supportive chords player. Joe was trying to do Jimmy a favor because Jimmy had asked Joe to play rhythm guitar on his first Delmark album, *Fast Fingers*. It seemed to me that Joe wasn't doing himself any favors by bringing in someone who wasn't as good at rhythm guitar as he was. I began thinking that some planning would make for a better record, even if it showed less respect for the artistic decisions of the bandleader. This revelation was probably the root of my reputation as a control freak in the production of Alligator sessions. A lot of musicians are surprised when I explain to them that Alligator is not prepared to release whatever songs and performances they choose to deliver and that (with the exception of a handful of artists who have proven themselves to me) all songs recorded and all accompanying musicians would be by mutual agreement between the artist and the label. This Alligator contractual provision has been a deal breaker for some artists.

At a recording session for Jimmy Dawkins's second Delmark album, *All for Business*, I learned that a session is only as good as its weakest player. If the drummer is mediocre, then everybody else is going to be limited by what that drummer can do. If your drummer can only play four different grooves, then you'll either make an entire album with those grooves or hope that your drummer can learn some new ones in the studio. But the studio is not a great place to learn how to play. At the session, Jimmy Dawkins asked me what I thought of the drummer he had chosen for the record. Knowing that the drummer regularly performed with him at club gigs, I said, "I think he's fine." "I think he walks like an elephant," Jimmy said. I thought to myself, "If you don't think he's the best possible drummer, why the hell did you bring him? Club gigs come and go; records last forever."

Bob's production approach—allowing the bandleader to choose the songs and band members and to guide the arrangements—could lead to brilliant results, like Junior Wells's *Hoodoo Man Blues*, Magic Sam's *West Side Soul* and *Black Magic*, and J. B. Hutto's *Hawk Squat*. But it was a risky way to make a record, and I wasn't as much of a risk taker as Bob.

4

It was probably sometime in the summer of 1970 that I first approached Bob Koester with the idea of my producing a Hound Dog record for Delmark. Having only seen him sitting in at jams, Bob was unimpressed, just as I had been at first. So when I began to feel him out about Hound Dog, he showed no interest. But ever since walking into Florence's that Sunday in the late winter of 1970 and hearing that primal boogie groove, I had become convinced that Hound Dog Taylor & The HouseRockers were something special. I returned to Florence's almost every Sunday after that to see them perform and to get to know Hound Dog.

Hound Dog told me he had been a farm worker in Mississippi—a tractor driver, which was a more valued position than field hand. He had first played a piano that he hauled around to parties in a wagon before switching to a more portable guitar. He told me that the Ku Klux Klan chased him out of Mississippi in 1942 because he had an affair with a white woman. Fleeing when a cross was burned in his front yard, he slept in drainage ditches and hid out at his sister's until he could get to Chicago. Once there, he took a series of labor jobs, including building wooden television cabinets, all the while playing on Sundays at the Maxwell Street Market for tips. Sometime in the late 1950s, he quit his job and started playing music full time. He performed more nights of the week than most bluesmen because Hound Dog Taylor & The HouseRockers were one of the cheapest blues bands in the city. In 1970, the band charged forty-five dollars (fifteen dollars a man) to play on weekend nights and thirty dollars (ten dollars a man) for weeknights. And those prices were negotiable.

A typical Hound Dog set began with Brewer Phillips playing raw, distorted lead guitar, squeezing the strings to the breaking point, performing instrumentals, and singing well-known blues songs in a voice that was as cracked as his dental work. Giving Brewer the spotlight, a low-key Hound Dog played the bass notes on his guitar because there was no bass player in the band. After he did two or three songs, Brewer would announce, "And now let's bring to the bandstand the star of the show, the one and only Hound Dog Taylor!" Then he'd take the single microphone stand over to Hound Dog. Of course, Hound Dog had been sitting there playing all along, but now the imaginary spotlight swiveled over and—surprise! It's Hound Dog Taylor! We didn't know he was here! At that point, Hound Dog took over and became the focus of the show.

A natural entertainer, Hound Dog loved being the center of attention, and he consciously projected a persona that said, "Don't take me seriously." He knew he looked funny; he knew he talked funny; he knew that if he smiled that big smile, people would smile back; and he knew that if they had a good time, people would buy drinks for him. It was clear that Hound Dog was a serious alcoholic. "I need my red water," he would say. He drank Canadian Club; he generally put a double shot of it into his morning coffee. He drank steadily through the day and was generally drunk by the end of the night. He usually smelled strongly of alcohol. Sometime in 1970, I saw Hound Dog open up for Howlin' Wolf at Big Duke's Flamingo, a West Side club on the corner of Roosevelt and Washtenaw. I told the waitress, "Get Hound Dog a drink on me." She came back and said, "That'll be two dollars and fifty cents." I was horrified. A shot of whiskey in those days cost only about fifty cents. "What did he order?" I asked her. "Half a pint," she said.

Everyone noticed Hound Dog's left hand. Just beyond the fifth finger was another finger, perhaps an inch and a half long, with joints and a fingernail.[1] His fifth finger, where he wore his slide, was un-usually long and strong. Whereas most slide players make their hand into a wedge to produce more pressure on the strings, Hound Dog could play with a heavy steel slide lined with brass, using just his fifth finger. As a result, he could move the slide quickly, creating a lot of vibrato. That's part of what made his sound.[2] But above all, it was his rhythms that were so infectious.

After he made a little money, Hound Dog had some matchbooks printed up. The cover read, "Hound Dog Taylor & The HouseRock-ers," and the spine, "Blues and Rock & Roll." For him, the slow songs were blues and the fast songs were rock and roll. That was the only difference. By that definition, Hound Dog played a lot more rock and roll than blues. He wanted to see people dance, and that meant he played a lot of shuffles, the syncopated beat that sounds like a horse cantering. He played fast shuffles, slow shuffles, and medium-tempo Jimmy Reed–style shuffles (known as lump-de-lumps), alternat-ing with driving boogies, grinding stomps, and romping up-tempo songs like his signature tune, "Give Me Back My Wig":

Give me back my wig
Honey, now let your head go bald
Really didn't have no business
Honey, buying you no wig at all.

He couldn't read music and probably could not have told you the names of the notes the strings on his guitar were tuned to, and, as he tuned by ear, they might be different on different nights. He

1. I later learned that Hound Dog had been born with six fingers on both hands, though the sixth fingers had no feeling. He told me that when he was a kid, the extra finger on his right hand kept getting caught on things, to the point that it often bled and became infected. He cut it off with a straight razor. On that hand he had a little nub where the finger had been.
2. I love slide guitar. For me, it represents the essence of the blues because to sustain the notes, you must keep the slide vibrating. This creates tension as the constantly moving notes circle the "correct" pitch without ever nailing it exactly. And there's the metal-on-metal excite-ment of the slide moving up the neck, like gunning a car, and the release when it descends down the neck, as in Elmore James's "Something Inside Me."

was entirely self-taught. Stylistically, he reminded people of the late blues giant Elmore James, but, though he played Elmore's songs regularly, Hound Dog always denied any Elmore influence. In fact, he sometimes claimed that Elmore had learned from him.[3]

As it became apparent that Bob wasn't going to take an interest in Hound Dog, I began thinking about producing the record on my own. Not only did I love the band, but I also wanted to show my mentor and father figure that I was ready to follow in his footsteps. As the year rolled on, I imagined starting my own label and financing a Hound Dog record using $2,500 I had inherited from my grandfather. By this time, Wesley Race had become Hound Dog's close friend and number one fan. When I revealed to Wesley that I was thinking about creating a label to record Hound Dog, he said he wanted to be involved and would contribute $1,000 toward the costs and become my junior partner in the new company. I was happy to say yes. Besides his financial investment, I thought his presence in the studio would be invaluable because Hound Dog loved and trusted him. Wesley and I shook hands on a partnership.

In early 1971, I stood with Hound Dog on the steps outside Pepper's Blues in the Loop and told him I wanted to record him. He knew me as a loyal fan because I had been to so many of his gigs. "I'd like to make an album with you," I said. "I'm wit' you, baby, I'm wit' you," he replied, without asking about any particulars like money or a contract. I'm sure he had received nothing for the two 45s he had cut for local labels. His only reward had been hearing his music on the jukebox. Now that he was being courted by a white "hippie," he must have thought that at least this record might lead to some gigs

---

3. Elmore James's technique on the slide guitar amazed me, and so did his passion as a vocalist. Singing at the top of his register, he seemed to deliver every song as though it was the last statement he would ever make. He brought a great depth of emotion to even the most prosaic lyrics, and his unfettered, raw intensity reflected everything a blues singer should be. I never saw him perform live, and there is nothing to show how he presented himself other than some still photographs and his studio work; no video clips or live recordings exist. Sometimes I think about the years of my life I would have given up to have heard him in person. Very few people make perfect records. Elmore James made perfect records. They weren't perfectly in tune, they weren't perfectly executed, they weren't perfectly recorded, but they were perfect emotionally. I never get tired of listening to him.

for a new audience of young white fans. Plus, with no other recording opportunities, what did he have to lose? I think he was shocked when I told him that I would pay him to record.

Although he didn't ask about money, he did ask, "Who's going to play bass?" "You don't need a bass player," I told him. "You've got a special sound with the two guitars and drums." "Everybody has a bass player," Hound Dog said. I knew perfectly well I wasn't going to record him with a bass player, but to placate him I arranged a rehearsal at Pepper's with Elbee Huggins, a solid bassman who sometimes played with Howlin' Wolf. As I expected, it was a musical disaster. Brewer Phillips had no idea what to do. Normally, the presence of a bassist would have freed him up to play chord-based rhythm guitar, but Brewer wasn't a chords man. His brilliance was playing driving, ever-varying bass patterns on a regular guitar. He struggled to find his way. "It's not the same with a bass player," I said to Hound Dog after the rehearsal. "You know it and I know it. Let's just record what you guys do every night." He didn't argue.

Just before we were ready to record, Wesley came to me and told me he had to back out of our deal; he had a family emergency and needed the money. Although he didn't join in my business, he more than earned his credit as coproducer. Over the weeks before the sessions, he made a list of virtually every song the band played. He and I put together a list of songs to be recorded. We knew that this was not a band that needed rehearsing. Through their many nights of performing together, each musician could feel the direction of a song and play what fit it best.

Following Bob Koester's example, I booked time at Sound Studios with engineer Stu Black, a former engineer for Chess Records who was Bob's first choice for Delmark sessions. Stu, whose catchphrase was, "I've done it all, from Howlin' Wolf to Steppenwolf," had recorded dozens of blues sessions. Hound Dog and I signed the first Alligator recording contract at the studio on Tuesday, May 25, 1971, just before the first session. The second session followed on June 2. I paid Hound Dog $480, plus royalties to come. I paid Brewer and Ted $240 apiece as sidemen ($120 per three-hour session; our sessions went longer than three hours but nobody complained). That was the studio-scale payment set by the musicians' union as Bob Koester had taught it to me. As was the norm, there were to be no royalties for Brewer and Ted since they were considered sidemen.[4]

We set up the band members in the studio just as they normally arranged themselves in a club—Hound Dog on the left, Ted Harvey in the middle, and Brewer Phillips on the right. They used their own equipment. Hound Dog played his Kingston Japanese guitar through his Sears Roebuck Silvertone amplifier. Although the amp was manufactured by Danelectro, a company famous for its inexpensive fiberglass guitars, it had six Lansing speakers, a good brand. Two of the speakers, however, were cracked, which created distortion that the cheap guitar only added to. Ted had his trusty Slingerland drum set. Brewer plugged his beat-up Fender Telecaster into a relatively new Fender Concert amplifier that he had recently bought.

We recorded simply, with one microphone on each guitar amp, one vocal microphone for Hound Dog, and four microphones for the drums (one on the bass drum, one on the snare drum, and a stereo pair overhead). Stu asked me if I wanted any reverb (the slight echo effect heard on most commercial recordings), but I thought it would sound too slick and "studio-ish." I told Stu, "No. Just make it sound like their instruments sound. Don't do anything fancy." My goal was to get a recording that captured as much as possible the spirit and feel of the band's performances at Florence's. I wanted to remove any possible barriers to making this happen in the studio.

Delmark sessions had taught me that musicians usually wore headphones in the studio so that they could clearly hear one another. I suggested to Stu that instead of using headphones, we point some smaller speakers toward the band, so it would seem much more natural to musicians who weren't used to being in a recording studio. I also thought this would make them feel less inhibited because they wouldn't be chained down by headphone cables. Brewer

4. Brewer and Ted did share in the royalties for the later albums, after they threatened to quit the band if they didn't.

Phillips always played standing up and dancing around and I didn't want to keep that from happening. I wanted them to feel as relaxed and loose as they did in Florence's.

I was excited and scared and worried that, without the enthusiasm of an audience to feed their energy, it would be hard to capture the spirit of their live performances. Hound Dog felt the same way. After the first couple takes, he said, "Send that boy [meaning Wes] in here," From then on, Wes stayed in the studio with the band while I sat in the control room with the engineer. That gave the band an enthusiastic one-man audience to play for. It took a little while for them to get loose, but once the alcohol was flowing and they realized they could just do what they knew how to do, they lost any studio jitters and began having fun making music together. As the sessions went on, Brewer and Ted even began to holler encouragement to Hound Dog during the performances, just as they did in the clubs.

Wes and I were determined to keep things moving along so that the band didn't grow bored. We worked from the song list we had put together. When Hound Dog said, "Hey, baby, what do you want to hear?" we could say, "How about '44 Blues'?" "I'm wit' you, baby, I'm wit' you," he would answer, and launch into the song. "Give Me Back My Wig," "Held My Baby Last Night," "Wild about You, Baby," "It Hurts Me Too," and "It's Alright" were all songs we had heard the band do live and included on our essentials list. Brewer Phillips was featured on a searing slow blues called "Phillips' Theme." Hound Dog also came up with a few surprises, like "55th Street Boogie," "I Just Can't Make It," and "She's Gone," all songs we had never heard him play before.

In the course of two evenings, we recorded twenty-five songs, with no more than four takes of any of them, and in many cases, one take only. To keep the budget down, we recorded directly to two-track, mixing as we went, which meant there would be no way to repair anything later. I knew when we left the studio that we had the record we had dreamed of. It was everything I wanted it to be, an album that captured the electric energy and exuberance I had first heard in Florence's. It was stripped down, emotionally honest, and true to the spirit of the band. After Wes and I chose the sequence of songs, the studio cut the master lacquers used for manufacturing LPs. The total bill was nine hundred and seventy dollars. That's pretty good for a record that went on to sell close to a hundred thousand copies in the United States alone.

There are musicians who can play all of Hound Dog's notes and who understand his technique. But they can't play with Hound Dog's attitude, rhythm, and drive. They can play his licks, but they can't play his music, because they haven't lived the life that created it. They haven't driven a tractor in Mississippi or seen a cross burning in their front yard or slept in a drainage ditch. I suppose most other musicians also can't play while drinking Canadian Club from morning to night.

There is a magic in doing something incredibly simple better than anybody else can do it. When a musician has the ability to stir the deepest, most elemental place inside the listener, that magic is even more powerful. In all my years listening to blues, I've rarely heard any electric blues that's simpler and more direct than that of Hound Dog Taylor & The HouseRockers. And I mean that as high praise.

Even before my first recording session, I tried to find just the right name for my fledgling label. Almost all of the names I toyed with were those of exotic animals, from armadillos to zebras. In the end I chose Alligator Records because my girlfriend, Bea van Geffen, had given me the nickname "Little Alligator." It was a reference to my unconscious habit of playing drum parts by clicking my teeth together as I listen to the radio or a record (I can play almost a full octave on my teeth).

There were other reasons that the name Alligator appealed to me. Alligators come from the South, just like the music and most of the musicians I love. Alligators have an image of being dangerous. I'm not dangerous, but I thought it would be good if people thought I was a tough, ruthless businessman. Also, an unpaid bill from a label with a name that started with *A* would be at the top of each distributor's payables pile. An illustrator named Michael Trossman designed the Alligator logo as a favor. He was trying to draw a realistic alligator, but I kept telling him to make it more of a cartoon, happier and more fun. Finally he came up with a smiling alligator that looked like it had just dined on a distributor who hadn't paid his bills. I loved it.

From the beginning, my goal had been to create something that would last, both as a body of music and as a business. Even before completing Hound Dog's record, I had decided that attention to packaging was going to be a priority. Most small-label blues album covers struck me as either garish or bland and uninspiring. I was prepared to spend money on a professional, eye-catching look that said something about the feel of the music and might generate sales. Why go through all the trouble of making a one-of-a-kind record and then package it like it's not important?

The sepia-toned, starkly lit cover of Chuck Berry's 1970 Chess release *Back Home* inspired the first Hound Dog cover photo. I had been introduced to a very talented, experienced, and eccentric photographer named Peter Amft, and discovered that he had taken the photo of Chuck Berry that I loved so much. As a favor, he agreed to take the cover photograph of Hound Dog at no charge. It was a masterpiece of simplicity—Hound Dog holding his cheap Japanese guitar, his hat perched on his head, grinning his infectious grin. I spent extra money on custom-mixed ink and special textured paper to achieve a classic look. Using Musical Products, the same down-at-the-heels pressing plant on the near South Side that Bob used for Delmark, I ordered a thousand copies of *Hound Dog Taylor and the HouseRockers* in August 1971.

Capturing the magic on a record was only the first challenge. Now I had to sell it, and I had a plan. Historically, radio airplay for folk, jazz, and blues LPs had been limited, but that began to change in the late 1960s, when the free-form format of progressive rock FM stations revolutionized the world of commercial radio. Before then, FM radio programming consisted primarily of classical music and news. Rock and roll radio was an AM format, hit driven and focused entirely on singles, not albums. But beginning with the Beatles (especially the *Rubber Soul* album) and the Rolling Stones, my generation began listening to albums instead of singles. Artists and producers began thinking of an album as a concept rather than just a collection of unrelated songs. Young baby boomers, inspired by visionary musicians and by their self-image as rebels, turned their backs on the inoffensive pap that most AM rock and roll radio was feeding them. College dorm rooms were filled with experimental rock, folk, jazz, blues, and other music outside the mainstream. Inevitably, the exploratory and eclectic tastes of 1960s music fans made their way to radio. The stations that played album tracks generally had no rules and no playlists. They mostly operated on a shoestring budget, selling inexpensive ads to local retailers, restaurants, and youth-oriented businesses.

In San Francisco in 1968, Tom Donahue, a disc jockey on FM station KMPX, began playing album rock tracks rather than hit singles. The format, called progressive rock or free form (because each DJ programmed his or her own show, often following individual tastes and playing an eclectic mix of music), spread from city to city within a year. Caught with their proverbial pants down, the record companies realized that there were album sales to be made to a young audience, but the labels didn't have ears for this new music. They signed many locally popular artists, recorded their debut albums, and then awaited public reaction. The major labels such as Columbia, Capitol, Decca, and RCA and the small or medium-sized independents were releasing albums by bands like Ultimate Spinach from Boston, the Flock from Chicago, Kaleidoscope from Los Angeles, and the 13th Floor Elevators from Austin. The records might do well or not sell at all, but the labels threw them into the marketplace to see what this mysterious new youth culture would embrace.

Because of the influence of English bands like the Yardbirds, John Mayall and the Bluesbreakers, Fleetwood Mac, and Cream and American bands like the Paul Butterfield Blues Band and Canned Heat, a new genre called blues rock, often built around guitar heroes, became popular. These bands developed followings and found a home at progressive rock stations.

The peak years of this radio format were 1970, 1971, and 1972, the same time I started Alligator. When progressive rock radio began to surge, I begged Bob Koester for promotional copies of new Delmark releases to send to these stations. "I give out two hundred promo copies," he told me, "and that's all." Because he had come into the blues world as a jazz fan (Delmark's blues series was called *Roots of Jazz*), Bob tended to send promotional copies to jazz radio programmers and jazz magazines like *DownBeat*, but not to rock radio programmers or new rock-centered publications like *Rolling Stone*. He had an established promo list, and every new blues release went to the same people. Bob was promoting to a small group of existing media and fans but not trying to reach new ones.

I knew there was a bigger audience out there just waiting to hear this music. It was an audience of young white adults like me who had discovered the blues in their dorm rooms rather than on commercial radio. Now they were listening to the new free-form progressive rock stations. But Delmark and other blues labels were ignoring those stations. When I started Alligator, I was determined to focus on this radio format to launch Hound Dog Taylor's record.

In late 1970, I had convinced Bob Koester to have the Jazz Record Mart sponsor a two-hour Wednesday night blues show on Triad Radio. I was the host. Triad was a small communal group that bought airtime from 10 p.m. to 2 a.m. every night on a powerful Chicago FM station, WXFM. A fascinating experiment in free-form radio, Triad played everything—psychedelic music by Tonto's Expanding Head Band, John Coltrane's exploratory jazz, folk tunes, and Beatles songs. Triad was looser and weirder than the other two free-form FM stations in the area, WGLD and WLS-FM. I began playing blues records on Triad and plugging Jazz Record Mart.

One night I arrived at the station and met Augie Blume, a colorful, experienced, independent radio promotion man who was traveling around the country, pushing a new release by Jefferson Starship. After mentioning to Augie that I was getting ready to start a record label, I asked him where I could find a list of stations and shows similar to WGLD, WLS-FM, and Triad. He told me about *Walrus*, a Philadelphia-based publication that listed what progressive rock stations around the country were playing. Discovering *Walrus* was like finding a treasure map.

As my plans to record Hound Dog and launch Alligator came together in spring of 1971, I began putting together a target list of stations. Having done a blues show on my hundred-watt university radio station, I had assumed that virtually every college station would consider airing a blues record. Now, with *Walrus* as a guide, I could also find progressive rock stations that might be open to a blues record like Hound Dog's. I knew that most of the DJs working these stations were within a year or two of my age. Most had heard the Paul Butterfield Blues Band, John Mayall, and Eric Clapton and maybe even Muddy Waters and Howlin' Wolf. I thought that I could relate to some of these DJs. Augie Blume had shown me how important relationship building was to the business of getting airplay. A little blues was part of the programming of most progressive rock stations, but I knew they were not getting releases from labels like Delmark and Arhoolie.

Radio airplay was necessary for publicizing the record and building demand, but it couldn't get the record into stores. For that I would need powerful distributors who could convince the major record stores and chains to stock my lone album. Most of Delmark's distributors were small companies that specialized in folk, jazz, and blues. But in Chicago, Delmark was distributed by Summit Distributors, an independent company that distributed fifty or sixty different labels, including big pop labels like A&M, Buddah, and United Artists. Delmark was a tiny part of their business. Whenever Summit put in an order for Delmark, I loaded LPs into my old Rambler and drove to the Summit office in Skokie, a Chicago suburb. Seymour Greenspan and Jack White ran Summit and were well respected among independent distributors. Seymour took a liking to me. I told him about my plans and asked for the names of distributors like Summit in other markets. He gave me a list of companies across the country that he thought I should approach and the names of his friends who ran them. By the time I finished Hound Dog's album, I had a list of target radio stations and a list of target distributors.

My simple plan was to visit a city, convince the progressive rock and college stations to play my record, and then visit the targeted distributor in the area. I would tell them that I had airplay on local stations and ask them to take on distribution of my one-record label. I already had friends at Chicago's larger progressive rock stations, WGLD and WLS-FM. Both stations began to play Hound Dog's record as soon as it was released, especially "Give Me Back My Wig." Hearing Hound Dog on the radio was an indescribable thrill. Of course I played it myself on my Triad show.

I took a leave of absence from Delmark, delivered a hundred LPs to Summit for local distribution, put the remaining nine hundred copies in the back of my newly purchased Chevy Vega station wagon, and hit the road with my girlfriend, Bea. For three weeks I drove from city to city, station to station, distributor to distributor, trying to create a market for *Hound Dog Taylor and the HouseRockers*.

The first day established the model for the whole trip. After visiting a couple of college stations along the way, we arrived in Ann Arbor, Michigan. There I talked WNRZ into some airplay. Later that night, we stopped at WABX in Detroit, where I met a DJ named Jim Dulzo. "I made a record of my favorite blues band," I explained earnestly. "I'd love it if you would play it." Instead of saying, "I have to consult my music director" or asking, "What other stations are playing it?" he said something like, "Far out, man." He brought me into the studio and played "Give Me Back My Wig" and "Taylor's Rock," then put me on the air to talk about Hound Dog. After visiting WABX we drove a few miles to WRIF. I pitched the DJ about to go on the air, gave a copy of the record to him, and then drove back to WABX to meet the DJ who came on after Jim Dulzo. I slept for a few hours in my car, then went back to catch the morning host at WRIF. I drove back and forth between these stations, meeting every DJ. Each one played Hound Dog at least once. Finally, I went to my targeted distributor, Record Distributing Corp., and met the owner, Armen Boladian. "I'm getting airplay on WNRZ, WABX, and WRIF," I told him. "Summit in Chicago is distributing this record. Would you be interested in distributing it in the Detroit area?" The radio airplay and the deal with

Summit gave me instant credibility. Boladian agreed to distribute the record and took a hundred copies from the back of my car.

From there we went on to Cleveland, Buffalo, Albany, Hartford, and Boston, repeating this tactic in each city. We slept in my car or at cheap motels. In Boston, I visited WBCN and stayed around the clock to meet each DJ going on the air. As a result of WBCN airplay, Boston became a major market for Hound Dog, who played there regularly over the next four years. From Boston I headed down the East Coast, visiting New York, Philadelphia, and Washington, DC. Everywhere I went the DJs were receptive (although New York was especially tough; the stations there were worried about higher ratings as they were trying to attract national advertisers).

As I traveled, I built credibility with broadcasters by naming stations in other cities that were already playing the record. The DJs loved Hound Dog's music, with its complete lack of slickness. The album cover, showing him grinning and playing his ultra-cheap guitar, was a funky image that helped reinforce the story. Before we could make it to Washington, I ran out of records for the distributors. Having talked the Cleveland distributor into advancing a little money to me, I phoned Musical Products and placed an order for a thousand more copies. By blues standards, I had a hit.

Besides targeting progressive rock radio, I tried to make an impact with a new kind of publication. As progressive rock radio was emerging, dozens of rock magazines and local entertainment newspapers sprang up. All these publications included record reviews, and all were directed at the same demographic as progressive rock radio. I had assembled lists of them, typed labels on my manual typewriter, and mailed out a copy of Hound Dog's album to each one before leaving on my East Coast promotional trip. As soon as I returned, I followed up on the phone, getting to know the music journalists personally. My persistence led to heaps of glowing reviews. The biggest early print media triumph came when *Rolling Stone* devoted a full-page article to Hound Dog.[5]

5. James Litke, "Hound Dog: Why I Rock the Blues," *Rolling Stone*, September 12, 1974, 28.

5

Shortly after returning from my three-week promotion trip, I received a call from Dick Waterman, the highly respected manager and booking agent for Buddy Guy, Junior Wells, Son House, Mississippi Fred McDowell, and a young Bonnie Raitt. Dick and some friends had founded the Boston Blues Society, and they wanted to bring Hound Dog and the band out for some college gigs in the first week of December 1971.[1] They offered shows for Hound Dog at Yale University, Harvard University, and the University of Massachusetts at Amherst. They would pay four hundred dollars a night, which was big money for Hound Dog. Plus, they would put up the band free of charge. At my suggestion, they also landed Hound Dog a gig at Trinity College in Hartford, Connecticut, with the help of a DJ at WRTC, the college station. This would be my first real road tour with a band. I was beyond excited.

Because of his day job working on the loading dock at Montgomery Ward's, Ted Harvey was unable to go. Scar-faced drummer Levi Warren agreed to fill in. We set out in his ancient Cadillac, which was large enough to carry a basic drum kit, two guitars (amps were being provided), luggage, the three members of the band, and me. I did most of the driving, generally being the soberest occupant of the car. The first gig was in a majestic, oak-trimmed dining hall at

---

1. The Boston Blues Society's board also included Peter Guralnick, perhaps the most acclaimed music author of his generation, and Scott Billington, who would become an outstanding producer for Rounder Records.

Yale in New Haven. Hound Dog quickly decided that it was his job to turn the hallowed halls of the Ivy League into Florence's Lounge. He succeeded. Within minutes, he had the students on their feet, boogieing. They never sat down again.

That night we stayed in the student apartment of Kit Rachlis (who later held top posts at the *Village Voice* and *LA Weekly*) and Jeff Boutwell (who became an expert in international nuclear security and served in the Carter administration). They had an acoustic guitar that Hound Dog borrowed for the night. When he came down the next morning, he proudly announced, "I wrote a song." Then he played and sang "Sadie," which went on to become one of his most-requested tunes. Hound Dog's songwriting usually started with a groove that he performed live, followed by a phrase or two of lyrics that would eventually develop into full verses. But "Sadie" was composed from start to finish, a big accomplishment for someone who could barely read or write.

Later that day, as we drove into Hartford for the Trinity College gig, both motor mounts on the Cadillac broke, and the car began shaking violently. We pulled into a service station, where the sympathetic owner guaranteed that the car would be fixed by the next morning. I called WRTC for help, and soon a VW Microbus full of students came to pick us up. (Four years later, I married one of the students, Jan Loveland.) The next morning, after another successful show, we returned to the service station to retrieve the car. We planned to continue on to Boston, where Hound Dog had been invited to perform live on WBCN early that afternoon. When we fired up the engine, we discovered that the car's oil pan had been dented while the mechanics were working to repair the engine mounts. The crankshaft balancer was banging against the inside of the oil pan, so the car wasn't drivable. We all scrambled to fix it, tearing out the steering gear to get to the oil pan and beating out the dent with a two-by-four. Then all five of us feverishly reassembled it.

Determined not to miss the broadcast, I drove on the Massachusetts Turnpike at literally a hundred miles per hour from Hartford to Boston. Brewer Phillips was so terrified that he got completely drunk and passed out on the back seat. At WBCN I had to dump water on his face to wake him up to play. Then it was off to Harvard, where the band set up in front of a Christmas tree in another dining hall. When they came out to play, Hound Dog was bareheaded. One of the students hollered, "Where's your hat?" Hound Dog went back to the dressing room to retrieve it. After that night, he rarely appeared hatless. In the Florence's spirit, Dick Waterman showed up with a jug of Wild Turkey to share with the band. At the end of the night, there was still some left. Much to the band's dismay, Dick took the partially full bottle home. It never occurred to them that it was not a gift to be consumed to completion. Boston became Hound Dog's most regular out-of-town stop, where he played week-long stands at a club called Joe's Place.[2] A smashing success, Hound Dog's first New England tour created a dedicated student audience that came out to see him whenever he was in the region. They had fallen in love with his Genuine Houserockin' Music just like I had.

In 1971, I knew of no booking agents who would be interested in representing an almost-unknown blues musician, so I reluctantly became Hound Dog's booking agent. Booking was not my greatest strength. I had a little plastic box of file cards on my "desk" (actually a coffee table that I found in a dumpster) where I worked while sitting on my mattress on the floor of my efficiency apartment. The cards had the names and phone numbers of club bookers and the few blues festivals. Some of the out-of-town clubs I called would book Hound Dog, but not many.

In the late winter of 1972, Roy Filson, a student at the University of Illinois in Champaign who later became Alligator's first employee, contacted me. The Student Activities Committee wanted to book a Hound Dog show at the student union. We named the event the First Annual Hound Dog Taylor Boogie-Rama, and two more Boogie-Ramas followed in 1973 and 1974. As a result, Hound Dog drew student crowds whenever he came to Champaign.

---

2. I later obtained a tape of the Harvard show. It was just as good as I remembered. Three of the best tracks appear on the *Release the Hound* album.

College towns became a staple of Hound Dog's touring. He developed a devoted following at the Kove in Kent, Ohio, and the Blind Pig in Ann Arbor, Michigan. He was a favorite at Friday's Child in Des Moines, Iowa. He played weeklong gigs at the El Mocambo in Toronto. He also performed at the occasional blues festival, although there were not many at that time. Hound Dog played at the Ann Arbor Blues Festival in 1970, and returned in 1972 and 1973, when his debut album had become well known to the audience. Hound Dog was thrilled to be performing at a national event with Muddy Waters, Bobby "Blue" Bland, and other musicians he admired. In 1971, Hound Dog had been a poorly paid South Side club musician. Suddenly he was sharing stages with the biggest names in blues. At the age of fifty-five, his life had changed dramatically.

Hound Dog wasn't touring all the time. He continued to play the Expressway Lounge, Florence's, and other South Side clubs. He was also performing now on the North Side of Chicago at places like Minstrel's Pub on Sheridan Road, the Wise Fools Pub on Lincoln Avenue, and Alice's Revisited on Wrightwood Street, just downstairs from the offices of the *Chicago Seed* where we typed *Living Blues*.

His life had changed, but his shows hadn't. Hound Dog still played the same kind of unrehearsed, fly-by-the-seat-of-your-pants shows for North Side and college town audiences as he did for the Florence's crowd. There were nights when he was pretty drunk and the music was extremely loose, but his fans tended to get wasted with him. If there was trouble, it was usually between Hound Dog and Brewer Phillips; their constant "just for fun" arguing sometimes turned all too serious. One night Hound Dog called me from the Kove at one o'clock in the morning and said, "I just gave somebody a hundred dollars to kill Phillips." Then he hung up. I hoped it was too low a price.

On another occasion, I left the band on their own for a weeklong gig at the Chicken Box, a club on Nantucket Island, while I took the opportunity to visit some East Coast radio stations. I returned on the last night and went directly to their gig. There I discovered

Hound Dog and Brewer outside the club in a standoff, with their knives out, circling each other. I had no idea what the argument was about. I stood between them and pulled the contract out of my jacket. "You can't kill each other," I said. "You've got another set." Relieved to have an excuse not to murder each other, they put away their knives and headed back into the club for the last set. By the end of the night, the argument was forgotten.

In 1973, Hound Dog fulfilled a dream by opening a show for B. B. King at a big theater in St. Louis. We drove down to St. Louis with Hound Dog listening over and over again to a B. B. King eight-track tape. Although they didn't know each other, B.B., with his remarkably gracious manner, came to Hound Dog's dressing room before the show to say hello. That's not something a headliner typically does. During his set, Hound Dog didn't play as much slide as usual and didn't boogie like he normally did, leaning more to slow blues. He must have been thinking, "I'm playing for B. B. King fans, so I should sound like B. B. King." It's hard to imagine any blues musician less likely to sound like B. B. King than Hound Dog Taylor. It wasn't his best show.

A few months later, B.B. was performing at Chicago's London House, a posh downtown supper club. It was the kind of upscale venue that B.B. often played at that time. After all, he was the only bluesman who had appeared on *The Tonight Show*. Hound Dog and I decided to go and stand at the bar in the back where there was no cover charge. From the other end of the club, B.B. spotted Hound Dog and said to the audience, "Ladies and gentlemen, we've got a wonderful blues musician in the house. How about a nice round of applause for the great Hound Dog Taylor?" Hound Dog was thrilled and flabbergasted to be treated like a star. Then B.B. started a slow blues. He sang one of the oldest blues lyrics known: *I can hear my black name ringing all up and down the line.* This is a lyric that goes back into the annals of time: if you hear your name ringing up and down the line of laborers picking cotton, that means trouble—people are talking about you.

In singing that song, B. B. King reached out over the hundred and fifty white businessmen in suits and women in gowns and spoke directly to Hound Dog Taylor. "Even in this slick place, where most people are just having dinner and being entertained," B.B. seemed to be saying, "there's something in this music that you and I understand and feel, something that nobody else here has an inkling of." I stand in awe of B. B. King for doing something that personal, something that bold. To speak of their blackness and their mutual heritage of oppression in that lily-white situation took both nerve and depth of being. I'll never forget it.

I certainly wasn't unique in starting an independent record label to record my favorite music. Three students living in a ramshackle communal house in Cambridge, Massachusetts, founded Rounder Records. They started by recording an obscure old-time banjo player named George Pegram. Rounder slowly turned into an independent powerhouse, eventually selling millions of records by George Thorogood and by the duo of Alison Krauss and Robert Plant. There were folk labels like Symposium and Red House in Minneapolis. John Fahey's Takoma label specialized in acoustic guitar music, and Gene Rosenthal's Adelphi label recorded blues and reggae. Chuck Nessa's Nessa Records specialized in avant-garde jazz. Blind Pig Records founders Jerry Del Giudice and Edward Chmelewski started their blues label out of a bar they owned in Ann Arbor. Bruce Kaplan ran his folk and bluegrass label, Flying Fish Records, from his run-down Chicago house. Other Chicago blues fans founded labels, such as Mark Lefens's Razor Records, Bob Corritore's Blues on Top of Blues, George Paulus's Barrelhouse Records, and Jim O'Neal's Rooster Blues.

Most of the blues labels were part-time operations that the proprietors ran while holding down day jobs. Alligator was one of the few that became a full-time business, but it was very much a hand-to-mouth business. For the first fourteen years, I ran Alligator from wherever I was living—first a one-room apartment, then a two-room apartment, and finally a small house.

Previous generations of niche music fans had created the models for small specialized labels. Delmark began in the early 1950s when Bob Koester, still a college student, recorded traditional jazz bands in St. Louis. His first blues recording was by Speckled Red, a piano player who had cut 78s in the 1920s. Arhoolie, the label founded by Chris Strachwitz in his home in Berkeley, California, in 1960, began with a recording by Texas country bluesman Mance Lipscomb, followed shortly by the Mississippi Fred McDowell album that my local record store in Wisconsin had searched to find.

All these independents found their niches as a result of historical changes in the record industry. In the early years of the record business, small labels were founded all over the country. Blues recording took place in such varied locations as Grafton, Wisconsin; Richmond, Indiana; Atlanta, Georgia; and New York City. Some labels sent representatives on field trips to record in the Deep South. During the Depression, many small companies went out of business, like Paramount in Wisconsin, which had recorded Son House, Skip James, and Charley Patton. Some were bought out by bigger companies, as when Columbia Records purchased the American Record Company, which had recorded Robert Johnson.

From 1942 through 1944, a musicians' union strike virtually halted commercial recording because the union realized that records (for which musicians at that time normally didn't receive royalties) were going to dominate radio, forcing live music off the air and thus putting musicians out of work. After World War II and the end of the strike, Columbia, Decca, and RCA ruled as the giants of the record industry, along with a few new upstarts like Capitol Records (founded in 1942). The big labels' emphasis on popular hits left openings in the marketplace for ethnic music and niche genres like blues, jazz, and country. A number of small independent labels sprang up to reach these markets. Immigrant Jews, often barred from executive jobs in larger corporations, founded many of the independents, especially in the blues and R&B genres.

Every major American city had its own independent labels, often recording local or regional artists. These labels would hustle for local airplay and hope that one of the larger indie labels would hear the buzz and license their local hit for national distribution. In Los Angeles, the Bihari brothers ran Modern, Crown, and RPM Records, and the Mesner brothers operated Aladdin. In New York, Bob Shad had the Sittin' In With label, Florence Greenberg operated Tiara (later the Wand and Scepter labels), and Hy Weiss ran Old Town. In Cincinnati, the colorful Syd Nathan ran King, Queen, and Federal Records, making "records for the little man" that included not only blues and R&B but also country and bluegrass. And of course, the famous Chess brothers in Chicago were recording bluesmen Muddy Waters, Howlin' Wolf, and Sonny Boy Williamson II, as well as doo-woppers like the Moonglows, jazz musicians like Ahmad Jamal and Ramsey Lewis, and rock and rollers like Chuck Berry and Bo Diddley. Not all the independent R&B record entrepreneurs were Jewish. Ahmet and Nesuhi Ertegun, two Turkish Americans, ran Atlantic Records, and Sam Phillips founded the Sun label in Memphis. Even underfinanced African American entrepreneurs succeeded, like Vivian Carter and Jimmy Bracken of Vee-Jay Records in Chicago; Bobby Robinson, who operated the Fire and Fury labels in Harlem; and, of course, Berry Gordy, who founded Motown in Detroit.

These labels competed for space in a musical landscape that the bigger labels didn't want to inhabit: black music for black people, "hillbilly" music for southern-rooted whites, jazz music for jazz fans, and foreign language recordings. From the point of view of the larger labels, these audiences were too small to care about; their music didn't have enough sales potential. The major labels wanted Perry Como, cast albums of Rodgers and Hammerstein musicals, Liberace, Johnny Ray, and, later on, Elvis. The burst of energy from independent record entrepreneurs in the late 1940s through the 1950s helped usher in rock and roll, a type of music that the big labels initially didn't perceive as having much commercial potential. Sam Phillips at Sun Records was just a small-time businessman recording blues and rockabilly until Elvis suddenly made it onto mainstream radio. Only then did the eyes and ears of the big labels open to rock and roll.

Most of the independent labels launched in the 1940s and 1950s were chasing that elusive hit, even if a "hit" actually meant selling only a few thousand copies as a result of radio play in their hometown. But not every independent label was searching for a hit. Beneath the radar, a folk music revival was growing. This music was recorded on little indie labels like Folkways and Stinson Records. A new recognition of traditional blues was part of this movement, with leftists bringing the Louisiana ex-convict Lead Belly to perform in New York and embracing veteran blues and gospel guitarist, singer, and songwriter Josh White. The hugely popular folk group the Weavers emerged from the organization People's Songs, and the folk music boom was born. Following in the footsteps of Moe Asch of Folkways Records, entrepreneurs created new labels like Elektra and Vanguard to record folk music, bluegrass, ethnic music, and sometimes blues. Usually operated by one or two fans who were seriously committed to the music, these folk labels were the precursors to my generation of genre-centered labels.

Distribution was one of the keys to success. Before the days of overnight delivery services and lighter, harder-to-break compact discs, having a national distributor with warehousing in one city that shipped to stores all over the country was impractical. Vinyl records were heavy and expensive to ship, and they warped if they got hot. And if the record label had a hit, inventory needed to be put into stores instantly. Every major city therefore had multiple record distributors selling singles and LPs to thousands of locally owned record stores and regional chains. The hit-driven independent labels like Chess were sought out by distributors whose business model was selling tens or hundreds of thousands of singles and albums. But the hit-driven distributors weren't interested in little labels catering to niche markets like folk, blues, bluegrass, and experimental jazz.

As the new generation of small genre-centered independent labels was born, new local independent distributors were established. Typically these were one-person companies that bought twenty-five or fifty copies of a record from an independent label and took them to local record stores, saying, "Let's put in a couple and see what happens." Companies like Riverboat Records in Boston, Adelphi Records in Washington, DC, Orwaka Records in the Pacific Northwest (the name stood for Oregon, Washington, and Alaska), Tant Distribution in Michigan, Silo Inc. in Vermont, and dozens more sprang up to sell labels like Delmark, Rounder, and Takoma. Some of the distributors were also retailers. These small distributors came and went, as their owners realized that selling nonpop LPs earned only small (or no) profits. They also discovered that retailers, who were operating on small profit margins, didn't want to get stuck with unsellable records, so they expected to have the right to return any unsold albums for credit, as they could do with the bigger distributors. If a record didn't sell, the store returned it to the distributor, which then returned it to the label. Record stores, distributors, and labels failed with depressing regularity.

When I founded Alligator, the only label that I had as a model was Delmark. There were a lot of new independent labels and independent distributors springing up at the time, each one facing similar challenges. If we could figure out how to share information and learn from each other's experiences, we would have a better chance of surviving.

In November 1971, the owners of eleven small, independent distributors and labels, including Alligator, gathered in the dank basement meeting room of a Minneapolis motel. Our goal was to form a self-help organization for the small independent labels and distributors. We first called it the National Association of Independent Record Distributors (NAIRD). Later, we added "and Manufacturers" to the name at the insistence of the labels. The organization quickly grew from eleven members to forty and then from forty to more than a hundred labels and distributors. Almost none of the large pop-oriented indie labels joined. Most members of NAIRD were niche labels specializing in jazz, folk, blues, bluegrass, and other nonmainstream genres. The majority of the distributor members were small operations that carried a hundred or more of these little labels.

The NAIRD conventions became essential opportunities for label owners to sit down with distributors and plot merchandising tactics and sales programs for upcoming releases. They were also essential forums for labels to share information with one another. In the 1970s and 1980s, labels like Alligator often had twenty or more distributors around the country; almost all of them attended the NAIRD conventions. As labels, we learned about key local stores from our distributors, who planted ideas with us for how we might achieve more visibility and sales, including discount programs and display contests. We discussed overseas marketing, radio promotion, and publicity. NAIRD also became a forum for new labels to learn the business from more experienced entrepreneurs. As the organization grew, the annual convention was filled with educational workshops and panels as well as deal making behind closed doors.

In the early years, NAIRD was a wild and woolly organization. Distributors in adjoining territories were constantly trying to steal retail accounts from one another (a practice called trans-shipping that wasn't illegal but was controversial). Feuds between competing companies became very personal, and fights occurred regularly at the conventions. At the Memphis convention in 1972, my Washington, DC, distributor, Gene Rosenthal, who also owned the Adelphi label, slugged Bill Barth of the Kicking Mule label. At our Kansas City convention, a distributor decked Gene Rosenthal's salesman brother, Howard. Along with the old-school violence, some of NAIRD's members also incorporated old-school sex into their business practices. At the Denver meeting, which was only the organization's third convention, one label owner brought in a couple of hookers to create goodwill with his distributors. We were shocked; this kind of practice had been normal in the hit-driven, cigar-chomping record industry of the 1950s and 1960s but was anathema to the young hippies and old hipsters at the core of NAIRD.

Chris Strachwitz of Arhoolie Records was elected the first president of the organization, but it quickly became apparent that no single person could run it. A board and an executive committee were created, but that arrangement didn't work either. The organization needed full-time staff, but with its tiny dues (so even the smallest companies could afford to join), the money wasn't available. Finally, Jerry Richman, an old-style record man who owned Richman Brothers Records, a distributor in Philadelphia, began taking money out of his company and pumping it into the organization. His wife, Sunny Richman, a smart, tough woman who often wore tiaras and had a background as a teachers' union organizer, became executive director. She and her staff, who were all Richman Brothers employees, ran the organization for a number of years.

Eventually NAIRD (which was later renamed the Association for Independent Music, or AFIM) grew large enough to be self-supporting. Pat Bradley, a former small-label owner, became full-time executive director. The organization's Indie Awards ceremony grew into a fancy evening event, and educational panels were staffed by industry bigwigs, not just fellow members. At its peak, about four hundred people attended the conventions. But beginning in the 1990s, the need to meet with multiple regional distributors lessened as most labels moved to national distribution. Membership shrank. The office closed and AFIM returned to being run by the board of directors.

I served on that board for twenty-six years, through the birth, growth, thriving, shrinking, and finally the shutting down in 2004 of NAIRD/AFIM. During that time, the organization helped hundreds of indie labels and dozens of distributors run their businesses more successfully. Alligator might not have survived without the business knowledge gathered from other members. As I matured from naive newbie to veteran record man, I was happy to share my experience. As I said to newer label owners, "I don't want you to make the same mistakes I made. I want you to make fresh, new mistakes."

I made my own share of mistakes, of course. I also learned that even when you try to do things right, you can run up against other people's preconceptions and grievances. One of the first things I learned when I entered the blues world was that every musician was suspicious of every record label. Basically, they thought label owners were crooks. Most were convinced their records had sold thousands (or millions) of copies and the record labels had become rich while they received nothing. Many musicians who had made records had never seen a royalty statement. Seeing a royalty check was even rarer. There have been plenty of crooks in the record business, and I believe a disproportionate number of black artists have been victims of these crooks. One of the most important things I ever did was to give Hound Dog his first royalties (in cash; he had no checking account) in early 1972. Within days, every blues musician in Chicago knew that "the hippie" paid royalties. It established my credibility all over the South and West Sides. I was determined to avoid getting a reputation as another rip-off record man. I vowed that Alligator would be scrupulous about royalty accounting. Since 1971, every Alligator artist and song publisher has received a royalty statement every six months, and, if money is due, a check.

Nonetheless, I've been accused of being a crook. As was probably inevitable, I've also been accused of being a racist. This happened when some critics, including some musicians, reacted to a remark I made in an interview in the *Chicago Reader* in May 2011. What they didn't see in the article was the full text of my conversation with the interviewer, especially the specific wording of the questions to which I was responding. Enduring those public accusations, which seemed patently unfair and based on a misunderstanding of my words, was perhaps the most painful episode of my career, and I won't rehash it here. I will say only that Alligator's business practices and our treatment of all our artists, black and white, should speak for themselves.

6

By late 1971, my approach to promoting *Hound Dog Taylor and the HouseRockers*, exhausting though it was, had paid off. In the first few months of release, I sold almost nine thousand records, which by the standards of Delmark or Arhoolie was phenomenal. This modest success gave me hope that with tireless promotion the audience for blues record sales could be greatly expanded. Alligator's next two albums, by Big Walter Horton and Son Seals, threw a lot of cold water on my hopes and plans for reaching that larger market. At the same time, both these albums helped me grow as a producer.

I knew even before making my first record what I wanted my second one to be. A couple weeks after seeing Hound Dog at Florence's for the first time, I returned with some Swedish blues fans who were staying with me. They had been in touch with harmonica player Big Walter Horton and asked me to pick him up on the way to the club. Although I didn't know Big Walter personally, I had seen him perform at the 1966 Mariposa Folk Festival (the same festival where I purchased the copy of *Hoot* magazine that led me to the Jazz Record Mart). I had bought a number of his records, including *The Soul of Blues Harmonica*, his rather disappointing album on Argo (a Chess subsidiary), and *Chicago Blues*, on Arhoolie, on which he was featured accompanying Johnny Young. I had also heard a reissue of Walter's classic single "Hard Hearted Woman" on *Chicago Blues: The Early 1950's*, an LP released on Arhoolie's reissue label, Blues Classics. Walter's delicate, melodic playing fascinated me.[1]

We picked Walter up outside his run-down three-story apartment building on 31st Street overlooking the Dan Ryan expressway. Battered and gray, with missing teeth and scars around his eyes, he was well known as a hard drinker. He looked much older than his real age of fifty-two. It was hard to believe he could still play. At Florence's we were joined by Walter's protégé, Carey Bell, who at thirty-four was one of Chicago's best younger harp players. A sweet-tempered, outgoing guy with a gap-toothed smile, he had cut his debut album for Delmark, *Carey Bell's Blues Harp*, in 1969.

Walter, always nervous in the company of strangers, was clearly happy to see his friend Carey. Hound Dog invited them both to sit in on a basic shuffle. Standing side by side, each with a harmonica, Carey and Walter passed a microphone back and forth as they began to compete musically. Carey played a lick and Walter would repeat and embellish it, each challenging the other to greater heights of spontaneous creativity. As the contest grew more intense, they wrapped their arms around one another's shoulders and, still playing, danced up and down the aisle of Florence's. I was riveted. I knew immediately that I wanted to capture the magic of their performance in the studio. This became one of my dreams, second only to my dream of recording Hound Dog. With the success of Hound Dog's debut album, I had enough money to take Walter into the studio in early 1972.

I knew that recording Walter was not going to be as easy as

---

1. Most blues fans would name four harmonica players as the greatest of all time. John Lee "Sonny Boy" Williamson (aka Sonny Boy Williamson I) was the first blues harmonica player to have hit records with black consumers. He was murdered in 1948 in Chicago. The more famous "Rice" Miller (aka Sonny Boy Williamson II), whose first name may have been Aleck or Willie, began recording for Trumpet Records in Mississippi in 1951 after performing the King Biscuit Time radio show in Helena, Arkansas. He later recorded for Chess in Chicago and toured Europe and the UK. Little Walter Jacobs, the visionary Chicago master, first gained fame as a member of Muddy Waters's band before recording as a leader in 1952. He was easily the most influential and copied blues harp player ever. The fourth was Big Walter Horton.

recording Hound Dog. Walter had a reputation for being erratic. Many fans thought he had passed his peak, his undeniable talent stolen by alcoholism. He was a physically and emotionally scarred man. Life had been hard on him, and he had developed ways of shielding his vulnerability. One was by drinking. Acting the clown was another. He said strange things, called everybody "grandpa," and told tangled, often indecipherable stories without any apparent point or conclusion. People thought he was just plain crazy. Like his personality, Walter's harp tone was vulnerable. It quivered with a warm, woody vibrato that distinguished him from most other harp players. "If Little Walter played harmonica like a tenor saxophone," somebody once said, "Big Walter played it like a bass clarinet."

Wanting to create an emotional safety net for Walter in the recording studio as well as capture the two harp masters' musical "father and son" chemistry, I first asked Carey to join the project before approaching Walter. Carey happily agreed. Even with Carey's participation secured, Walter was willing but anxious. He had no band and was not a natural bandleader. His most regular gig was with famed songwriter and bass player Willie Dixon's Chicago Blues All-Stars, a band that didn't perform regularly in clubs. They played mostly festivals and European tours. When I asked Walter whom he wanted to record with, Walter immediately named guitarist Eddie Taylor, a childhood friend from Walter's years in Memphis. Eddie was a highly respected Chicago blues player who was always in demand as a sideman and who had made some classic recordings on his own. I knew Eddie would put Walter in his comfort zone. Walter also named the capable Frank Swan, the drummer who was playing with Willie Dixon's band. I suggested Joe Harper, the bassist from Carey and Eddie's West Side aggregation. Wanting a piano on the record, I proposed respected blues veteran Sunnyland Slim. Walter adamantly disagreed. As he explained it, Sunnyland played "those opera changes." Never having heard Sunnyland play *La Traviata*, I had no idea what Walter was talking about. He suggested instead Aaron "Slim" Moore, a musician I had never heard of and couldn't

locate. I later found out he was Koko Taylor's garbage man. In the
end, we recorded without a piano player.

I planned to cut the album in two evenings, the same way I had
recorded Hound Dog. We rehearsed a couple of times, with Walter
pulling out some obscure songs that I didn't know. But once we got
to Sound Studios, Walter didn't want to record any of the rehearsed
songs; he hardly seemed to remember them. He insisted on cutting some songs he had recorded before, like "Have a Good Time"
and "That Ain't It," a familiar Jimmy Rogers composition. He also
chose a song he had been performing for years called "Little Boy
Blue," supposedly a Robert Johnson composition that Johnson had
never recorded. So our rehearsals went out the window, along with
my confidence, and the sessions became uncomfortably improvisational. I didn't know what was going to happen. I was downright
scared. Walter was nervous about everything, especially his singing;
he wanted to cut primarily instrumentals whereas I was hoping for
more vocals. Walter's voice was scarred like his face, but it made him
a soulful singer with intense blues feeling. I had to keep encouraging
him to sing. I was trying to be a psychologist at the same time I was
trying to be a record producer, prodding and begging Walter to deliver while complimenting him every time things went well.

Fortunately, Carey Bell stepped in whenever Walter got scared.
Each time recording threatened to come to a halt, Carey sat down
next to Walter and blew a riff in his ear. "Bet you can't do this, old
man," he would say. With the gauntlet thrown down, Walter would
step up and start *really* bearing down. That's when he and Carey began to play off each other, re-creating the magical interaction I had
witnessed down at Florence's.

The session's most magical moment came during a break on the
second night. Sitting together in a corner of the studio, Walter and
Eddie began playing the old folk blues standard "Trouble in Mind,"
performing it with beautiful delicacy. At Stu Black's suggestion, we
recorded the song just as they had played it, with only the two of
them. In two takes we captured a magnificent musical love affair

between two old friends. I ended the record with that performance because nothing else could follow it. It will stand as one of the most memorable recordings of Walter's career and of Alligator's legacy.

As I prepared the release of the album, titled simply *Big Walter Horton with Carey Bell*, it became clear that I would no longer be able to work for Bob Koester and Delmark while also working for myself and Alligator. For a start, I was doing Alligator business on Bob's time. In 1972 Bob had moved Delmark to 4243 North Lincoln Avenue. He put in a little store in the front and a warehouse in the back, where there was room and ventilation enough to operate a plastic shrink-wrapping machine. Bob and his family lived upstairs. I came in every day, ran the shrink-wrapping machine, typed invoices, packed orders, and fielded phone calls for Delmark. But I also would arrive with cartons of Hound Dog albums ready to ship. When I went to the post office for Bob, I'd take the Alligator boxes and ship them at the same time. Bob even allowed me to receive some Alligator calls there. The only way I could do Alligator business during the day, especially booking dates for Hound Dog, was to take calls at Delmark. Bob was aware of all this, but amazingly, he kept paying me even while I was doing my own business under his roof.

Finally, in May of that year, Bob said, "Let's go to lunch." At the restaurant he laid it out for me by saying, "It's time for you to make a decision. Either you're working for me or you're working for yourself." I knew I couldn't stay. I needed to show Bob, show the world, and prove to myself, that there were thousands more people who would buy a blues record if it were publicized, marketed, and packaged properly. I said, "I've got to go work for myself." I stayed another week or two and then I was out on my own. Bob had carried me longer than I had any right to expect. I can't imagine him being more considerate, especially after having been such a tough taskmaster over the two and a half years I had worked for him. Perhaps he had begun to see me as his spiritual son, just as I considered him my spiritual father.

When I released Walter's album in June, I had a much harder time getting commercial rock airplay than I had with Hound Dog's.

Between fall 1971 and the summer 1972, progressive rock radio had begun to retract its free-form tentacles. Blues, jazz, traditional folk music, and twenty-minute psychedelic jams were all being pushed out as stations sought higher ratings and national advertisers. Plus, Walter's record was much more a traditional blues record than was Hound Dog's. Hound Dog's music was distorted, loud, energetic, and rocking. Rock fans could relate to it instantly. Walter's record was subtle; it revealed its wonders more with each listen. Subtlety is the enemy of commercial radio.

The 1973 record that followed Walter's, Alligator's third, was a shift in gears — the debut of Son Seals. If I had ever had the talent to be a bluesman, the one I would have chosen to be is Son. There are other musicians whose music I also love, but Son's music speaks to me like no one else's. I think it's because Son released a huge amount of anger through his music. Like Son, I've got a certain amount of anger and frustration that I've never quite resolved. He helped me let it out and let it go. His music does to me just what the blues is supposed to do: wring you out emotionally and leave you feeling cleansed. It's that quality of blues usually described as tension and release.

There was a lot about Son himself that I could relate to. He was only a few years older than I was and of a completely different generation than Hound Dog and Big Walter. Although he had grown up in Osceola, Arkansas (described by guitarist Michael Burks as "the most racist town in the Delta"), there wasn't much about him that was "country" in the way that Hound Dog and Walter were country. He didn't speak slowly or have that loose country way of walking and talking. He walked with a city swagger. Although he was a man of few words, he obviously had more formal education and was better spoken than the older musicians. Son had an air of confidence that I found very appealing. For me, a mark of many of the most charismatic blues musicians is how comfortable they are with themselves.

I first heard about him in 1971, when Wesley Race, my coproducer on Hound Dog's album, started raving about a fiery young guitar player named Son Seals whom he had seen sitting in with Hound

Dog. He played a reel-to-reel tape for me of Son performing "Mother-in-Law Blues" live at a club. It was an energized, raw performance of the Junior Parker song with super-aggressive guitar. Son's gruff singing completely abandoned Parker's smooth vocal approach. Then, one night that summer, while I was working in the Jazz Record Mart, Wes called me from a South Side club and had me listen to Son over the club's pay phone. Even over the phone, Son's passion and energy were obvious.

A few weeks later, I finally had a chance to see him live at the Expressway Lounge, where he was filling in for Hound Dog. A small club that had once been a store, the Expressway Lounge had no stage. With the drummer sitting in the display window, Son stood on the floor in front of the tables, playing for about thirty people. He was skinny, with a disheveled Afro haircut. His polyester pants didn't reach down to his shoes, and it looked like he had outgrown them years earlier. There were just three players: Son, a bass player, and a drummer. Most of the vocals were performed by Son's cousin Charles Turman, a singing mechanic known professionally as Mr. Leo. Son played with slash-and-burn physical intensity, his sound drenched in the kind of distortion only a cheap guitar can make. Although he didn't look threatening, he sounded like a guy you wouldn't want to meet in a dark alley. Unlike Hound Dog's music, which was such great fun, and unlike Big Walter's music, which was subtle and multilayered, Son's music was a brash, bold slap in the face. I became an instant fan. It was the beginning of a relationship that would last for more than thirty years and produce eight memorable albums.

I went back to see him a few weeks later and asked if he had any original songs. "I've got a whole notebook full of them," he told me. Though he was well aware that I had recorded Hound Dog, Son never tried to sell himself to me. As I got to know him, he told me his story. Jim Seals, his father, had been a trombone player and guitarist who had performed with the Rabbit Foot Minstrels, one of the most successful of the traveling tent shows that toured the South. He eventually settled in Osceola and raised thirteen children, with Son being the youngest. The family ran a juke joint called the Dipsy

Doodle Club out of their house.[2] On the weekends his family moved the furniture out of the front room, hired local musicians (with Son often acting as the house drummer), and served up white whiskey along with gambling. Son's first paid drumming gig was with Robert Nighthawk, a well-known southern blues musician who had been recording since the 1930s.

Son learned the ins and outs of gambling from his father. He told me that when he was first learning to play cards, he was too short to reach the table in the club without standing on something, and for his first poker game, he stood on a dead body. True story? I don't know. He became a masterful cards and dice player and won a lot of money gambling. In his teen years, Son took up guitar. His first road gig was playing rhythm guitar with the legendary Earl Hooker, a brilliant guitarist who rarely sang.[3] Son had also drummed with Albert King.[4]

Early on in our relationship, Son had a diabetic seizure in his basement apartment while I was visiting him. As we talked, his eyes suddenly rolled up and he fell, writhing and incoherent, to the floor. I was terrified. A friend and I took him to Cook County Hospital, where staff members strapped him down to a table to control his convulsions. I had never seen anything like it. I didn't know anything about diabetes, and looking back, I suppose he could have died right then. As with many blues musicians, alcohol was a regular part of Son's life. He didn't always drink, but when he did, his blood sugar could skyrocket. With his diabetes, his off-again, on-again drinking was a constant mortal danger.[5]

2. Son wasn't the only Alligator artist whose family ran a juke joint down south. Years later I signed Michael "Iron Man" Burks, whose family had built a club outside of Camden, Arkansas. Michael's father and grandfather were also bluesmen.

3. Earl was truly an itinerant musician. He moved back and forth between Chicago; Cairo, Illinois; Clarksdale, Mississippi; and various places in the Delta, putting together packages of musicians and promoting his own shows. He'd walk into a club and say, "I want to play here. I'll take the door, you can have the bar." Everybody knew him because he had done this for decades.

4. Son told me that he was the drummer on Albert's famous album *Live Wire/Blues Power*. This assertion has been disputed, but I did see him play drums, and he was a good drummer.

5. The musicians weren't the only people in the blues community who struggled with alcohol. Over my years of spending many nights in bars, alcohol became more and more a part of my

Son was a serious guy with a gruff manner, and some people were scared of him, which he found hilarious. As a teenager, Son had worked as a projectionist at the local movie theater in Osceola. It was segregated, of course, and black people were only permitted to sit in the balcony. Son loved westerns. His favorite cowboy actor was Bob Steele, whom he described as "a little guy who never walked away from a fight. And when he fought, his hat never came off." When I met Son he had an Afro, but soon he took to wearing cowboy hats. I think Son saw himself as the John Wayne of the blues, a man of few words, a man very comfortable in his own skin, a tough guy. There is a photo of Son in a cowboy hat next to life-size cutouts of the Lone Ranger and Tonto; he looks right at home.

I wouldn't describe Son Seals as one of the technically best blues guitar players. He was a unique stylist with a personal, distinctive sound and an aggressive attack. Like Albert King, he had his signature licks that showed up in a lot of his songs. But technique is not what blues is about. Touching the emotions is what blues is about, and that's what Son could do. Bumble Bee Bob Novak, one of the first generation of white Chicago blues players, once said, "The thing about the black guys, unlike the white guys, is that they play every note like they mean it." That was true for Son Seals. He played every note as though it was the most important note he was ever going to play.

Soon after I first saw Son perform live, I began talking to him seriously about recording. I met with him to look over his lyrics. He lived in the bare concrete-floored basement apartment of a run-down South Side four-story building. Son showed his notebook of songs to me, and we chose half a dozen for possible inclusion on the album. I wanted him to cut "Mother-in-Law Blues" because that was a high point of his live show. He had worked out fresh arrangements for "Going Home Tomorrow," a Fats Domino song, and "I'm a Lonely Man," a Little Milton tune. Besides his father, Son's big influences were Albert King on guitar (some people say Son played like

---

life. Eventually I was drinking every night, whether in a bar or by myself. I am happy to say that I've been clean and sober since 1995. It wasn't easy.

Albert King on speed) and Little Milton on vocals. Son also loved Junior Parker, though both Parker and Milton were much smoother singers than Son.

Son wasn't gigging enough to keep a steady band. For the studio, Son recruited bass player John Riley, who had played with him when he was with Albert King, and a good drummer named Charles Caldwell. I wanted keyboards (this would be the first time I would be recording them) and suggested Johnny "Big Moose" Walker, an outgoing, hard-driving player who was well known on the Chicago scene. Moose had been a member of Ike Turner and the Kings of Rhythm and had also toured with Earl Hooker. He was called Moose because he had a gigantic head and a flowing processed hairstyle that looked like a hurricane was blowing through it.

Moose had a friend who ran a dry cleaner in Chicago's Old Town neighborhood. He arranged to let us rehearse there after hours amid the clothes hanging on racks in plastic bags. In rehearsal, Son delivered all that passion that I had heard at the Expressway Lounge, including an ultra-raw guitar tone produced by his Norma guitar, a cheap brand sold by Montgomery Ward.[6] Son described his playing as a "scuffling" guitar style. He got a thick, dirty sound that filled up a lot of space, and he sang with that rough-hewn intensity I loved so much. He also had a dramatic falsetto that he sometimes used for effect when he was bearing down in the most intense part of a song.

We recorded *The Son Seals Blues Band* in two evening sessions at Sound Studios. Because they had rehearsed, Son and the band pounded through the songs in one or two confident takes of each. Some of them became signature tunes for him—"How Could She Leave Me?" and "Your Love Is Like a Cancer." They were dark, angry songs in minor keys. He cut another wonderful minor-key slow blues called "Now That I'm Down" that begins with the lyric, *When I had money / I was the talk of the town / But now I'm broke and raggedy* [he pronounced it "rag-i-ly"] / *And you don't even want me around.*

---

6. As soon as he was making a little money, Son traded in his Norma for a Sears & Roebuck Silvertone. Soon after, I found a Guild Starfire IV for him that he played for decades. In later years he played a Gibson ES-345.

On the word *even* he hits a strong falsetto. "Cotton Picking Blues" was another original. The song starts with a strong metaphor: *The little bee sucks the blossom, the big bee makes the honey / I do all the hard work, but my boss, he takes all the money*. I asked Son whether he had ever picked cotton. He told me he had picked cotton for half a day, just long enough to know he never wanted to do it again. His songs were episodes from his own life and also from the lives of others he had known.

Son created his signature instrumental, "Hot Sauce," in the studio, at my request. My concept was inspired by "Busy Bee," a fiery, up-tempo showcase by Texas guitarist Bee Houston. "I want it to be fast," I told him. "I want it to be flashy, and I want you to put breaks in it, where the band stops and you play by yourself." "Give me ten minutes," he said. When I returned he told me to roll the tape. He might have cut two takes, no more. The song he had created was much more exciting than the one I had imagined. There was some fantastic guitar playing, fast and super-confident, full of energy, aggression, and attitude; it was thrilling. I said, "Do you have a name for that?" He said firmly, "That's got to be 'Hot Sauce.'" He knew what it was to be called, and it was not open to discussion. "Hot Sauce" became the trademark song that he used to end sets. We recorded another searing version of it on his *Live and Burning* album a few years later.

As the second session came to a close, I was worried that we had recorded too many shuffles with similar grooves. Then I had another inspiration. I asked Son, "Do you know 'All Your Love' by Magic Sam?" Sam's biggest hit, the song was released in 1957, when Son was a teenager. It had been played on black radio down south, so Son was familiar with it. He picked a key and counted it off. He only needed one take. I walked out of the studio after two nights, knowing that I'd gotten the record I wanted.

I was slowly gaining more confidence as a producer and giving more input and ideas to the musicians. With Hound Dog and Big Walter, I didn't suggest songs. I recorded their existing repertoires. With Son, I was encouraging his songwriting and choosing which of his originals to record. Asking Son to compose and record an instrumental to my specifications is something I never would have done with Hound Dog. Before producing Son, I don't know if I would have had the nerve to suggest a cover song to an artist.

I believed that Son could be an important bluesman, one of the best of his generation. But he was brand new and totally unknown outside of the South Side. Both Hound Dog, who had been to Europe as part of the 1967 American Folk Blues Festival tour, and Big Walter, who was one of the iconic Chicago blues harmonica players, were known to hard-core blues fans. Introducing Son to the world was going to be a huge challenge.

I released *The Son Seals Blues Band* in spring of 1973 and immediately hit the road, traveling back to the East Coast to visit radio stations and distributors. Many of the stations had moved from the progressive rock format, which allowed DJs to program their own shows, to the Album Oriented Rock (AOR) format with a playlist created by the station's music director. Programmers were polite about Son's record, but it failed to generate the enthusiasm that Hound Dog's had received. Hound Dog's record was full of infectious boogie energy. Son's record was a more serious blues record, and the AOR format wasn't the home of serious blues by black musicians. Blues was falling victim to the continuing morphing of progressive, free-form radio into the less adventurous AOR format.

When progressive rock stations had depended on a small but devoted audience and local advertisers, there was less pressure to standardize a playlist. But once stations became focused on building a larger audience and getting higher ratings as a way to attract more lucrative national advertising, playlists that repeated the most popular songs became the norm. AOR radio was consciously committed to an audience that was young, white, and affluent. "They're the people who are making lifelong brand and product decisions," the thinking went. "We need to hook them on these brands now."

AOR stations were increasingly relying on national consultants to choose songs for their playlists. They supposedly knew everything that was going on in the format and could foresee trends. Album rock radio was not only tightening up the playlists; it was whitening them up. Sometime in the early 1970s, one such consultant famously said, "Black music is the kiss of death to rock and roll radio." He meant, of course, black music other than oldies and dead artists like Jimi Hendrix. It was okay to play a Motown or Stax classic, but if you were going to play something bluesy, it should be something familiar to rock fans, like Eric Clapton, not a song by little-known and black Son Seals. With that attitude came the elimination of most black blues from the AOR format.

Black-oriented radio wasn't any friendlier to us than AOR, and the few blues records heard on those stations had a much slicker sound than anything on Alligator. In the early 1970s, black-oriented radio stations played blues songs like "Little Bluebird" by Little Milton, "You Made Your Move Too Soon" by B. B. King, and "As Soon as the Weather Breaks" by Bobby "Blue" Bland. Songs like these blurred the line between blues and R&B. An artist like Little Milton could easily record or perform a traditional twelve-bar blues and then turn around and do an up-tempo version of an R&B tune like "Grits Ain't Groceries" or "Just a Little Bit." The production on these records often included horns and background singers, and even strings and synthesizers. The producer's goal was a hit record, with a catchy, danceable groove and a sound that appealed to the broadest possible (black) audience. Alligator's records were considered old-fashioned, unsophisticated, and "down home." The black-oriented stations sold advertising just like the white rock stations, and the music director's job was to attract as many black listeners (and potential consumers) as possible to sell that advertising. There was nothing that sounded like Hound Dog on any black radio station that I heard as I drove around the country. Son Seals's style was a little more contemporary, but his raw sound was not the kind of blues that black stations were playing. Even with the shrinking of progressive rock radio, Alligator releases had more chance for airplay on rock stations than on black stations.

In promoting Son to rock radio, I quickly learned that I couldn't rely on any momentum I thought I had built with Hound Dog. My struggle to get rock airplay for Son's record made me understand the luck I had had by starting with Hound Dog, whose music was so accessible to rock fans, and how fortunate I had been by starting when radio was at its loosest ever. I founded Alligator in *the* moment when my vision could succeed. If I had started a year or two later, or started with Big Walter or Son, I probably would have failed. It was a hard realization to accept.

7

As I tried to promote and sell Son Seals's record, I was getting anxious about the future. The Big Walter album had sold enough to break even, and Hound Dog's LP continued to sell. Some money was flowing through Alligator, but my expenses were bare bones; I was still the entire label staff. I was still cutting records in only two evenings in the studio. I was still paying union scale for recording, $480 for the leader and $240 for the sidemen. I was paying royalties, but I wasn't paying any larger advances.

Originally I had thought that the Chicago blues talent pool was so deep that I'd record one album by each of my favorite artists. I realized that my initial vision wasn't going to work. I was going to have to act like a "real" record company and continue to make records with my "stars," even if my one and only star wasn't exactly a star by the standards of the entertainment industry. In late 1973, I somewhat reluctantly began planning Hound Dog's second release, *Natural Boogie*. I was afraid that we had already recorded his best material. What was I going to do to make a record as good or better? I called again on Wesley Race to be my coproducer, and we began choosing material. Among the songs we recorded were "Sadie," which Hound Dog had written during the 1971 New England tour, and "See Me in the Evening," a song that took shape on the bandstand, as most of Hound Dog's originals did. We decided to remake a song called "Take Five" that he had originally cut as a 45 for Cadillac Baby's label Bea & Baby. We also chose some songs that featured Brewer Phillips. Brewer could be an astounding guitar player, and you could always hear how much fun he was having. His playing was wonderfully aggressive. He took chances and made many mistakes, but they were great, funky mistakes.

We cut the album in Sound Studios with minimal rehearsals. Stupidly, I allowed Hound Dog to bring his girlfriend (not be confused with his wife). Her presence encouraged Hound Dog to show off, and he got too drunk instead of just drunk enough. He kept asking her opinion of the performances rather than listening to Wesley and me. She loved everything, which made it hard to convince him to record second takes. The session became tense and unproductive, and I called it off for the night. We had to return to the studio for a third session to complete the album, which meant spending hundreds of extra dollars out of Alligator's tiny coffers to pay studio costs. We finally got the songs and takes that we wanted, but it took a while (and the absence of the girlfriend) to get the band back to playing with their normal "Let's have some fun" attitude. I was horrified to have spent the additional money, but I was happy with the record. I was also aware that we had come close to exhausting Hound Dog's repertoire as well as my slim cash reserves.

In preparing *Natural Boogie* for release, Alligator faced a new, unexpected hurdle. The LPs were being readied for pressing at the Capitol Records pressing plant in Jacksonville, Illinois, which was owned by the giant Capitol label. At the time, the OPEC oil embargo was causing a shortage of vinyl, a petroleum product. One day I received a call from the pressing plant and was told that because of the shortage, only Capitol label records would be pressed there. To get back the essential metal masters for my three albums, I would have to pay off all my pressing bills in full. Things were already financially shaky for Alligator, and this expense could kill the label. I managed to scrape up the money to get my masters back, but with vinyl in short supply, I also had to find somewhere else to press LPs.

The first pressings of *Natural Boogie* were done at a plant in Cincinnati called Queen City Album. I left a party at Brewer Phillips's home and drove out to the freight company in Cicero, Illinois, to pick them up. Standing on the loading dock, I opened an LP and discovered a pressed-in scratch across at least three songs. It was on every album I opened. Clearly, the scratch was in the metal stampers they had made. I stood there in tears and thought, "I'm going to lose my company." I taped up the boxes and told the freight company to ship them back. I had to delay the release until late summer of 1974. Weeks passed before Queen City Album was able to produce good enough pressings for me to put the record on the market. (I changed pressing plants immediately afterward.)

I had already taken three promotional trips to the East Coast for each of the previous Alligator releases. With the second Hound Dog record, I decided to travel west. I loaded up my red Plymouth Duster with a thousand LPs and headed off to St. Louis, Denver, El Paso, Albuquerque, Phoenix, and various destinations in California and the Pacific Northwest. I went north as far as Seattle and then headed back to Chicago through Idaho, Montana, and North Dakota. I drove seven thousand miles in three and a half weeks, visiting stations and distributors all along the way.

Because many of the AOR stations I visited had played Hound Dog's first album before tightening up their playlists, at least some of them were open to playing Hound Dog's second album, although not with the same level of enthusiasm or frequency. To encourage them, I mailed out all kinds of promotional materials—lists of other stations playing the record, magazine and newspaper reviews, gig reviews, tour schedules—whatever I could think of. Nobody else was promoting blues records to these stations. The few major labels that had blues artists under contract didn't heavily promote their blues releases, and other small specialty labels didn't seem to have the same vision or drive that I did.

If 1974 was partly about playing it safe by releasing another Hound Dog record that stood a decent chance of getting some airplay on AOR radio, it was also a year of risk taking. Releasing a second Hound Dog record was a smart business decision. Releasing Alligator's fifth album, Fenton Robinson's *Somebody Loan Me a Dime*, was a gut decision and a big risk. The two albums couldn't have been more different. With Fenton, a polished guitar player and singer only known to the hardest-core blues fans, I was taking a long step away from the raw boogie blues of Hound Dog.

I had first heard of Fenton shortly after I moved to Chicago, when Jim O'Neal played for me the original version of "Somebody Loan Me a Dime." It had been released as a 45 on Palos Records, a little local label, in 1967.[1] The unusual introduction to the song grabbed me immediately. Fenton started the song on what blues musicians call the raised five (correctly called the sixth chord) instead of the usual fifth chord, then jumped unexpectedly to the fourth chord, his fingers flowing smoothly down the neck of the guitar. He sang in a big, beautiful, effortlessly soaring voice with a little falsetto, and his style was smoother and less rough edged than most Chicago blues singers. The record fascinated me. Jim educated me about Fenton's career, playing singles Fenton had cut in the late 1950s for the Duke and Meteor labels down south. I was surprised to discover that Fenton had recorded the first version of the blues standard "As the Years Go Passing By." I knew Fenton lived in Chicago, but in the ensuing months, I could never find a club where he was performing.

My search for Fenton led me to the Burning Spear, a large South Side club at 55th and State, where he was scheduled to appear one night along with half a dozen other artists. Originally opened in the 1930s as the Club DeLisa, the Burning Spear probably held a thousand people and charged an exorbitant eight dollars at the door (the cover charge at neighborhood blues clubs was only fifty cents or a dollar).[2] As though that weren't enough to brand it an upscale establishment, the club served hard liquor only in cocktail setups: for two dollars and fifty cents, patrons could order a little plastic bowl with ice and tongs, a bottle of mixer, and a carafe of whiskey, gin, or

1. Later on, Boz Scaggs cut a popular version of "Somebody Loan Me a Dime" with Duane Allman on guitar. Boz put his own name on it as writer, not because he was trying to rip off Fenton, but because he didn't know who wrote it. I was able to get the rights back for Fenton some years later and pay royalties to him for the song. Fenton's version also appeared in the background of a scene in *The Blues Brothers*, earning thousands of dollars for him.
2. The Burning Spear booked all kinds of black music. I went there to see blues and R&B artists like Bobby "Blue" Bland, Albert King, Little Milton, and Junior Parker. The club was also an incubator for future stars. One night, the opening act for Junior Parker was a skinny guy with a huge Afro. He had just a guitar player, not a full band, and hired Junior Parker's rhythm section for the show. His name was Al Green.

vodka. Long cloth-covered tables ran from the back of the room to the stage, part of which could be lowered to serve as a dance floor. Admission to the Burning Spear was way beyond my means as a Delmark employee making thirty dollars a week, but I spent the money anyway because I was so eager to see Fenton. Many musicians performed that night, but not Fenton. The emcee never even mentioned his name.

I finally caught up to Fenton at Pepper's Lounge, where he was booked on a series of Tuesday nights. A handsome, well-dressed, serious man in his late thirties, he played a beautiful, semi-hollow blond Gibson ES-125 guitar, a model more popular with jazz musicians than blues musicians. Supremely confident, he clearly knew more guitar than almost all of the other blues players around town. His playing ran the gamut from raw down-home blues to sophisticated jazz stylings. He avoided obvious clichés and never mimicked the popular B. B. King and Albert King styles. In the midst of his melodic, single-string soloing, he occasionally threw in big, lush, jazzy chords, sometimes stacking those chords one after another rather than picking individual notes. He sang with a rich voice, and his vocal note bending was smooth and easy, like the jazz and blues singer Joe Williams. His music wasn't that shake-your-fist, sweaty, soul-baring blues that Son Seals and Buddy Guy delivered so well. Although Fenton said crowd-pleasing things like, "We're going to have a good time," and "Let's have a party up in here," I could tell that he actually wished the audience would sit quietly and pay attention. If they did that, he was going to make it worth their while.

I went to see Fenton regularly after that and slowly got to know him personally, sometimes driving him home after gigs because, strangely, he didn't own a car. He never had much to say, but he was clearly intelligent, well spoken, and well read, even though, he told me, he had little formal education.[3] Private and self-disciplined, he didn't drink, he rarely smiled or laughed, and he never hit on women. He told me he jogged every day to stay in shape. His sophisticated

---

3. My friend Dick Shurman visited with Fenton once and found him reading *One-Dimensional Man* by the German political philosopher Herbert Marcuse.

musicianship and reserved, rather formal demeanor earned the universal respect of his peers. I was thinking of him as a possible future Alligator artist when, after playing at Pepper's for some weeks, Fenton abruptly moved to Indianapolis and I lost touch with him.

When I had first met him, Fenton was under contract to Seventy 7 Records, a Nashville-based label owned by the influential DJ John Richbourg.[4] In early 1974 I ran into Fenton at Lovia's Lounge. He sounded as good as ever and was now out of his contract. I quickly made an offer, and he agreed to sign with Alligator. Fenton didn't have a good regular band at the time, so we mutually decided to hire Mighty Joe Young's band for the sessions. Joe was a well-respected West Side guitar player whose band included Cornelius "Mule" Boyson on bass and Tony Gooden on drums. To augment the band, I recruited a Pittsburgh-based piano player named Bill Heid, whom I had heard sitting in with Fenton. In rehearsal and in the studio, Fenton proved himself to be a master professional. He knew what he wanted to hear from the band, showed Joe specific and sometimes unusual rhythm guitar parts, and made the recording sessions remarkably easy. In two nights, we cut eleven songs, including a new version of "Somebody Loan Me a Dime" and five other Fenton originals. It was an easy decision to name the album after his most memorable song.

With Fenton's record, I agreed, for the first time, to use horns. I associated horn sections with the kind of slickly produced R&B that was the antithesis of the raw blues bar music I had fallen in love with. But Fenton was adamant, and, since they were to play on only a few songs, I agreed. Rather than recording the horns live with Fenton and the band, I decided to add them in later, despite having no experience with overdubbing (adding musical parts to a song after the initial recording). With two tracks available for the horns, I delivered a tape of the rough mixes to Dave Baldwin, the horn arranger Fenton had requested. Dave wrote the horn charts (sheet music was

---

4. Richbourg, under the name John R., broadcasted on WLAC, a 100,000-watt AM station that blanketed the entire South and played blues, R&B, and gospel all night long. Its sponsors included three successful mail-order record stores. Getting airplay on WLAC almost assured that a 45 would be a good seller, and the mail-order companies could get the records to rural areas where there were no record stores. Excerpts of WLAC's colorful broadcasts are available online.

also a new concept for Alligator), created tastefully spare and simple arrangements, chose the players, and supervised the horn session. Fenton was right: the horns enhanced the album.

Fenton's record sounded a lot more like the blues being played on southern black radio than any previous Alligator release. Some of Fenton's earlier 45s had been played on these stations as well. When it came time to load up my Plymouth Duster and hit the road to visit radio stations, stores, and distributors, I decided to take *Somebody Loan Me a Dime* south, through St. Louis and into Oklahoma and Texas, then east to New Orleans, Jackson, Memphis, Atlanta, and Miami. Besides visiting college stations and the few remaining progressive rock radio stations, I also made a point of visiting black-oriented stations. Most of the DJs and program directors listened politely but never played Fenton's record. I was a young white stranger representing a label they had never heard of. Traditionally, the promo men visiting the black stations were themselves black and had long-standing relationships with the programmers and radio hosts.

One station that did play Fenton's record was WYAZ in Yazoo City, Mississippi, a funky little station located in a house trailer in the middle of a cornfield. A DJ known as the Mighty Scrap Iron played Fenton's record while I was at the station. I was thrilled. About two weeks later, Scrap Iron called me, saying that his rent was due and wondering if I could help him out. I think this was the first time anyone suggested to me that I give something in exchange for airplay. I politely declined, and I'm sure that Fenton received no more airplay in Yazoo City.[5]

---

5. Although no rock programmer ever asked me for cash, it was not uncommon for rock stations to ask labels to pay for programmers' attendance at industry conventions by purchasing air tickets or hotel rooms, or to pay for contest prizes given to listeners, or to make a contribution to the station's "promotional fund." The request for promotional money rarely came directly from a station; instead, it would come from an independent promoter that worked closely with the station and had knowledge of the songs being considered for airplay. The station might add a contributing label's song to the playlist, but doing so was never presented as payola, or "pay for play" (insert wink and nod here). Labels claimed these contributions as business expenses, and the stations reported them as income.

8

As radio airplay became harder to secure, live performances became an increasingly important way to get exposure for Alligator artists, expand the audience for the music, and increase record sales. When it came to booking my artists, I definitely worked the white side of the blues street. A few black-owned clubs, like the Burning Spear in Chicago and Governor's Inn in Buffalo, still booked some touring blues musicians. But just like the black-oriented radio stations, most of these clubs weren't interested in what Alligator had to offer.

As mentioned earlier, I was a reluctant, unenthusiastic booking agent. It was boring work, with a lot of repeated calls to unresponsive club owners who usually said no. Disco was beginning to replace live music in clubs, and blues festivals were rare events. Blues had also lost some of its hipness for college students, and fewer college bookings were available. With the exception of Hound Dog, it was a struggle for me to find good-paying gigs for my artists.

I did have some booking success locally. Although the Chicago club scene on the South and West Sides was shrinking in the early 1970s, a healthy blues scene was developing closer to my home on the North Side. White audiences patronized new blues clubs such as the Wise Fools Pub, Elsewhere, and Kingston Mines, all on Lincoln Avenue. Kingston Mines is now on Halsted Street, opposite B.L.U.E.S. on Halsted, which is a later incarnation of Elsewhere. At the Wise Fools, a good piano player from Wisconsin named Bob Riedy convinced Dave Ungerleider, the club's owner, to book Riedy's blues band. Then Riedy began to invite black musicians like Johnny Young and John Littlejohn from the South and West Sides to play with his band as guests. As Riedy began finding gigs for his own group elsewhere, he arranged gigs at the Wise Fools for other South and West Side artists and their bands, most of whom had rarely played on the North Side before.

With Alligator beginning to occupy more and more of my time, I found myself going to the conveniently located North Side clubs more than to the South and West Sides. Set times were predictable, and more of the bands were well rehearsed and performing original material. But the atmosphere of the North Side clubs was very different.

The South and West Side clubs had always been looser and more spontaneous. You might hear a great set or a mediocre one; the band might be tight and rehearsed or thrown together for a single gig. The best nights in those clubs were wonderful; sometimes completely unexpected things happened. I remember driving down Ogden Avenue with my car windows down, listening for a band, and unexpectedly finding Big Mojo Elem playing in a club. Big Mojo was a singing bass player with a high voice whose signature song was J. B. Lenoir's "Mojo Boogie." At the climax of the song, he would put down his bass while the band kept grooving and run around the club, singing "Ow, ow, ow" on the same note over and over again. It was hilarious and fun. Nothing like that happened on the North Side.

Neither did running into a character like Dogman (whose real name was Art Jackson), a good swing drummer who trained horses for a living and often mounted a saddle over his drum stool. Muscular and good looking, he shaved his head, leaving just enough hair for a little ponytail, and wore a Fu Manchu mustache. Perhaps the most eccentric thing about him was that he talked like Tarzan. He liked to walk into a club with a bottle of Wild Irish Rose (it's not good protocol to bring your own bottle into a bar), put it down in the middle of the table, order a glass of ice, and then declare loudly to everyone else, "Drink wine, be strong like Dogman." He was called Dogman because he always had three or four dogs in his car. He only had one command for his dogs—"Pacey, Pacey"—which, according to him, meant "Do it" in Swahili. The order could mean "guard the car," "attack this man," or "be friendly." Sometime in the mid-1970s, I traveled to a blues festival at Beloit College in Wisconsin with Carey Bell, who had hired Dogman to play drums. Dogman talked in his usual Tarzan style until we were alone and I said, "I always thought there was something else going on with you besides 'Drink wine, be strong like Dogman.'" "Well," he replied, "actually I'm studying pathology at the University of Illinois Circle campus." Then one of the other musicians came by and he immediately went back to "Drink wine, be strong." One night I drank Wild Irish Rose with him at the Rat Trap, and the next week I developed a prostate infection. I never touched the stuff again.

It was clear to me that the white audiences for blues had a different upbringing from that of the black performers they were coming to see. Almost all of the blues artists had poor or working-class backgrounds. Few had much formal education. Many of the white audience members came from comfortable upper-middle-class families. They were not only of college age, but often college educated. Many didn't have much experience interacting with black people, just as I hadn't.

The black and white audiences responded to the music in vastly different ways. In the black clubs, the musicians and the audience were members of the same community. Many of them had grown up down south and knew the same repertoire of songs, having first heard them on southern radio stations and small-town jukeboxes. Whether in neighborhood clubs that held seventy-five people or in bigger places like the Burning Spear that held a thousand, black audiences interacted with the musicians and spontaneously responded to the music. There would be a lot of enthusiastic back-and-forth between the audience and the musicians that energized the performers, much like the interaction between a preacher and congregation in an African American church. When the music hit them, black blues fans might stand up and raise their right hands like they did in church to testify to the soulfulness of the performance, yell encouragement to the musicians, or even walk up to the stage to stuff dollar bills in the musicians' shirt pockets. Koko Taylor once complained to me that her new preacher didn't like to get so much response from the congregation. "Why would you go to church if you couldn't holler?" she asked. For black audiences, the question was the same: Why go to a blues club if you can't holler?

In the white clubs, people might dance or occasionally shout something during a song, but audience response was much more restrained, usually only applause and whistles when a song ended. Many in the white audience hadn't grown up with the blues; they didn't share the same touchstone songs as the black audiences did, and they didn't necessarily feel the same grooves. Because most white people were introduced to blues as a form of rock and roll, the flashy guitar solo became more of the center of the performance.[1] Often the lyrics and vocals ended up taking a back seat. This is not to say that white audiences didn't enjoy the music. They just enjoyed it in a different, less interactive way.

Sometimes it was hard for the black artists to learn how to communicate with the white audiences. Hound Dog loved to clown and could make any audience smile along with him. Son Seals had a more serious demeanor and was a less experienced communicator. It took Son a long time to find his own way to reach the white audience between songs. At first, the things he said were the clichéd "Let's have a party" and similar lines copied from better-known musicians, and there was no sense that he was speaking spontaneously. The energy and momentum he built with each fiery performance seemed to dissipate between songs. This is a typical blues band problem,

---

1. These days, a lot of guitar players, black and white, seem to want cram as many notes as possible into their solos. Many of them seem to have no idea that different notes can have different values, or that a pause or rest can create tension or the release of tension. I often suggest to soloists that they listen to the best black preachers, who know how to use both loud and quiet passages, as well as pauses, and repetition of key lines, to move their congregations. Those preachers never try to cram in so many words that the emotional or spiritual impact gets lost. Both in black churches and in black clubs, I would hear the audience encourage either the preacher or the musician by saying, "take your time; take your time." I wish more guitar players got this message. All the great blues guitarists know how to take their time.

especially when the band isn't tightly rehearsed, as was often the case at local club gigs. Sometimes between songs there's a little band huddle to decide what song will be played next and what key it will be played in. That works fine in a neighborhood bar on the South Side where the audience has paid a dollar at the door, but not so much when a North Side audience member has paid ten or twenty dollars and expects a rehearsed show.

As he gained experience, Son tightened up the time between songs and said less and less. Finally one night at the El Mocambo in Toronto, he found his presentation style. Before the last chord of a song had died, he launched into the next, not even giving the audience a chance to applaud. He did this song after song, like winding an alarm clock tighter and tighter, bearing down on his strings harder and harder. Finally, after four or five songs in a row, he paused. The audience exploded with applause and cheers. His intensity, not his between-songs banter, *forced* the audience to pay attention. That was the way he presented himself for the rest of his career—a man of few words and unrelenting energy, so confident that he never had to exhort the fans.

I began to realize that in addition to being the record company owner, record producer, record promoter, booking agent, and tour manager, I could also help my artists project what I thought was the right image. As I first began booking club dates for Son, who could seem a bit menacing, I encouraged him to dress differently. Son had come up in the era when the blues musicians he admired—B. B. King, Little Milton, Albert King—performed in suits and ties. "You're of a younger generation," I told him. "You're playing for a younger audience. They'll relate better to you if you dress more casually." For a time he followed my advice. Then one night, Son showed up for a gig at the Wise Fools Pub wearing a three-piece suit. Never one to bite my tongue, I said, "Son, I thought we had agreed you were going to dress more casually. Why are you wearing a suit?" He responded, "Do you know what a suit looks like when you sweat through it?" Then he showed me. By the end of the first set, when he took off his guitar, his sweat had soaked right through his shirt and vest, and there were big wet stripes across the back of his suit jacket. Now the audience could see exactly how hard he was working for them. From then on, he generally dressed up, and I had no objections.

Having Hound Dog and Son on the road was a crucial part of my audience-building strategy. After the release of *Somebody Loan Me a Dime* in 1974, getting Fenton on the road turned out to be impossible. Just before the album's release, Fenton revealed to me that he was going to prison, convicted of vehicular manslaughter. Some years earlier, he had been in a bad auto accident, apparently while drunk, and had killed a pedestrian. So, instead of Fenton being out on the road touring, Fenton was going to be touring Joliet Penitentiary. I realized in retrospect that this was the reason that Fenton seemed to have such an opaque personality and why he didn't drink or own a car. I couldn't imagine someone less suited for prison life than this private and thoughtful man, and I felt sure that Fenton had already punished himself more than any prison term would. I was determined to get him out at the first opportunity.

During the nine months before Fenton's first parole hearing, I wrote to every individual, club, college, and European promoter that had ever booked one of my artists and asked, "Can I get a letter from you saying that if Fenton Robinson were a free man, you'd have a gig for him?" When it came time to make my presentation to the parole board, I trimmed my beard, cut my hair short, put on my only suit, and drove down to Joliet. I gave each member of the board a copy of Fenton's album and the letters and offers of employment. Somehow I convinced the parole board to release Fenton. As soon as he was free, I began booking him.

But as good as Fenton was, we were never able to advance his career as much as either he or I wanted. With his talent, he should have risen to stardom in the blues world. Eventually, after the release of his second album, *I Hear Some Blues Downstairs*, Alligator ceased managing and booking him by mutual agreement. However, a gig we had booked for him in Springfield, Illinois, led to his being offered a high school music teaching residency there. He loved working with students and stayed in Springfield for some years. After that, he performed relatively little, more often overseas than in the United States. He had developed a cult following in Japan, where he was known as the Mellow Blues Genius, and was able to perform there and in Europe as a concert artist. Fenton died in 1997 at the age of 62.

Alligator was born of my love for the music. I continued to be a fan, but I was also finding my way as a businessman. There were moments when the roles dovetailed, but there were many more moments when they conflicted. Alligator profits were so thin, and during the early years the day-to-day operations so tenuous, that one serious mistake could send the company crashing down around me. Of course, the most difficult decisions were choosing which artists to sign. As a one-man company with only one or two releases a year, every bit of energy I put into one artist was energy I couldn't put into another one. Signing Koko Taylor was one of those tough decisions.

I met Koko Taylor at the Wise Fools Pub in the early 1970s. She was sitting in with Mighty Joe Young's band. Joe introduced us. Almost immediately she said, "I know you're making records. What about recording me?" I knew who Koko was, of course, and I was familiar with her trademark powerful, growling vocal style. She had scored a hit in 1966 on Chess Records with "Wang Dang Doodle," written and produced by her mentor and "discoverer," Willie Dixon, the famed producer and songwriter. The single had reached number 13 on the national black radio charts, but she never had a follow-up song that did nearly as well. By the end of the 1960s, Chess had been sold and blues was disappearing from black radio. No longer in demand, Koko had returned to her day job working as a cleaning woman and nanny for white families on Chicago's wealthy North Shore while making guest appearances with established bands.

Most fans now assume that when I signed her, Koko was already a blues star, but that fame was years in the future. At first, I wasn't very interested in recording her. I viewed her as a one-hit wonder with a strong but rather repetitive vocal style. She didn't have a band and wasn't performing regularly. I didn't know if she had a repertoire other than blues standards and her Chess recordings. I also doubted my ability to effectively promote a female artist in the male-dominated blues world. But most of all, I was afraid of trying to promote a standup singer who didn't play an instrument. The white blues audience expected musicians to be guitar or harmonica heroes as well as singers.

Recording a vocalist like Koko would also mean challenging myself as a producer. The musicians I had worked with could use their instruments to explain a song's arrangement to the band. I didn't play an instrument and was a mediocre singer. I feared that my musical limitations would hurt my ability to produce a vocalist's record. That type of record required me to become more involved in helping to create and direct arrangements and shape the music, and I doubted that I had these skills.

But Koko was persistent. At our first meeting, I had given my phone number to her. She called me frequently, always asking politely about recording. After hearing me say, "I don't think so," "No, not right now," "I'll think about it," or "I've got other priorities" quite a few times, Koko finally asked, "Could you help me get some gigs?" This was a different question. "Sure," I told her. "I'll try getting you some gigs, but you need a band." A week later, she called back. She told me she had a band in rehearsal and had made a down payment on a van. This impressed me. Koko was a businesswoman; she was taking care of business. I booked a few dates for her that went well. My respect for her professionalism grew, and at her gigs, I began to hear in a few songs (especially slow blues) that she could do more than growl and holler. Perhaps I could bring out that subtlety in the studio. So I crossed my fingers and committed to making a record with Koko. In the long run, it turned out to be well worth the risk.

Koko's real name was Cora Walton, but she had been called Koko from a young age because she loved sweets, particularly chocolate. Like everyone I had recorded up until that time, Koko was from the country. She was born on a farm in Bartlett, Tennessee, just outside of Memphis. Her mother died when she was young, and she and her brothers were raised by her father, a poor sharecropper. From time to time, when things got tough, she was sent to live with other relatives around northern Mississippi. It was a hard life. She worked in the fields, cleaned homes, took care of other people's children, and went to school when she could, only finishing the third grade. Koko always loved blues, inspired by the recordings of Bessie Smith and Memphis Minnie. She and her brothers sang in church, but her father, a religious man, discouraged her from singing blues. Like many churchgoers, he considered blues to be the devil's music.

Koko fell in love with her future husband, Robert "Pops" Taylor, while still in her teens. Pops drove a truck that took laborers to work in the fields. Older and more sophisticated than Koko, Pops was a part-time gambler who helped operate clubs in the West Memphis area. He often took Koko to hear blues musicians like Muddy Waters and Howlin' Wolf. Sly and smart, there was a bit of the trickster in Pops.

Koko and Pops came to Chicago in 1951 in the back of a Greyhound bus with only, as Koko said, "thirty-five cents and a box of Ritz crackers." They stayed with relatives on the West Side, and she got a job working in a laundry. Pops drove a cab, worked in the steel mills, and did anything he could to make a living. Fairly soon, Koko began getting jobs as a domestic. She went to night school to learn grammar, handwriting, spelling, and some arithmetic. That was typical of Koko. She didn't go back to school to get a better job. She did it out of pride. She was embarrassed that she couldn't read or write well.

On the weekends, Pops and Koko made the rounds to various blues clubs, especially Silvio's on the West Side, where Howlin' Wolf and Elmore James held court, and the Zanzibar on the Near West Side, not far from the Maxwell Street market, where Muddy Waters played. Pops knew a lot of musicians from down south, and, eager to promote Koko's singing talent, he began asking them to let her sit in.

It was at Silvio's around 1962 that Willie Dixon first heard Koko. After producing her first 45 for the USA label, Willie brought her to Chess, where he had produced blues hits by Muddy Waters, Howlin' Wolf, Sonny Boy Williamson II, and many more. Koko became

Willie's pet production project. Between 1964 and 1968, he produced nine Koko 45s for Chess's subsidiary Checker. Songs from those sessions were collected on two LPs, one titled simply *Koko Taylor* and the other called *Basic Soul*. But only "Wang Dang Doodle" sold.

We recorded *I Got What It Takes*, Koko's first Alligator album, on January 21 and 22, 1975. Koko was not a prolific songwriter, so I had suggested a number of songs that had been recorded by other artists. She chose six of my suggestions, songs originally cut by Elmore James, Ruth Brown, Magic Sam, and Bonnie "Bombshell" Lee, and remakes of one of her Chess tracks (the album's title song) and one of her USA label cuts. Willie Dixon gave her a new song, "Be What You Want to Be," and she also brought one of her own compositions, "Voodoo Woman." She suggested Jimmy Reed's "Big Boss Man" (which she often performed live) and songs by Otis Spann and Denise LaSalle.

With the exception of Vince Chappelle, her devoted drummer, Koko's road band wasn't quite good enough to use on the recording. Instead we brought in three musicians she knew who had contributed greatly to Fenton's album: her close friend Mighty Joe Young, the sophisticated R&B guitarist whose wide musical vocabulary included blues, and his bass player, Cornelius Boyson, as well as keyboard ace Bill Heid. With Koko's approval, I recruited Sammy Lawhorn, the deeply soulful and musically elegant house guitar player at Theresa's. I wanted to feature some horn solos, and Joe suggested saxophone player Abb Locke, who could growl on his horn like Koko growled with her voice.

As I feared, *I Got What It Takes* required me to give more direction about how the songs were to be played than anything I had produced before that time. With Joe Young's help, I learned to speak in clearer musical terms that the band members would understand. I was starting to become an arranger, but my self-consciousness about this role was heightened by the fact that we conducted rehearsals at Willie Dixon's storefront studio at 77th and Racine. Dixon wasn't there every minute, but he occasionally observed the rehearsals. I wondered whether he thought he could have done a better job directing Koko's band than I was doing. He may have wondered why I wasn't hiring him to produce records, which would have been a fair question given how much production knowledge and experience he had. In truth, Willie intimidated me. As a result I missed out on an opportunity to nurture a relationship from which I might have learned a lot.

Although it wasn't a big seller, *I Got What It Takes* garnered Alligator's first Grammy nomination. Producing it made me feel better about my own abilities. But more important, the album revealed a side of Koko that hadn't appeared on her other records. The crucial track was the Magic Sam song "That's Why I'm Crying." When I suggested it to her, I knew that it would be a stretch. Instead of her usual power player approach, she sang parts of it quietly and wistfully, with a little sigh in her voice, a little expulsion of air, and a lot of pain. She built the intensity slowly from verse to verse. Full of despair, her singing fit the meaning of the words:

> *I walk the streets at night with you on my mind*
> *All I do is run around crying*
> *Whoa now, baby, baby, what is wrong*
> *Someone told me you wanna get your baby back home*
> *Stop crying*
> *Yeah, yeah, stop crying*
> *You have someone new but I'm still in love with you*
> *That's why I'm crying.*

She delivered it perfectly. Sammy Lawhorn played a beautiful, simple solo that featured his signature tremolo bar vibrato. Bill Heid played organ rather than piano so that we had the chords sustaining behind her, creating a stark, late-night feel. It was the most mature, subtle performance Koko had recorded up to that time.

We issued the album that spring, Alligator's only 1975 release. This time there was no need to visit out-of-town radio stations in person. By then, I had established enough relationships with the few remaining blues-friendly AOR music directors that I could pick up the phone and call them. As usual, I prepared copies of reviews and lists of stations giving the album airplay and mailed them to every valuable programmer, store, and distributor. I did anything I could do to create credibility with radio and give programmers and my distributors the impression that this was a "happening" record. Yet even with a Grammy nomination, *I Got What It Takes* didn't sell well. There wasn't much marketplace excitement, nor was there the sense of revelation that some media and fans had felt discovering my other artists. It was with her next album, 1978's *The Earthshaker*, that Koko earned her reputation as the Queen of the Blues. Alligator took on Koko's management and eventually found a good booking agent for her. She performed around the world until almost the age of eighty, never losing the ability to pitch a wang dang doodle. Koko stayed with Alligator until her death in 2009, recording nine albums. She said she felt that she and Alligator went together "like red beans and rice."

In the spring of 1975, I married Jan Loveland, a fellow Cincinnatian whom I had met in Hartford while I was on the road with Hound Dog in 1971. Jan loved the blues. After moving to Chicago in 1973, she had thrown herself into my life and my lifestyle. She got to know the wives of Hound Dog, Brewer, and Ted. Together they started the HouseRockers' Social Club and presented occasional live music events featuring the band, including a memorable evening at a South Side YMCA that featured a fashion show by drag queens (one of whom was Hound Dog's best friend). We bought a small run-down house in Chicago's Edgewater neighborhood. I ran Alligator from the spare bedroom, using the basement as my warehouse. After our wedding, Jan and I took a blues honeymoon in the Mississippi Delta, visiting towns where Chicago blues musicians had grown up—places like Tchula, the hometown of Jimmy Dawkins, and Coila, Brewer Phillips's hometown, which was little more than a crossroads with a general store.

One day toward the end of my honeymoon, I called my home office from northern Mississippi. "There's trouble," my only employee, Richard McLeese, told me. "Hound Dog shot Phillips." I was stunned. I never thought that the childish animosity they acted out so often could become real. He told me that Hound Dog had shot Phillips in the forearm and in the thigh in Hound Dog's own living room. Apparently, Phillips had made a remark about having sex with Hound Dog's wife. This kind of teasing wasn't unusual. Traveling to gigs they joked constantly about their successes with one another's wives or girlfriends. It was almost a routine: "Your wife was telling me just the other night that you can't get it up anymore." It was a way of playing "the dozens," the traditional African American game of trading insults. But it was a breach of their code to suggest that somebody's wife was unfaithful to him within her earshot. Outraged, Hound Dog went into another room and came back with a .22 rifle. After two shots were fired, Son Seals, who was there visiting, wrestled the rifle away from Hound Dog.

Phillips insisted on pressing charges, and Hound Dog was arrested for attempted murder. Jan and I cut short our honeymoon and returned to Chicago. By that time, Hound Dog was out on bail and didn't want to talk about it. Phillips, not severely wounded, was out of the hospital. I was sure that at some point, Phillips would drop the charges rather than send Hound Dog to jail. Even though they argued constantly, they had been friends for almost twenty years. But Phillips was angry and wanted to make life hard for Hound Dog. Pressing charges was his way of doing just that.

My first job was to find another guitar player for Hound Dog. I approached Magic Slim, but he chose to remain with his own band even though that meant making less money. (By that time, Hound Dog was probably paying one hundred or one hundred fifty dollars per night, a grand sum for a blues sideman, whereas Slim was probably making only forty bucks per night working in town.) We finally recruited Lefty Dizz, who turned out to be a good choice. He was a jovial, reliable guy and an exuberant showman who could also match Hound Dog drink for drink.[2] From time to time I talked to Phillips on the phone, pushing for reconciliation with Hound Dog. "You may

2. One of the first gigs Dizz played with Hound Dog was at Milwaukee's Summerfest. That afternoon I chatted briefly with a fascinating woman named Jo Kolanda, who was dating a friend of mine. Twenty years later Jo and I were married.

want to kill each other," I argued, "but that doesn't mean you don't love each other." Phillips wouldn't budge.

Then suddenly, in September 1975, Hound Dog was in Cook County Hospital, diagnosed with lung cancer. We had worried so much that his liver would go to hell because of his drinking; instead his lungs went to hell when all those Pall Malls caught up with him. "I'm going to die," he told me when I went to visit him. I stupidly (and wishfully) said, "No, you're not." Eventually, he required an oxygen mask to breathe. I had to accept the fact that things were not going to get better. I didn't know what to do or what to feel. I knew how to make a record. I knew how to book gigs. I knew how to deal with fights in the band. I didn't know how to deal with cancer, and I didn't know how to deal with death. I hadn't thought about Hound Dog dying. I hadn't thought about *any* of my artists dying. As the years have passed, dealing with the deaths of my artists has become a far too regular occurrence for me.

The last time I saw Hound Dog alive was on December 15, 1975. Jan and I had stayed with him until the end of visiting hours. While we waited for the elevator, the door to the service stairs opened, and there was Brewer Phillips, his usual smiling self. "I'm going to see Hound Dog," he said. He told me later that Hound Dog hugged him so tightly that Hound Dog's fingernails cut into his back. They talked and made up. Within forty-eight hours, on December 17, 1975, Hound Dog died. I believe that he had been keeping himself alive because he needed to make peace with the one person who was most like a brother to him. Strangely, I don't remember Hound Dog's funeral. I must have been too numb.

Hound Dog's death brought Alligator to a crossroads. Alligator releases were outselling Delmark and Arhoolie, and the company had outlived other startup blues labels like Razor and Barrelhouse. But now, my best-selling artist, the man who had sparked the creation of the company and had given it its public identity, was dead. Sales of each new release were less than the one before. I was still giving away more free albums to radio stations, press, and stores than anybody else in the blues business and was spending more on advertising and marketing. I'd created a business model that was more expensive to run than that of my competitors. But I didn't want to backtrack, lower my expectations for the label, or give up my goal of growing the blues audience. I had to keep doing what I was doing. With Hound Dog gone, I wasn't sure how.

9

Hound Dog was dead. But the blues in Chicago was still very much alive, and I wanted to make sure the rest of the world knew it. Before starting Alligator, I had been inspired by the *Chicago/The Blues/ Today!* series that Sam Charters had produced for Vanguard Records. Those crucial records helped turn my generation on to Chicago blues. They featured three bands per album, each given about the same number of tracks. This digestible format was a perfect way for a record company to introduce new artists and could prompt further sales if any of the artists were signed to the label later on (as happened with Junior Wells, Buddy Guy, James Cotton, Otis Spann, and Charlie Musselwhite, all of whom recorded full albums for Vanguard). I dreamed of a similar series to show off the musicians who were playing the Chicago blues clubs in the late 1970s.

When I first envisioned this series, I made a list of forty unrecorded or underrecorded Chicago blues musicians who deserved national and international recognition. These were musicians I was seeing in the clubs almost every night — people like Jimmy Johnson, Lonnie Brooks, Left Hand Frank, Carey Bell, Magic Slim,[1] Eddie

1. Magic Slim (born Morris Holt) and Magic Sam (Sam Maghett) are often confused. Both were born in 1937 near Grenada, Mississippi. Magic Sam was the brilliant West Side guitarist and singer whose recording career began in 1957 at age twenty, when he cut the popular "All Your Love" for Eli Toscano's short-lived (1956–1959) but influential Cobra label. (Cobra was also the first recording home for Otis Rush, Buddy Guy, and Guitar Shorty.) "All Your Love" was produced by Willie Dixon, who was working for Cobra while feuding with his long-time boss, Leonard Chess. Sam went on to cut a number of singles for various labels and

Shaw, and Pinetop Perkins. But to launch such a project, I would need capital that Alligator didn't yet have. Even if I cut every corner, nine sessions would still require a lot of studio time and tape. And, of course, the musicians all had to be paid. It would be a significant financial gamble for me to record artists who were not going to burn up the world with record sales. Nonetheless, I wanted to show just how vibrant the blues scene in Chicago still was; I wanted to call the series *Living Chicago Blues* for a reason.

Because the blues scene was invisible to the general public, a lot of people thought the blues was dying in Chicago. Back when I was working for Delmark, a visiting writer for one of the British blues magazines had stopped by the Jazz Record Mart on a Thursday or Friday. When he came in the next Tuesday, I assumed he had been spending time in the clubs, and I asked him, "Who'd you see over the weekend?" "Nobody," he replied. "I spent the weekend buying and trading records. Blues is dead in Chicago." Horrified by this blasphemous declaration, I took him out that night to hear J. B. Hutto at Rose and Kelly's. It was J.B.'s birthday, and I presented him with a guitar-shaped cake. When I brought the writer up to meet J.B., I said, "J.B., this is a writer from England, and he tells me blues is dead in Chicago." Then I turned around and walked away, leaving a very much alive J.B. to explain to the writer that he and the blues were not, in fact, dead.

Clearly, the current generation of blues musicians was not being publicized well enough. It was my mission to correct that, but money was the problem. Although most record companies in the United States neglected blues, I knew that there was a solid market for blues recordings in the UK and Europe. Maybe those places held the

---

two classic albums for Delmark, *West Side Soul* and *Black Magic*. He died in 1969 at the age of thirty-two. Magic Slim, who was given his nickname by Magic Sam, began his career as a bass player before switching to guitar. Slim emerged as a popular South Side bluesman in the 1970s, cutting albums for half a dozen labels. Some of his earliest recordings are on Alligator's *Living Chicago Blues* series. Magic Slim and the Teardrops were Hound Dog Taylor's favorite band. Magic Sam was blessed with a soul-inflected tenor voice and a soaring, clean-toned guitar sound, whereas Magic Slim had a lower and gruffer voice and a rougher, gritty guitar style. Both artists are essential listening for any fan of Chicago blues.

answer to my financial problem. Blues artists had been touring there since the early 1950s, starting with Big Bill Broonzy. European and British jazz organizations and jazz bands had arranged these tours, as had European tour promoters fascinated with American jazz. They all considered blues to be part of the jazz tradition.[2] In the United States, blues musicians typically played in bars; in Europe, they were treated as concert hall artists. Tours by Broonzy and Muddy Waters had inspired the British blues movement of the 1960s, and European jazz festivals regularly featured blues artists. Although the number of British and European fans was never as big as the American artists or American public thought, there was a steady market in Europe for both touring artists and blues records.

About the time I released Son Seals's first album, I received a letter from Dag Häggqvist, owner of Sonet Records in Sweden. He expressed interest in licensing the rights to manufacture and release Alligator records in Europe. I had never heard of Sonet, but I soon learned that Dag had become a legend in the European record business starting at a very young age. He had begun distributing American jazz labels in Sweden at the age of fifteen and produced his first album at sixteen, establishing his own label to release it and other jazz recordings. When he was nineteen, he joined the four-year-old Sonet label as a one-third partner. Though jazz and blues were his passions, he began releasing pop records as well. As Sonet became a successful pop label, Dag brought together independent distributors and labels in Norway, Denmark, and Finland to form a Sonet conglomerate, with each company distributing the records of the others.

By the time Dag reached out to Alligator, he was one of the best-known record men in Europe. He had become a key figure in the International Federation of the Phonographic Industry, the European equivalent of the powerful Record Industry Association of America.

---

2. German promoters Horst Lippmann and Fritz Rau, who were business partners, created the American Folk Blues Festival, which toured packages of American blues musicians across Europe and the UK almost annually from 1962 to 1982. The musicians for these tours were often chosen by Willie Dixon.

He had set up an international Sonet office in England and placed Rod Buckle, an experienced British record man, in charge. It amazed me that this successful record company, with offices in Sweden and the UK and pan-European distribution, wanted to license my tiny label. Sonet even offered a financial advance to be deducted from future royalties. Of course I said yes.

Licensing was a new concept for Alligator. It gave Sonet the exclusive right to manufacture Alligator recordings for sales in the UK and Europe. Sonet would press and distribute Alligator albums throughout Europe, and because the records were pressed locally, retailers could buy them at a wholesale price that allowed the stores to price them like European records. European media would pay more attention to Alligator releases because they were available on a European label, not hard-to-find imports. Both the Alligator and Sonet logos would appear on each record. The Alligator records that Sonet licensed would be domestically priced in Europe but also have the cachet of being branded as the product of Alligator, a cool American label. Sonet would handle all European promotion and advertising, at its own expense. Sonet also would pay the song publishers under local copyright law. Then Sonet would pay a royalty to Alligator for each sale, and Alligator would pay the artists their share. By the end of the 1970s, Alligator made a little less than two dollars for the sale of each LP licensed to Sonet.[3]

As the deal with Sonet was being finalized, I traveled to London to meet Rod Buckle, who would be my key day-to-day contact. He was charming, self-confident, talkative, and physically imposing. Rod had come up through the British pop industry and was a younger

---

3. In contrast, if Alligator had chosen to export a recording (which we now do more than licensing), we would have negotiated a per-LP price with a foreign distributor. Under an export deal, we would pay the song publishers here in the United States. We would cover the cost of advertising in the foreign markets, and we wouldn't expect the foreign distributor to do more than send some promotional copies to radio and press. In the late 1970s, an album that we exported to a foreign territory earned about three dollars of profit for Alligator. But exporting also meant that Alligator had to pay the pressing costs as well as the artists and song publishers, so the per-LP costs were higher. If we licensed, our per-LP profit dropped, but our costs also dropped and our chances for greater sales numbers in foreign territories improved.

equivalent of the old-school American record men, aggressive, fast-talking deal makers like Leonard Chess. Whereas Dag was about the art, Rod was about the commerce. He gave seed money to producers he thought might develop popular acts, in exchange for a piece of the action if they had success. He was uninterested in the boring nuts and bolts of distribution, but he was very interested in shrewd deal making. Rod was in charge of the distribution of Sonet outside of Scandinavia.

From 1974 to the end of the 1990s, Sonet was Alligator's licensee for Europe, and I developed close personal relationships with Dag, Rod, and their staffs. I admired Dag's boyish, energetic style. Rod was always full of good spirits and seemed to make deals with the right European companies, ones that were eager to promote Alligator releases. Sonet's powerful sublicensees, like Virgin Records in France, Intercord in Germany, Indisc in Benelux, and Ricordi in Italy welcomed me when I came to Europe on tour with my artists, as I often did.

In early 1977, Dag came to Chicago. While we had dinner, I made a proposal to him: Would Sonet help finance the *Living Chicago Blues* project? Dag naturally asked, "How much would it cost?" I plotted out the costs for him on a paper napkin—the sessions, the mixes, even the packaging, all of which totaled about eleven thousand dollars. To me, this was a daunting amount of money. I was cutting records for three or four thousand dollars, including advances to the musicians. Dag didn't hesitate. "Let's do it," he said. Of course his investment would be an advance to be deducted from the royalties the series could earn for European sales. But Dag was taking a leap of faith; the series might never earn back his investment.

Armed with the promise of Swedish money, I looked over my list of about forty possible musicians and created a short list of the priority artists I would approach about recording. All of them agreed immediately. They had few other opportunities, and I wasn't asking anyone for an exclusive contract. The recording began in early 1978 and went quickly, with the first three LPs released by fall of that year.

It was incredibly exhilarating and challenging for me to work with all these artists. Some led well-rehearsed bands that were gigging regularly. Others needed a lot of help and guidance. For example, Jimmy Johnson and his band were an experienced unit with an established repertoire. Jimmy was a veteran R&B musician who had reinvented himself as a bluesman. He had been creating a lot of excitement on the Chicago scene. Jimmy's gospel-inflected high tenor voice and soaring guitar were perfectly matched. These would be Jimmy's first recordings for a US label. He went on to prove himself to be one of the best, but least heralded, Chicago bluesmen of his generation.

On the other hand, my old friend Carey Bell was freelancing at the time, and I had to assemble a band to back him up, as well as help him choose songs. It was the first time that his brilliant guitar-playing son Lurrie, who was only eighteen, had been in the studio. Because I had an inexperienced newcomer in the band, I wanted a rock-solid rhythm section. Along with veteran West Side bassman Aron Burton, whom I had met when he played with Luther Allison, I recruited Odie Payne Jr., one of the most respected Chicago blues drummers of the 1950s and 1960s. Odie was what I call a conversation drummer. Rather than playing tightly rehearsed parts, he played differently on each take as the song was being recorded, improvising fills and accents spontaneously to fit with what the other musicians were playing. Laughing and joking with everyone and playing with incredible ease, he created an aura of relaxed confidence. Odie, like Fred Below, was a graduate of the famous music program at DuSable High School in Chicago.

The exuberant Eddie Shaw was the only sax player leading a blues band in Chicago. He had a big voice and a brash, aggressive horn sound. Eddie didn't play a wide range of melodies, but if you heard one note, you knew it was Eddie Shaw. Eddie led the Wolf Gang, Howlin' Wolf's last band, which included the famed guitarist Hubert Sumlin. Eddie also had Johnny "Big Moose" Walker in his band at the time, the same keyboard player who had appeared on Son Seals's Alligator debut. Moose had played with Ike Turner, Earl Hooker, and Elmore James. At Eddie's session, I was so impressed with Moose's two-fisted piano playing that I invited him to cut a *Living Chicago Blues* session of his own.

Billy Branch had already established his reputation as the most dynamic young blues harmonica player in Chicago, and he seemed to have a bright future. He had recently put together his first band, which we rehearsed in the basement of his apartment building. Billy didn't have a name for the band. We decided that, with Carey Bell's son Lurrie on guitar and Willie Dixon's son Freddie on bass, plus Billy being the spiritual son of James Cotton and Junior Wells, we'd call it the Sons of Blues, or the SOBs for short. Billy's kept that band name ever since, and he's become the most visible Chicago harp master of his generation.

The revelation of the *Living Chicago Blues* series was Lonnie Brooks. Lonnie was one of the most popular musicians on the West Side. When I met him, he was playing at the Avenue Lounge, on the corner of West Madison Road and Mozart. The place drew a rough crowd, including lots of pimps and hookers.[4] Lonnie's job was to play anything that was on the jukebox, including some blues. But he had to know his Stax material and his James Brown songs, too. He also had to back up a "shake dancer" (a very athletic stripper) named Miss Shaky Bottom who had no trouble living up to her name. Lonnie had an energetic, jovial onstage personality and a big voice with a gritty edge that reminded me of Memphis-style soul singers like Otis Redding. He would occasionally even throw some mock-Elvis gyrations into his show. He struck me as a strong though not very original guitarist and a good-time entertainer.

Lonnie Brooks was born Lee Baker Jr. in Louisiana, but his career started in the mid-1950s in the oil refining boomtown of Port Arthur, Texas. Known in those days as Guitar Junior, he had a basic blues

---

4. One night at the Avenue, somebody approached me and said, "Will you do me a favor? Hold this," and handed me a gun. Then he disappeared back into the crowd. I sat there with this gun in my hand thinking that it undoubtedly had just been used to murder somebody. Now my fingerprints were all over it. I was terrified. I put it on the floor under my chair. An hour or two later, he came back and reclaimed his weapon. I was never happier to see somebody leaving a club with a gun. That was the kind of place the Avenue Lounge was.

vocabulary but was more of a rocker than a bluesman.[5] He had cut Gulf Coast regional rock and roll hits like "The Crawl" and "Got It Made in the Shade" for the Goldband label, run by Eddie Shuler out of his record store and TV repair shop in Lake Charles, Louisiana. After a few years, Lonnie's Gulf Coast career dried up. He came to Chicago in 1959 and reinvented himself as a blues and R&B musician with the stage name Lonnie Brooks.

I considered Lonnie to be a middleweight journeyman who would be playing gigs like the Avenue Lounge forever. But in 1975, he went overseas on tour. European blues audiences didn't want to hear popular jukebox songs; Lonnie was expected to play real blues. After he came back, I saw him late one night at Pepper's Hideout playing a rearranged version of the Lowell Fulson standard "Reconsider Baby" that sounded fresh and different. Realizing there was more originality in Lonnie than I had thought, I asked him to cut four songs for *Living Chicago Blues*. At the first rehearsal, Lonnie started playing a strange, infectious, funky "backward" rhythm guitar part that had the band and me guessing where the downbeat was. The song was called "Two Headed Man," and it became a highlight of the *Living Chicago Blues* series. The lyrics began, *Going back to Louisiana / Gonna renew my mojo hand*, and continued, *Two headed man / Won't you make my roots a little stronger this time?* I loved the image of Lonnie going into the mojo store with his warranty and saying, "My mojo isn't working properly anymore, and women aren't falling at my feet." That was the song that sold me on Lonnie Brooks. The strength of his *Living Chicago Blues* session inspired me to offer him a full contract. Between 1979 and 1999, Lonnie cut seven full albums for Alligator, each with one or two of his signature "voodoo blues" songs. He became a crucial member of the Alligator family.

Producing the *Living Chicago Blues* series was exhilarating. I was

---

5. Lonnie's biggest hit was 1957's "Family Rules." It's in a Louisiana style called swamp pop—medium-tempo songs that go back and forth between the I and IV chords. Phil Phillips's "Sea of Love," with future Alligator artist Katie Webster on piano, is an archetypal swamp pop song, with the piano triplets that were an intrinsic part of the laid-back swamp pop sound. People would do line dances like the Stroll to swamp pop songs.

proud of the quality of these recordings; they raised my level of self-confidence as a producer. I was spending a lot of money on them, unsure how they were going to do in the marketplace. But I had my financial safety net; I couldn't have done it without Dag Häggqvist's faith and financing. The series ultimately earned back both Alligator's and Sonet's investments. Three of the six albums won Grammy nominations. (There was no blues category in the Grammy awards in the 1970s and 1980s; the albums were nominated in the "Best Ethnic or Traditional Recording" category.)

With the *Living Chicago Blues* series, I had announced to the world that the blues was still alive and well in my adopted home city. Alligator had become an iconic label for Chicago blues. Now it was time to become an iconic label for the blues, period.

In 1978, Alligator took a giant step forward with the signing of the label's first non-Chicago artist—Albert Collins. Known as the Master of the Telecaster, Albert had a bigger reputation than any artist I had previously signed. He had been one of the few bluesmen in the national spotlight during the late 1960s and early 1970s, though his career had slumped since then. He was a Texas-born electric guitar hero whose stinging, ultra-percussive, echo-laden style had been dubbed "the cool sound."[6]

Back in the early 1960s Albert had cut a series of danceable instrumentals that received a lot of airplay on black-oriented radio stations. Originally released on the small TCF Hall label, they were reissued in 1969 as *Truckin' with Albert Collins* on the popular, well-distributed Blue Thumb label. At the urging of Canned Heat, the successful white blues band, Albert had relocated to California in the late 1960s, where he played at rock venues, including the famous Fillmore Auditorium. He had gone on to record three albums for the powerful Imperial Records, but none had been exciting enough

6. Part of Albert's sound came from tuning his guitar in a very unusual way (in open F minor) and playing with his thumb and first finger rather than with a pick. He also liked to play with the volume and treble on his amp set at maximum level and his midrange and bass turned to zero. It made for a sound that cut like a razor blade.

to catch the attention of the young white blues audience. I had read about Albert in *Rolling Stone* but didn't hear his music until I was working at the Jazz Record Mart. There I came across the original version of his 1965 album of instrumentals, *The Cool Sounds of Albert Collins*, with song titles like "Frosty," "Sno-Cone," "Don't Lose Your Cool," and "Shiver 'n Shake." I bought the album for $1.77 and fell in love with it.

I first saw Albert live in 1974 at Ruby Gulch, the club in Champaign, Illinois, where Hound Dog played regularly. Albert's music was so powerful that I had imagined him to be a tall, imposing man. Instead I found that he was slight, wiry, and soft spoken, with an angular face and high cheekbones that suggested his family included not only African Americans but also Native Americans. He played a lot of instrumentals, and when he sang, he sang quietly with a Texas drawl, almost speaking the lyrics. But when he turned up his guitar, it felt like it was going to rip my head off. The club he was playing in was small, but he put on a fiery, physical show. Like Freddie King and Luther Allison, Albert Collins played with his whole body, from his toes up. He made faces, stomped around, and threw himself into the music. You could see the muscles swell in his arms as he squeezed the strings. He ended the show covered in sweat. He left me exhausted, my ears ringing. I was entranced.

Our relationship was nurtured by Dick Shurman, the producer, writer, and blues music expert who became one of my most important collaborators and a good friend. I had first met Dick in the early 1970s. After he moved to Chicago permanently in 1974, I would see him often in the blues clubs. Dick had befriended Albert in Seattle, Dick's hometown, where Albert played regularly. In early 1978, Dick had helped Albert land a European tour where he was backed by a Dutch band. By this time Albert had so few gigs that he had no steady band of his own, so when he gigged on the road, he'd hire a local band to back him. Dick and I arranged a couple gigs for him in the Chicago area, one backed by Lonnie Brooks's band and the other by Jimmy Johnson's. Again, I was overwhelmed by his intensity and energy level. Dick pushed me to sign Albert.

When Dick broached the subject of making a record for Alligator, Albert asked for one thousand dollars as an advance, to be deducted from his future royalties. That was a terrifying sum for my little label. Typically I was still advancing only about five hundred dollars to a bandleader. I briefly dismissed the project, but Albert's music was too compelling. It triumphed over my financial fears. Looking back, after having sold one hundred thousand copies of the first Albert Collins album, *Ice Pickin'*, I realize that a much larger advance would have been appropriate.

We arranged for a preproduction meeting at Dick's home. Albert was driving in from Los Angeles with his wife, Gwen. He had told us he would have original songs ready for us to hear, but when he arrived at Dick's house, we discovered just how unprepared he was. All he had was an idea for an instrumental, a set of lyrics written by Gwen that seemed more like a story than a song, and some mediocre lyrics written by his cousin. Not the least bit worried that we were planning to record in only a week and a half, Albert asked us to suggest some songs previously recorded by other artists. Sitting up well past midnight listening to Dick's record collection and identifying songs that might work on the album, we chose tunes by fellow Texans like Johnny "Guitar" Watson, T-Bone Walker, and Freddie King. I soon learned that Albert could master and personalize songs with incredible ease.

Because Albert didn't have his own group, Dick and I solicited a top-notch Chicago band co-led by Casey Jones, a singing drummer, and Aron Burton, a singing bass player. Their chemistry with Albert was instant. The sheer physicality of his music inspired them, and his self-effacing personality and sly sense of humor made them warm to him immediately. Before going to the studio, we had arranged for them to play four nights at the Wise Fools so that they would be more comfortable with each other musically. I invited veteran Chicago saxman A. C. Reed to sit in one night. Albert loved his playing so much that he wanted A.C. to play on the album, exactly as I had plotted.

For the recording, I sat in the control room at Curtom Studios with the engineer, Freddie Breitberg, while Dick worked in the studio with the musicians. Working from his notes on the arrangements, Dick reviewed the rehearsed parts with each musician before each song was recorded. I listened to the playback of every take and decided if we needed another performance. Everyone worked quickly in the studio, and the entire recording was completed in three days.

Albert liked doing everything live in the studio without overdubs, including the vocals and solos. Unlike any other musician I have ever worked with, Albert sang in the studio without wearing headphones because he could hear the vocal pitches in his head. Although we had some technical challenges trying to keep Albert's super-loud guitar from being picked up by every microphone, the spontaneity of Albert's solos was thrilling. The other musicians fed off his energy.

It took Albert a little while to adjust to Casey Jones. "I'm not used to these boogaloo drummers," he said. Casey played a funky Chicago shuffle rather than a swinging, jazzy Texas shuffle, and his bass drum playing had a cool syncopation that was a little different from what Albert was used to. Albert was able to adapt rhythmically, and Casey and A. C. Reed became members of Albert's touring band, the Icebreakers (as Aron Burton named them), for years.

We released *Ice Pickin'*, a title inspired by the "cool" names of his earlier singles, in December 1978. Albert quickly became Alligator's most visible and popular artist—even more so than Koko Taylor and Son Seals—and he brought many new fans to the label. I took on the job of managing him and often personally road managed his foreign tours. Albert went on to record five more albums for Alligator (two of them live), including the Grammy-winning *Showdown!*, which I discuss in chapter 13. His albums have proved to be enduring classics that continue to sell, year in and year out.

From the very beginnings of the label, I realized that our artists needed help if they were going to have performing careers outside of their home cities. At first, I acted as booking agent for Hound Dog, Big Walter, Son Seals, Fenton Robinson, Koko Taylor, Lonnie Brooks, and Albert Collins as each one joined the label. Thankfully, by the early 1980s, I had placed each of them with professional booking agencies that could do a much better job than the tiny Alligator staff could.

But the artists still needed help. Someone needed to field every offer from the booking agent, assess the profitability of each potential gig, and discuss with the agent if other shows could be booked within driving distance. Someone needed to pressure the agents to deliver more dates, suggest potential venues and routing, and do tour planning. Someone needed to contact the venues to establish load-in, sound check, and performance times. Someone needed to book motel rooms for the bands. Most of our bands traveled by highway and had no road managers, so, in those pre-GPS days, someone needed to sit with a road atlas, plot out the best possible routes, and create a printed guide (we called them "running sheets") for the band to get from one gig to the next, with each highway and local street designated. For overseas dates, flights needed to be booked and often a member of the Alligator staff needed to be on tour with the artists, dealing with travel from foreign city to foreign city, doing business in a foreign language, handling foreign cash, and taking care of unexpected emergencies.

The artists needed help with their bookkeeping too. The booking agents often received advance deposits from the venues. After deducting their commissions, the balance went to the artist. Someone needed to make sure that the commissions had been calculated properly and help the artist get this information summarized for tax preparation. In many cases, our artists had operated on a cash basis when playing locally; some had not been scrupulous about reporting cash income. Once they were touring nationally and internationally, they had to learn correct tax preparation and filing.

All these tasks were the job of a personal manager. After we placed our artists with booking agents, some of them asked Alligator to take on the role of management. In addition to the tasks mentioned above, management involved advancing artists' careers in other ways—for example, placing them in films and on television or helping to arrange for them to make guest appearances on other artists' albums. When one of our managed artists had a film appearance, as Albert Collins did in *Adventures in Babysitting*, as Koko Taylor did in David Lynch's *Wild at Heart*, and as both Koko Taylor and Lonnie Brooks did in *Blues Brothers 2000*, one of the Alligator staff was always with them to take care of their needs. One of us also traveled with them when they made TV appearances on *The Tonight Show with Jay Leno*, *Late Night with David Letterman*, *Late Night with Conan O'Brien*, and *Austin City Limits*. For example, I traveled with Albert Collins when he recorded with David Bowie for a movie soundtrack and filmed a TV commercial with Bruce Willis, as well as on his first few European and Australian tours.

From the early 1980s on, Alligator had one staff member dedicated to artist management. Longtime staffers Nora Kinnally and Matt LaFollette both served in this role. It was a grueling job. They had to be available to the artists on nights and weekends if something went wrong (like vehicle breakdowns, canceled flights, emergency health problems, or problems with payments after shows). They were held responsible for every detail of tour planning. I remember a musician calling from a thousand miles away to yell, "Have you *seen* this filthy motel where you booked us?" Of course, the answer was no. Our head of artist management had found it in a motels directory.

Our longest-running managed artists were Koko Taylor and Lonnie Brooks. We managed Koko from 1975 until her death in 2009. We managed Lonnie from 1978 until his retirement in 2012. They were our friends and part of our daily lives. The commissions we earned from their gigs never did more than cover Nora's or Matt's salaries. But they needed us. For decades, management was one of Alligator's essential jobs.[7]

Overseas tour management in particular was an endless adventure. There were great triumphs for our artists, like when the virtu-

---

7. Some people perceive a conflict of interest when the artist's manager is also employed by his or her label. The main conflict, however, arises because managers normally take a piece of the recording royalties, as do producers. Neither Alligator nor I ever took a commission on any of the managed artists' Alligator recording royalties, so there was no conflict.

ally unknown Son Seals opened for B. B. King in Paris and London and won multiple standing ovations. And there were times when we ended up in the emergency room. This included the night when Koko Taylor had an attack of diverticulitis in Buenos Aires and the only emergency room we could find had feral cats wandering around looking for food. The doctors wanted to do surgery, but we declined; Koko recovered. And there were nights of danger, like at a concert in a basketball arena in Thessalonica, Greece, in 1980, when I was road managing the first blues tour of Greece with Albert Collins and the Icebreakers, Koko Taylor, Billy Branch, and Lurrie Bell. Without warning or provocation, for no apparent reason other than the fact that thousands of young people were gathered there, the riot police showed up fully armed and formed a line between the stage and the audience, billy clubs and shields at the ready. With his 150-foot guitar cord, Albert Collins walked right through the row of police and into the audience. Nothing was going to keep him from bringing the music to his fans! Fearful of the police, I herded all the musicians into the bus heading back to the hotel about thirty seconds after the last song ended. Thankfully there was no riot.

Though this was a harrowing night, nothing in my road management experience was more terrifying than the incident that ended Son Seals's tour of Scandinavia in 1978.

1. Hound Dog Taylor & The HouseRockers, 1974. *Left to right:* Hound Dog Taylor, Ted Harvey, and Brewer Phillips. Photo by Bob Keeling. Courtesy of Alligator Records.

2. Bob Koester at Jazz Record Mart, 1970. Courtesy of Delmark Records.

3. Luther Allison concert poster from Lawrence University, 1969

4. Florence's Lounge with musicians likely to show up any weekend, 1978. *Left to right:* Nick Holt, Byther Smith, Junior Pettis, Joe Carter, unknown, Johnny Junius, unknown, unknown, possibly Bonnie Lee, Louis Myers, Larry Cox (*background*), Little Willie Anderson, Bob Myers (*far right*), Joel Poston (*kneeling*). Photo by Erik Lindahl.

5. Junior Wells outside Theresa's Lounge, 1978. Photo by D. Shigley. Courtesy of the
D. Shigley Collection curated by Scott Shigley.

6. Big Walter Horton at the home of pianist Jimmy Walker, 1975. Photo by D. Shigley. Courtesy of the D. Shigley Collection curated by Scott Shigley.

young bluesmaster

THE SON SEALS BLUES BAND

Son Seals plays blues for today — and for tomorrow. At 30, he's been a professional musician for fifteen years. He's learned from Albert King, Earl Hooker and Robert Nighthawk. But Son has his own style, combining his youth and energy with a lifetime in the blues. His incredibly fast, raw guitar and urgent, intense vocals mark him as something special. And Son isn't content to rework other bluesmen's material . . . he insists on writing and performing his own songs.

Son Seals' blues doesn't need any fancy overproduction, background singers, corps of studio sidemen or overdubbing. This is his own band, direct from Chicago's South Side, playing his music. It's an amazing, fiercely original debut album by a man destined to become a major figure in the blues world.

Alligator 4703
List price: $5.98

Alligator Records

P. O. Box 11741
Ft. Dearborn Station
Chicago, Illinois 60611

7. Son Seals's 1973 debut album announcement sent to record stores and distributors. Courtesy of Alligator Records.

8. Fenton Robinson (guitar) and James Cotton (vocals) with Nate Applewhite (drums) at Theresa's Lounge, 1976. Photo by Hans Andréasson.

9. Son Seals at the Mill Run Theatre, Niles, IL, late 1970s. Photo by Steve Kagan. Courtesy of Alligator Records.

10. Train wreck outside Moss, Norway, 1978. Courtesy of NTB scanpix/SIPA USA.

11. Koko Taylor with Son Seals and Lonnie Brooks at the Mill Run Theatre, Niles, IL, late 1970s. The concert was sponsored by WXRT-FM. Photo by Steve Kagan.

12. Mailing piece promoting Lonnie Brooks's *Bayou Lightning* to radio programmers, 1979. Courtesy of Alligator Records.

13. David Lee Watson, Professor Longhair, Dr. John, and Bruce Iglauer at Sea-Saint Recording Studio, New Orleans, 1979. Photo by Michael J. Smith. © The Historic New Orleans Collection.

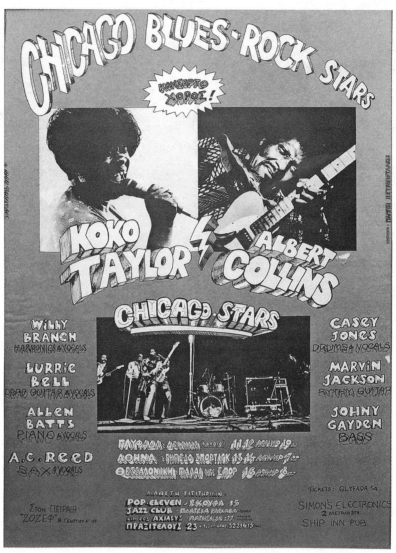

14. Poster advertising the first blues tour of Greece, 1980. Courtesy of Alligator Records.

15. Koko Taylor at ChicagoFest, 1979. Photo by Jim Quattrocki.

16. Albert Collins and James Cotton sitting in with Johnny Winter at the Park West, Chicago, 1984. Photo by Paul Natkin.

17. Albert Collins, Lonnie Mack, and Roy Buchanan at Carnegie Hall, New York City, 1986. Photo by Ebet Roberts.

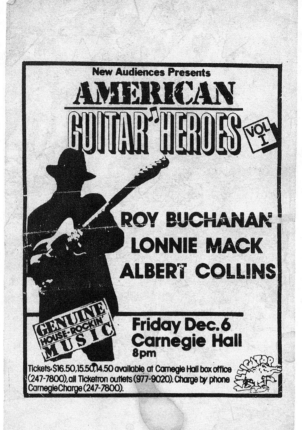

18. Carnegie Hall concert poster, 1986. Courtesy of Alligator Records.

19. Albert Collins, Johnny Copeland, and Tinsley Ellis at Tramps, New York City, 1990. Photo by Lisa Seifert.

20. Alligator Records 20th Anniversary Tour poster. Courtesy of Alligator Records.

21. Albert Collins, Bruce Iglauer, and Dick Shurman at the Chicago Blues Festival, 1992. Photo by John Brisbin.

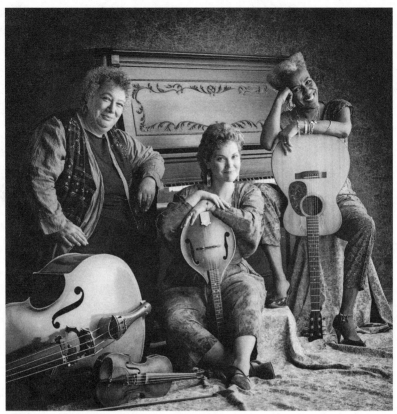

22. Saffire—The Uppity Blues Women. *Left to right:* Ann Rabson, Andra Faye, and Gaye Adegbalola. Photo by Marc Norberg. Courtesy of Alligator Records.

23. Shemekia Copeland and Michael Burks at the Chicago Blues Festival, 2011. Photo by Jennifer Noble.

24. Marcia Ball, C. J. Chenier, and Lil' Ed Williams at the Rawa Blues Festival, Katowice, Poland, 2011. Photo by Aigars Lapsa.

25. Lil' Ed and Corky Siegel with James "Pookie" Young (*background*) at the Chicago Blues Festival, 2016. Photo by Paul Natkin.

26. Tommy Castro and Toronzo Cannon at the Chicago Blues Festival, 2016. Photo by Howard Greenblatt.

27. Lonnie Brooks and Rick Estrin at the celebration of Alligator's forty-fifth anniversary, the Chicago Blues Festival, 2011. Photo by Marilyn Stringer.

28. Shemekia Copeland at the Chicago Blues Festival, 2017. Photo by Howard Greenblatt.

29. Lil' Ed & The Blues Imperials, thirtieth anniversary celebration at B.L.U.E.S. on Halsted, Chicago, November 17, 2017. *Left to right:* Lil' Ed Williams, Kelly Littleton, Michael Garrett, and James "Pookie" Young. Photo by Eric Kreisant.

30. Selwyn Birchwood and Jarekus Singleton at SPACE, Evanston, IL, July 2014. Photo by Roman Sobus.

PART II

Son Seals's October 1978 tour of Europe began in Scandinavia, with dates in the UK to follow. Traveling with him was the band he had used on the Live and Burning *album: his longtime bass player, Snapper Mitchum, along with drummer Tony Gooden, sax player A. C. Reed, and rhythm guitarist Lacy Gibson. As Son's agent, I had helped arrange the tour and was traveling on the trip as tour manager and friend. The tour opened with a few dates in Sweden. In Gothenburg, the last gig before we caught the train to Oslo, Norway, the band played at a community center. Son was fired up and played more than ninety minutes without a break. Tony had had quite a bit to drink, and as the performance rolled on, he signaled repeatedly to Son that he desperately needed to go to the bathroom. Son ignored him. As Son launched into the last song, Tony, unable to wait any longer, wet himself. I grabbed Tony's coat from the dressing room and tossed it to him so that he could hold it in front of himself when he left the stage. Son was furious, but the only private place he could chew Tony out was in the dressing room, which we were sharing with the Swedish opening band. The Swedes were in a foul mood because all their equipment had been stolen the night before. I had to ask them politely to vacate the room. The bandleader, who was far from sober, refused and angrily challenged me to go outside and settle things like a man. I'm no fighter and, afraid of taking a beating, I quickly backed down. The band finally left us alone, and Son yelled at Tony for a while before we all went back to our hotel. All the next day, I felt like a coward for having backed away from a fight.*

In the evening, we boarded a four-car electric-powered train to Oslo. It was a typical European train, with an aisle along one side of the car and compartments with sliding doors that seated six, with three passengers facing three others. We sat in the last two compartments of the last car. Son and members of the band noisily played cards in one compartment while I read in the one closest to the back of the train. Wanting to sleep, Tony came into the compartment where I was sitting with an elderly American couple and an old Norwegian woman. The old woman started yelling at Tony in Norwegian, making it clear that she didn't want a tough-looking dark-skinned man anywhere near her. Deciding that nothing could be done about an elderly racist, Tony shrugged and went back to the compartment where the rest of the band was playing cards.

Soon after, as the train rounded a curve, I felt the rear wheels derail and bounce along the tracks. The car lurched sideways, and the old woman sitting across from me jumped up out of her seat. Realizing that the car was tipping over and she would be hurt, I let go of my arm rests, jumped up, and pushed her back down into her seat. At that moment, the car started turning over. I was thrown out the open door of the compartment and into the aisle just as a large, heavy trunk fell from the overhead luggage rack and landed hard in my empty seat.

I assumed that the train would turn over and land on its side. Night had fallen, and in the darkness I hadn't realized that we were high atop a steep embankment above a fjord. Instead of coming to a stop, the car rolled over until it was almost upside down. Then it started skidding downward toward the water. People screamed and the lights went out. I slid down toward the rear of the train on the ceiling of the car. The train kept sliding down, finally coming to a halt with the rear end of the car much farther down the embankment than the front. Everything stopped, and in a moment of silence, I could hear the water of the fjord flowing outside. Shaken but not injured, I called to each of the band members and heard their voices in reply. But when I called to Tony, there was no immediate response. Then he started screaming. Tony had been asleep when the train started turning over. He was thrown from his seat, and the heavy door to his compartment slammed down on his right forearm, cutting it to the bone. He was bleeding profusely.

Fearing that at any moment the train car could slide into the water, I looked for an exit. One side door and set of windows were blocked by the embankment, and the other side door and windows were overhead and out of reach. The back door of the car, facing the water, was the only way out. A.C. and Snapper slid down to the back of the car, where I was, and together we tried to open the back door of the car. Normally the door slid sideways, but at this angle it needed to be pushed upward and to the right to open. We fought with the door, but it was off its runners and wouldn't budge. Water from the fjord, meanwhile, was seeping into the car around our feet. I called to Son for help, but he was desperately digging through his luggage to find his insulin. A.C. and Snapper (who had been a highly decorated paratrooper in Vietnam) crawled back to try to slow Tony's bleeding by using Lacy's belt as a tourniquet. I was left by myself, staring at the jammed door. I tried it again, and, for one moment, I found more strength than I thought I had. I pushed the door up, and it opened. I could feel the night air and see the water of the fjord outside. I placed my feet in the corner where the back wall of the train met the ceiling and the side wall, and stood, making my body rigid. I lowered the door slightly and allowed it to rest on my shoulder so that it would remain open. I knew that if I moved at all, the door would come down like a guillotine.

As the train car inched further into the water, it became clear to me and the band that we had to get everyone out of the car. Son and A.C. clambered out the door and into the water, holding on to the back of the train. Lacy and Snapper got Tony out of the car, and Son, Lacy, and A.C. dragged him out of the water and onto the little bank of the fjord. Snapper stayed in the train car with me. Nobody was coming to help us. The engine and first two cars were still on the track, but people were afraid to slide down the almost-vertical slope for fear of plunging into the water.

I didn't know how long we had before the car might slip into the fjord. I called to Snapper, who had the coolest head, perhaps because of his military training. He crawled from compartment to compartment, helping semiconscious people down the length of the car and through the door into the fjord. Son and A.C. stood chest-deep in the cold water and grabbed people as they evacuated the train. The darkness made it difficult to see anything. We worked for more than an hour to get dozens of people off the train and onto the bank. With the car emptied, Snapper climbed out. Now, I was the last person in the car. I knew that if I moved, the door would come down and trap me inside. It seemed that I was in an impossible position. I was pretty sure I was going to die. I had been angry with myself all day, feeling I had been a coward the previous night in Gothenburg when I had backed down from a fight with the Swedish bandleader. Now, when I had to be brave for a good reason, I refused to give in to fear. If I was going to die that night, I was going to go out like a man.

As I stood inside the car in about ten inches of water, I felt my aluminum briefcase bump up against my ankle. I managed to reach down, grab it, and wedge it in the open door. Now I could get out. But I knew I couldn't leave that briefcase behind. The contents were too important. I thought, "We're obviously not finishing this tour. We're going to be lucky if Tony is alive tomorrow. We don't have the cash to buy airline tickets to get back to the United States. I'm going to need the contracts in that briefcase to prove our loss when we sue the Norwegian national railway system." I clambered out into the fjord. Immediately my cowboy boots filled with water and I felt myself being dragged down to the dredged bottom of the fjord and into the channel. Thankfully, Son or A.C. grabbed me and hauled me up toward the bank. As I was being pulled up, I reached for the briefcase and yanked it out. The door slammed down, sealing the train car. But I had the contracts, and I was alive. And so was everyone else.

By this time, somebody on the tracks had made his way out to a road and summoned help. The volunteer fire department from the nearest town arrived, and after lowering ropes and forming a human chain, they began bringing people up the steep embankment. The fire brigade took us into Moss, Norway, about forty-five miles from Oslo. Twenty-seven passengers were hospitalized. Tony had suffered the worst injury. Although the bone of his arm was intact, the flesh, muscles, and nerves had been severed. Surgeons were called in from Oslo to try to save his arm.

That night in Moss, the uninjured were put up in a small hotel. In the morning I took a long taxi ride to the US consulate in Oslo. An experienced consular official took me to the offices of the Norwegian national railway system, where I was promptly given a "you can ride the trains free" pass. I discovered that the band and I couldn't sue the railway system because we weren't Norwegian citizens. On the other hand, Norway had socialized medicine, so there would be no medical bills for all the doctors' work on Tony and on A.C. (who had been hospitalized as well because of chest pains). But nobody at the railway office was offering tickets for us to return to the United States.

I reluctantly rode back to Moss that evening on a train. There was still enough daylight for me to see our railroad car at the edge of the fjord down below as we went past. I traveled back and forth to Oslo for a number of days. Finally the consular official was able to convince the railway that it was going to have to pay for our airline tickets. We decided that Son, Snapper, Lacy, and A.C. would fly back to Chicago while I stayed in Moss until Tony could travel. Happy to be alive, nobody complained to me about the lost income.

Tony Gooden was never the same. He regained feeling in his hand but the muscles atrophied, and he wasn't able to grasp a drumstick well enough to play again. For a while, I helped him out financially as best I could. Then one day, a year and a half after the train wreck, as he was moving into a third-floor apartment, he leaned against a back porch railing that gave way. He fell to his death. If both his arms had been working properly, perhaps he could have held on and saved himself.

10

It's fair to say that I like to be in control—I'm often described as a control freak—but I don't think Alligator would have lasted had I not obsessed over every detail from the start. The reason is simple: the career I had chosen was full of uncertainty. Every day I was dealing with something unexpected, from a shipment of defective LPs to Hound Dog's shooting of Brewer Phillips. Each day seemed another test of my abilities. But nothing I had experienced in keeping the label afloat could compare with the challenges I faced during the train wreck. That was a life-and-death situation for which no amount of planning or obsession to detail could have prepared me. I don't want to overstate its significance or make it seem overly dramatic, but the experience changed me. In those moments of mortal danger I found an inner strength that I didn't know I had. In starting Alligator, I had taken a leap of faith, but the train wreck represented the first time in my life I had been brave. I don't know if it ultimately made me a better record company owner, or less controlling, or less demanding of perfection, but it did give me self-confidence and perspective. The most obvious lesson I learned was that life is short: you'd better do something now if you're going to do it.

As the 1980s rolled in, I knew I had to get Alligator in a more secure financial position if we were going to take more chances with new, unproven musicians or spend more money on recordings. With its tenth anniversary approaching, Alligator was moving in the right direction. The catalog was growing (twenty releases by the beginning of 1980) and generally selling well. Although operations were still based in my house, the label's staff had grown to four. Hound Dog's recordings continued to sell almost a decade after his debut album and half a decade after his death. Son Seals was touring quite a bit, and we had already released his fourth album. Koko Taylor's second album, *The Earthshaker*, was a success. The risk I had taken with Albert Collins had paid off handsomely. We were quickly becoming a major player in our musical niche.

At the time, we didn't have much competition. Rounder hadn't started its Bullseye Blues label yet, and its blues output was small. The Blind Pig label had been founded in 1977 and was just beginning to become a competitor. A few blues artists like B. B. King were signed to major labels, and others, like Little Milton, found success on independents like Malaco that were directed primarily at black fans. Delmark was continuing to release records, but without much promotion. For Alligator, promotion, publicity, and booking continued to be a major part of the business model. We kept our artists gigging locally and on the road. We worked hard to develop relationships with distributors, record stores, press, and radio. With a foothold in Europe through our deal with Sonet, as well as distribution and licensing deals in Canada and Australia, Alligator was tapping into the international market. We were making a small profit. I was beginning to feel I could take some chances and make some mistakes without sinking the company.

One cost-effective way to build the catalog was by licensing and releasing records that had already been produced and, in some cases, released by other labels. The first record I licensed was by Blind John Davis. John was a charming, urbane, elderly piano player who lived alone in a small apartment only two doors from Ma Bea's club on the West Side. A colorful character, John played and sang muscular boogie-woogie, old blues, and pop tunes. In the 1920s and 1930s, he had been in great demand as a studio musician, playing on dozens of popular blues 78s on the powerful RCA Bluebird label. In the 1940s, he had fronted a six-man combo traveling through Arizona and New Mexico playing hotel gigs. He had also played Chicago-area gay and lesbian bars, places in which he told me the patrons tipped so well that he tied his pant cuffs to his legs and cut out the bottoms of the pockets. He would fill up his pants with coins and go home and untie the cuffs while standing in a washtub. By the 1970s, John didn't gig much in the United States, but he was popular in Europe and traveled there often. European audiences loved his music, which blended blues, traditional jazz, and boogie-woogie, and he had a fascinating life story steeped in blues history. While in Germany he had recorded an album for Ornament Records, a small label run by a tour promoter named Siegfried "Ziggy" Christmann. In 1977, I licensed the record from Ziggy and renamed it *Stomping on a Saturday Night*.

In 1979, I licensed and released two records that had first appeared on my friend Bruce Bromberg's label, Joliet Records, which was going out of business.[1] The first was a Phillip Walker recording titled *Someday You'll Have These Blues*. Phillip Walker was a sophisticated, jazz-inflected Texas guitarist who had relocated to California in the late 1950s. The second was *Been Gone Too Long* by Lonesome Sundown, a solid, down-home Louisiana bluesman who had recorded for the Excello label in the 1950s and 1960s. I licensed both of them for a small advance. I didn't promote them with the same intensity that I poured into new releases, but blues fans were glad to have them back on the market and sales were reasonably good.

That year I also bought some live tapes by a deceased pianist named Johnny Jones, who had been one of Chicago's most in-demand sidemen, recording and performing with legends like Tampa Red and Elmore James. I loved Johnny's hard-pounding style. Heavily influenced by the great Big Maceo Merriweather, he had played on some of my favorite Elmore James records and had cut some singles of his own in the late 1940s and early 1950s. Sometime in the 1960s, a blues fan named Norman Dayron had recorded

---

1. Bruce is one of my favorite producers. I met him for the first time when I went to California in 1974 to promote my second Hound Dog record. Bruce and I hit it off when I mentioned my fondness for Bee Houston's self-titled album, which had the track that inspired Son Seals's "Hot Sauce." It turned out Bruce had produced it. One way to create a lasting friendship is to compliment somebody else's production skills without realizing you're doing so.

Johnny, accompanied by the harmonica player Billy Boy Arnold, at a folk club.[2] Before I bought the tapes, Norman assured me that Johnny and Billy Boy had been paid. I tracked down Billy Boy and he said, "Yeah, we were paid—for a gig. Not to make a record." He led me to Johnny Jones's widow, Letha, and I negotiated advance payments and royalties with both of them. Norman later licensed some of the same material to other labels. Apparently, my exclusive ownership wasn't so exclusive.

Our most successful licensed masters came from the French label Isabel, owned and operated by Didier Tricard, a successful European blues tour promoter. Didier regularly brought Buddy Guy and Junior Wells to tour in Europe, and they were happy to record for him while there. (Didier named the label Isabel at Buddy's suggestion; it was Buddy's wife's name.) In 1981, Alligator licensed a Buddy Guy album from Isabel that we called *Stone Crazy!* Though cut in the studio, it was the closest album to Buddy's almost-out-of-control live shows, with Buddy improvising lyrics and playing explosive solos. A decade later, we licensed another album from Isabel, an intimate acoustic duo session by Buddy Guy and Junior Wells that we called *Alone and Acoustic*. Each has sold more than one hundred thousand copies. In addition, we licensed a fine Magic Slim album from Isabel called *Raw Magic*.

The Alligator catalog wasn't only growing; it was also pushing beyond the geographic boundaries of Chicago and musical boundaries of "pure" blues. In the early 1980s, two projects in particular helped establish Alligator's reputation as more than a Chicago blues label—albums by New Orleans piano master Professor Longhair and Los Angeles R&B giant Johnny Otis.

Many people consider Professor Longhair's *Crawfish Fiesta* to be the best album Alligator has ever released; it's an album I never

2. Billy Boy Arnold is a Chicago blues artist who began playing harmonica as a child, inspired by Sonny Boy Williamson I. His career began in the 1950s when, barely out of his teens, he recorded classic singles for Chicago's Vee-Jay label, including "I Wish You Would" and "I Ain't Got You." In the 1990s, Alligator released two albums by Arnold, *Back Where I Belong* and *Eldorado Cadillac*. As of this writing, he is in his early eighties and still actively performing and recording.

thought I'd make. I had discovered Professor Longhair (known to his fans as Fess) through a marvelous, early 1970s album called *New Orleans Piano* that compiled all the 78s he had cut for Atlantic in the late 1940s and early 1950s. I listened to it constantly. Fess was one of a kind, a musician that only the Crescent City could have produced. He was a marvelously quirky piano player who meshed highly syncopated New Orleans Afro-Cuban rhumba rhythms with old-school R&B, blues and boogie-woogie while throwing in unpredictable flourishes and unexpected snippets of familiar songs. His complex playing seemed like more than anyone could do with just two hands. He sang in a slurred voice that cracked from time to time. He sang a lot of funny songs and smile-inducing nonsense lyrics. His records were full of energy; clearly everybody in the studio was having a wonderful time.

Fess's real name was Henry Roeland Byrd. In addition to Atlantic Records, he had recorded singles for Mercury and small New Orleans labels like Watch and Ebb. He had recorded under a number of names. On one of the early records, the band was billed as Professor Longhair and His Shuffling Hungarians. Professor Longhair was the name that stuck. Some of the New Orleans piano teachers who taught the children of wealthy families were skilled classical players who could, of course, read music. They were called piano professors. Calling a self-taught musician who couldn't read music Professor Longhair was a sardonic comment on those highbrow musicians. Fess was a professor in his own way. He didn't give lessons, but he inspired protégés. His most famous pupils were the Crescent City's ambassador to the rock world, Mac "Dr. John" Rebennack; famed songwriter and producer Allen Toussaint; flamboyant keyboard wizard James Booker; and Huey "Piano" Smith, whose band the Clowns had dozens of local hits and a few national ones, like the original "Rocking Pneumonia and the Boogie Woogie Flu" and "Don't You Just Know It."

Fess had performed and recorded throughout the 1950s and then virtually disappeared. He got a job as a janitor at a record distributorship, made some money as a gambler, and played infrequently. When the New Orleans Jazz and Heritage Festival started in 1970, the festival's producer, Quint Davis (selected by George Wein, who had founded the Newport Jazz and Newport Folk Festivals), located Fess and brought him out of virtual retirement to play that first festival. He was an immediate sensation and was quickly adopted by the city as a symbol of their music. Tipitina's, the famous New Orleans music club, was named after his song "Tipitina."

Fess skated on the edge of a major label deal for years. He cut some sessions in the early 1970s for Bearsville, a label owned in part by Albert Grossman, who had managed both Janis Joplin and Bob Dylan. In 1974, Fess's national profile grew when the public television show *Soundstage* brought him together with Dr. John, the Meters, and Earl King for a show dedicated to New Orleans music. The buzz through the 1970s was that Quint Davis, who was managing Fess, was close to having a major label record deal that would bust Fess wide open and make him a household name. But it didn't happen. I dreamed of signing Fess to Alligator, but Quint was shooting for the big leagues, not for a tiny independent blues label.

In August 1979, Perry Aberli, the organizer of the Midwest Blues Festival at Notre Dame University, asked me if I could arrange for Professor Longhair to perform there. I contacted Quint, who told me that his friend Allison Kaslow was now managing Fess. I called her, and after negotiating the agreement for Fess to come to Notre Dame, I said, "I know that Quint was always waiting for that major label break. But if Fess would ever like to cut an album for an independent label that would truly value his music, promote the album well, and keep it in print forever, please give me a call." She said, "Thank you." I figured I would never hear another word about it.

A couple of days later Allison called me back. "We're interested in talking to you about recording," she said. "Fess has a gig this weekend at Tipitina's. Could you come down?" I dropped everything and flew to New Orleans. Fess was just as good as I had hoped. He had a well-rehearsed band that included Andy Kaslow (Allison's husband) and Tony Dagradi on tenor saxophones; Johnny Vidacovich, who was considered one of New Orleans's best, on drums; and Alfred "Uganda" Roberts on congas.

On the first night, I sat in Tipitina's, taking notes and listening for songs that Fess might want to record. I knew much of his repertoire because he had cut some of the songs for other labels. But there were a few surprises, like "It's My Fault, Darling," an obscure tune recorded by the R&B singer Little Johnny Taylor. The next day, I met with Allison at her home. Fess was there, but he was reserved and quiet. He would take care of the singing and the piano playing; Allison would take care of the business. That afternoon we hashed out a deal. I was thrilled. As with recording Albert Collins, another of my dreams was becoming reality.

Recording sessions were scheduled for October. The project was given a huge boost by my friend Tad Jones, a scholar of New Orleans music whom I had first met at the Jazz Record Mart. Tad called Fess's longtime friend and protégé Dr. John, who was living in New York. Since Fess didn't have a regular guitar player, Tad suggested that Dr. John come and play guitar on the record. (Guitar was Dr. John's first instrument.) He agreed instantly. For my own sense of security, I brought Freddie Breitberg down from Chicago to engineer. By that time, Freddie had cut eight albums for me and he knew the kinds of sounds I liked.

Dr. John arrived for rehearsals carrying a rusty-stringed Gibson guitar he hadn't touched in years. He made it clear that he had no desire to play solos; he wanted to be the rhythm man. In rehearsals, he proved invaluable, especially in directing the three-man horn section. He knew Fess's style backward and forward, and with his experienced ears he could hear nuances I would have missed. With music as funky and syncopated as Fess's, precision playing and exact phrasing were essential. The horns could either emphasize the unique character of Fess's playing, or they could play generic parts you could hear on other records. We wanted something special. Dr. John was on top of that.

We recorded in Allen Toussaint's studio, Sea-Saint. The "Saint" referred to Toussaint; the "Sea" referred to his business partner Marshall Sehorn. A longtime record man, Marshall had a mixed reputation. He had come up during the era when record men had to use whatever tactics they could, clean or dirty, to succeed. Fess didn't trust him. On the first night of recording, Fess instructed me, "I want you to take the master tapes to your hotel room every night because I think Marshall will copy them." So each night I hauled heavy reels of 24-track tapes to my hotel and brought them back to the studio in the morning.

We cut the band sessions in the studio in two long, intense evenings. A tough critic of his own performances, Fess would record a take that we thought was perfect and then would say, "I can do it better." At his request we would call another take and he would show us what he meant. Sometimes the difference between a final take and a rejected one was simply the subtle timing difference of one piano phrase, but he was a perfectionist. Although his solos sounded improvised, he seemed to have plotted them out in his mind. When he did alternate takes, the solos were almost identical, and he'd crack his voice at the same spot in the song each time as well. Everything he played was arranged in his head; our job was to get it on tape.

The songs were mostly ones he performed every night, like Earl King's Crescent City anthem "Big Chief" and Solomon Burke's hit "Cry to Me," which he had turned into a New Orleans–style rhumba. In Fess's hands, "Got My Mojo Working" became "Got My Red Beans Cooking." Allison suggested two instrumentals that I had never heard. One was "Willie Fugal's Blues," which Fess occasionally played live but had never recorded. It was inspired by the music of Louis Gottschalk, a French composer who lived in New Orleans in the 1800s and became famous writing music for a dance known as the quadrille. The song was made up of ten-bar verses, a very unusual structure for blues or R&B. We cut it on the last afternoon of recording with just piano and congas. The other tune was an unnamed instrumental that combined strains of the calypso "Rum and Coca-Cola" with the melody of Ella Fitzgerald's Latin jazz version of the nursery rhyme "A-Tisket, A-Tasket." Dr. John suggested using a tuba for the bass line, in the style of New Orleans marching bands. He also suggested taping a piece of corrugated cardboard to the top of a snare drum and playing it with brushes; this provided a more percussive sound than a normal snare drum and helped create a marching feel that fit with the tuba. Uganda played congas. It was a unique sound. We recorded it in a couple of takes, with the studio darkened to help everyone concentrate.

We were done with the recording, but the instrumental was still untitled. Earlier in the week, Dr. John had told us that when Fess played gigs in the 1950s and early 1960s, he often told audiences, "Next week we're going to have a big crawfish fiesta." Then he would point at somebody and say, "You'll be bringing the potato salad." Then he would talk more about this crawfish fiesta before pointing to someone else and saying, "And you'll be bringing the chitterlings." It eventually became clear that Fess was telling the audience, "I'm throwing a party, except it's going to cost me nothing to invite all of you because you're going to bring the food and drinks!" I loved the story, so I suggested we name the instrumental "Crawfish Fiesta." It also became the title of the album.

On that last day of recording, Fess and I arrived at the studio early and played pool as we waited for the others. Throughout the sessions he had said little to me. I think he was suspicious of record men, believing that they paid musicians a little money to make a record, released it, made a mint, and never paid the artists anything more. Over our relaxed games of pool, however, he opened up. He told me how much he hated leading a band and being the boss, how he didn't like the road, and that he preferred just living at home in New Orleans. He also told me that while he was in the Civilian Conservation Corps (a Depression-era government jobs program) in the 1930s and 1940s, doctors had done a medical experiment on him that had destroyed the muscles in his knee. This was the reason he walked by swinging his upper leg forward and then locking his knee so that he could put weight on it. By the end of our game, we had a good feeling about each other. I think he finally understood that I was a true fan, not just someone trying to make a quick buck, and that I had a deep love for his music and would protect his legacy. He told us at the end of the session that he was happier with this album than any recording he had ever done because he had never been given so much artistic control. He felt it was really *his* record. Freddie and I took the tapes back to Chicago and mixed the album at Curtom Studios. We sent cassettes of the mixes to Fess for his approval.

On the morning of January 31, 1980, the day we were releasing *Crawfish Fiesta*, I played back a message on my answering machine. It was Tad Jones, weeping uncontrollably. I could just make out the news that Fess had died of a heart attack the night before. He was fifty-nine. Later I learned that he had spent the previous week visiting with various old friends. One visit was to the undertaker, to make sure that the arrangements for his funeral were in order. I couldn't help but wonder if Fess knew he was ill, and making the record that he had always wanted to make allowed him to accept the end of his life. At his funeral, in a small house that had been converted into a funeral home, I sat with Jerry Wexler, the producer of Fess's classic tracks for Atlantic Records in the 1940s and 1950s. Allen Toussaint and Art Neville were among those who performed. Allen performed a beautiful song he had written for Fess, employing strains of Fess's piano melodies and Allen's simple, original lyrics thanking God for Fess's life. When I spoke with Allen many years later and reminded him who I was, he told me, "Fess is with me every day." Me too, Allen.

I'll always be grateful to Fess for trusting me and giving his best music to Alligator. It had never crossed my mind that his style of New Orleans R&B rhumba wouldn't fit on the label. Recording this legendary artist gave me a sense of triumph and historical importance. So many older musicians were dying that I began thinking that if I didn't record them, it wasn't going to get done. I began seeing the label not only as an extension of my being a blues fan, but also as a mission to capture and preserve an endangered form of music.

As with Professor Longhair, recording Johnny Otis represented a significant step in Alligator's evolution. A Renaissance man of R&B, Johnny had begun his career in the late 1930s as a drummer. Over the years he had become a piano and vibraphone player, songwriter, talent scout, producer, bandleader, newspaper columnist, author, preacher, DJ, television host, and (although he was not

African American by birth) spokesman for the Los Angeles African American community. When I met him, he seemed larger than life, fearless and confident. Because he had dealt with a lot of racism, he was very race conscious. Although he was of Greek origin—his family name was Veliotes—people assumed he was black. He *felt* black. Touring the South in the 1950s and 1960s, he had been forced to order food at the back doors of restaurants, drink out of colored drinking fountains, and stay at black-run hotels. If I had called him white I'm sure he would have slapped me.

By the time he was thirty, Johnny Otis had probably been in the studio a thousand times. He had discovered Little Esther, Big Mama Thornton, the Robins (who became the Coasters), and dozens of other artists, and produced R&B radio hits by all of them. He had run talent shows in the Barrelhouse Club in Los Angeles, in the early 1950s. In 1957, he had his own rock and roll hit single, "Willie and the Hand Jive." I owned dozens of records he had produced, including albums of his multi-artist revues. When I met him in the mid-1970s, he was doing a radio show on KPFK-FM, the noncommercial Pacifica Foundation's radio station in Los Angeles. Veteran blues journalist and DJ Mary Katherine Aldin introduced us. She took me to Johnny's church, which was located in his home, a dilapidated mansion on Vermont Avenue that obviously had belonged to some rich white folks decades before. Not only was his church in his home, so was his recording studio, built for his own small label, Blues Odyssey. Plus, he had converted his multicar garage into an aviary where he raised rare birds.

His church was located in the large parlor of the house. There he preached and directed a small choir. Charismatic and dignified with a stentorian voice, he had thick black hair with a widow's peak and he spoke with great eloquence and conviction. His services were filled with music and celebrated the hope of the *now* and the hope of the future. "I don't care where you were last night," he preached, "or who you were having sex with, or what drugs you were using. I don't care whether you're an addict or a hooker. I only care that you're not going to be one tomorrow." Johnny's famous guitar-playing son, Shuggie, played in the church band, as did his drummer son, Nicky.[3]

In 1981, I decided I wanted to make a record with Johnny Otis, and he accepted my offer. Although he had cut albums in the 1970s for various labels, including his own, Johnny wasn't under contract. There weren't a lot of recording opportunities for him. But he could still call on great musicians when he performed and recorded. Everybody on the Los Angeles R&B scene knew him; he was a revered figure.

I flew out to LA for the recording sessions and turned the production reins over to Johnny. I had never watched another producer besides Bob Koester work in the studio. As I had done with the Professor Longhair sessions, I brought my favorite engineer of the time, Freddie Breitberg, who gave me confidence that everything would be OK sonically, so that I could concentrate on the music. We chose a well-established, modest studio in Hollywood called Sage and Sound. Johnny assembled the band. Johnny didn't propose to be the only vocalist on the record. He knew he wasn't a polished singer with a big range. But he knew how to deliver a lyric that told a story, especially on a novelty song.

For some of the album's vocals, he brought in his old friends, like Delmar "Mighty Mouth" Evans, who had appeared with Johnny's live revues and on some of Johnny's other records. He also shone the spotlight on singers from his church choir. Charles Williams, the choir's young featured singer blessed with a beautiful, high voice, performed many of the lead vocals. Besides Johnny on keyboards, the band included master drummer Earl Palmer. He had virtually invented rock and roll drumming as a member of the house band at Cosimo Matassa's studio in New Orleans, where he recorded behind seminal musicians like Little Richard and Lloyd Price. The bass

---

3. Shuggie already had quite a reputation, both for being a guitar prodigy and for being not quite earthbound. While still a teenager, he had cut a couple of highly regarded solo albums and been a featured artist at the legendary Fillmore Auditorium. In 2017, Shuggie made a comeback as a touring artist.

player, Edgar Willis, had toured for years with Ray Charles. Plas Johnson, who played tenor sax, was one of the key R&B horn players of the jump blues and early rock and roll era of the late 1940s and early 1950s. It was quite an array of talent, and they all deferred to Johnny.

We made the record in two and a half days, using various combinations of vocalists. Everyone followed Johnny's instructions, and as he directed them, he called them "children." ("Tighten up those harmonies, children." "Pay attention, children.") We started with a Johnny vocal feature, a version of "Drinkin' Wine Spo-dee-o-dee," a well-known song that had been a giant hit for Stick McGhee in the late 1940s on Atlantic Records. The lyric is about a group of men trying to hustle up enough money to buy a bottle of wine. The original "street" lyric for the chorus was, "Drinking wine, motherfucker, drinking wine," but Stick McGhee couldn't sing that on a record, so "Spo-dee-o-dee" became the substitute. At the end of Johnny's version of the song, somebody ad-libs, "Look, there's a dime on the sidewalk." Then Johnny quips as the music fades, "That ain't a dime, that's spit." That kind of spontaneous improvisation was typical of how Johnny Otis brought extra life to a song.

For Johnny, there was no line separating blues and R&B. Some of the songs used the massed voices of the entire church choir. Some were humorous male-female duets. Some were intimate, like "Every Beat of My Heart," a sentimental ballad sung by Charles Williams that Johnny had written in the 1950s for the Royals and that became an early hit for Gladys Knight and the Pips. It was one of the most romantic tracks ever released on Alligator. When I was courting my wife, Jo, I made a mix tape for her of songs that I thought would win her heart. That was one of them.

All the tracks were recorded without guitar. Shuggie Otis came in on the last night of recording at about 9 p.m. and laid down guitar parts for each song, both rhythm and lead, in a period of five hours, learning the songs as he went. Johnny kept pushing Shuggie to record faster and faster, with no breaks between songs. We finished his parts at 2 a.m. Then Johnny said, "I've got to take Shuggie to his job." "What kind of job does he have that starts at two o'clock in the morning?" I asked. "He throws newspapers," Johnny said. I was shocked that Shuggie Otis, a musician that some people considered to be one of the most creative guitar players of his generation, was delivering newspapers off the back of a truck in the middle of the night.

During the sessions, Johnny was the life of the party. He was always out in the studio, encouraging everybody, keeping the energy up. He was consistently positive and never seemed upset, even when he was calling for extra takes and being critical of performances. He wasn't one of those producers who had to make sure each note is perfectly in place. At one point, the vocal group cut a performance of "So Fine," an old rock and roll song written by Johnny that was originally recorded by the Fiestas. At the end of the take he turned to me and asked, "How'd that feel?" I said, "It felt good to me." "If it feels good, it is good," he said. "Let's go on." Even for a producer as musically knowledgeable and experienced as Johnny, the primary way to judge a performance was to ask, "Does it feel right?" rather than "Was everything precisely done as we hoped or as was rehearsed?" It was fun, inspirational, and instructional watching Johnny Otis work with musicians. Freddie and I were in awe.

We called the album *The New Johnny Otis Show with Shuggie Otis*. Unfortunately, it filled a nonexistent niche in the marketplace. For blues fans, it had a little too much R&B; for R&B fans, a little too much blues. I disappointed Johnny by not releasing "Every Beat of My Heart" as a single for black radio, as he wanted me to do. Alligator had no credibility with black radio, and the singer Charles Williams wasn't under contract to my label. Media wasn't interested in the album; Johnny had recorded other albums recently enough so that there wasn't a comeback story to tell the press. Sales were mediocre. Nonetheless, it was a thrill for me to be in the presence of a musical hero who represented what I wanted to grow up to be. As I do with Bob Koester and Lillian Shedd McMurry, the founder of Trumpet Records, I walk a little bit in Johnny Otis's footsteps.

11

During the 1980s, Alligator grew from a struggling business into an established label. In 1984, I bought a run-down three-flat building on Chicago's North Side, converted it into offices, and moved the label out of my little house.[1] The staff soon grew to more than a dozen. The label was gaining a national profile, helped along by three white guys who rocked the blues: Johnny Winter, Lonnie Mack, and Roy Buchanan. Like Albert Collins, they came to Alligator with established reputations and signature sounds. Each had his own personal and musical style, and each had earned rabid fans in the 1960s or 1970s from among the audience for blues-based rock. That audience had been revitalized and expanded in the early 1980s, thanks primarily to the popularity of Stevie Ray Vaughan. Blues rock was coming back into fashion just about the time we signed Johnny Winter.

Stevie Ray Vaughan was the first white blues-rocker to have a significant impact on black blues musicians. When I came to Chicago in 1970, a period when young white people were discovering and playing the blues, I found no black blues musicians on the South or West Sides who had listened to a record by Paul Butterfield, Johnny Winter, Eric Clapton, or John Mayall. The black musicians were lis-

---

1. By the time we made the move, seven people were arriving at my house every morning for work. The basement was full of LPs, and seven thousand cassettes were being warehoused in the kitchen. A copier occupied the dining room. My office was also my bedroom; when musicians came for private meetings, they sat on my bed. My brief marriage to Jan Loveland had ended in early 1978. There would have been no room for anyone else to live in that house.

tening to established artists who were popular on black-oriented radio, like B. B. King, Albert King, and Little Milton. They knew Muddy and Wolf, Etta James, and Ray Charles. White blues musicians and blues-rockers were simply not on their radar.[2]

However, for the generation of African American blues musicians who came up in the 1980s playing for mostly white audiences, Stevie Ray Vaughan made an impression. Flashy guitar solos had become the centerpiece of the kind of blues white people listened to. Stevie had masterfully juiced up blues by incorporating the stylistic creativity of Jimi Hendrix. In an era of stylish, synthesizer-centered British pop "haircut bands" like Flock of Seagulls and Depeche Mode, Stevie got the raw passion of the blues back on the radio by playing blues with rock and roll energy and attitude.

One result of Stevie's skyrocketing popularity was that I began receiving scores of demos recorded by Stevie imitators. They even dressed like he did; I called them "kids in flat hats." Most of them had nothing fresh to say and were mediocre (or worse) singers. But as Alligator artist Tinsley Ellis once said, "The only thing worse than a world filled with Stevie Ray Vaughan imitators is a world without Stevie Ray Vaughan imitators," which is exactly the world we are living in now. A successful crossover musician, Stevie almost single-handedly stimulated the creation of tens of thousands of new white blues fans. His popularity definitely helped expand Alligator's audience. In the early 1980s, we suddenly had twenty-year-olds showing up at our artists' gigs. Before that, most of the fans were members of my generation, then in their thirties or early forties.

To my everlasting embarrassment, in 1979 I turned Stevie down for a one-record deal that probably would have made a pile of money for Alligator. Stevie just didn't impress me; I couldn't hear what made him special. I thought he was the world's loudest Albert King imitator. Later, he would be a crucial factor in the tremendous success of Alligator's first Lonnie Mack album. But Alligator's first

2. However, many blues artists I met during the 1970s and 1980s expressed their admiration for white Country and Western Swing artists like Jimmie Rodgers and Bob Wills. Lots of blues artists remembered enjoying the Grand Old Opry in their youth.

foray into recording a major blues-rock musician was signing Johnny Winter. Then we brought Roy Buchanan, the eccentric guitar genius, to the label. These musicians would test our ability to expand beyond Alligator's traditional audience—and, in Johnny's case, would test my ability to suffer the consequences of my own stubbornness.

I had known Johnny Winter since the 1970s, when Son Seals's second album, *Midnight Son*, had garnered a rave review by music critic Robert Palmer in *Rolling Stone*. As a result of the review, Son got an offer to open for Mose Allison at the Bottom Line in New York City.[3] Even though he would lose money driving to the East Coast and playing for a low fee, Son eagerly accepted. Playing the Bottom Line for the first time was a major step forward for any artist. As Son and I waited in the rabbit warren of tiny dressing rooms just prior to the show, we were told, "Johnny Winter is here. He'd like to come meet everybody." I was shocked. At that point Johnny was a little past his peak of popularity, but he had been the biggest arena rock draw in the country in the early 1970s, and his name was known to every rock fan. To be honest, I hadn't been a big Johnny Winter fan. I thought he played too many notes, and I wasn't crazy about his signature vocal growl. But he had turned many of my generation on to the blues, and I was excited to meet him. Here was a major star paying attention to Son, my emerging artist, and to my little label. When Johnny met us, he turned out to be charmingly boyish and self-effacing, almost shy. As we talked, I found that he was a fellow blues geek, eager to talk about other musicians and old records, not about himself. He was excited about having recently produced Muddy Waters. We exchanged phone numbers, and I felt I had made a new friend.

We kept in touch, and in the winter of 1978, Johnny flew to Chicago to stay with me for a long weekend and sit in with Son Seals at the Wise Fools Pub for a live recording.[4] We spent most of our time

---

3. Located just off Washington Square at the edge of Greenwich Village near New York University, the Bottom Line was, at that time, *the* showcase club in New York.

4. Although they recorded some songs together on the first night, they showed so much musical respect for each other that the set produced no fireworks. A major blizzard hit the next day and the rest of the nights we planned to record were snowed out.

visiting the clubs. He even helped people in the neighborhood push their cars after a heavy snowfall. We talked endlessly about blues records and our favorite musicians. Johnny had a fabulous musical memory; he could remember the arrangements and lyrics of songs he had heard years before. He talked about growing up in Beaumont, Texas, listening to local Gulf Coast records, including those of one of his heroes, Guitar Junior, who had become Alligator artist Lonnie Brooks. A considerate houseguest and night owl, he stayed up all night smoking pot and listening to my record collection over headphones while I slept. He knew that I didn't want drugs in my house, so when he was finished, he carefully put his pot back in the baggie, washed the ashtray, and put his dope back in his suitcase.

After his visit in 1978, we saw each other only occasionally until 1984, when Teddy Slatus, Johnny's fast-talking, obsequious road manager, phoned me. "Johnny is interested in recording for Alligator," he said. I was amazed. I flew to New York to meet with Teddy and Johnny's manager, Steve Paul, who was getting ready to retire. Teddy was taking over the management job. The Blue Sky label, which had been set up by Columbia Records for Johnny, was being shuttered, and Johnny was looking for a new label. As we talked, I thought to myself, "Johnny Winter is still a household name in the rock and roll world. How low are their financial expectations if they're looking at tiny little Alligator?" I later learned that Johnny had actually put his hands around Teddy Slatus's throat and said, "Get me a contract with Alligator Records." Sick of making records that were halfway between blues and rock and roll, he wanted to be on a real blues label.

At this time, with the exception of Johnny Otis, who was black in everything but skin color, the only white musicians I had recorded were sidemen. To record my friend Johnny Winter would be a huge commercial move for the label. But it was also a move away from recording black musicians who had grown up in the blues community. I knew some of Alligator's purist blues fans would say I had sold out. Ironically, as I was worried about accusations of being too commercial, Johnny wanted to join Alligator because he saw the label as the home of pure, noncommercial blues.

I went back to Chicago and brooded. It was a risky proposition. Although I was slowly making inroads into the commercial marketplace, Alligator was still a niche market label. I had never tried to release an album that would get us into the mainstream rock market. If Johnny demanded a big-money advance and recording budget and sales were disappointing, I could lose the company. After more than a few sleepless nights, I finally decided to offer Johnny ten thousand dollars as an advance on royalties. (Only six years earlier, I had sweated giving Albert Collins one thousand dollars.) I managed to pull together the money with the financial backing of Sonet Records. I knew this would be only the beginning of my expenses. We would have to assemble an all-star band, and Johnny would want more studio time than I was used to paying for. I typed up the contract on my portable typewriter and officially made the offer. It was immediately accepted. Dick Shurman, my collaborator on the Albert Collins records, agreed to coproduce. He and Johnny had bonded during Johnny's visit to Chicago.

I chose to record the album at Red Label Recording, a small studio located in the basement of a suburban North Shore mansion. I didn't like it as much as other studios. I thought the space was too small, the ceilings too low for good sound, and the location too remote. But my trusted engineer, Freddie Breitberg, had taken a job at Red Label, and working with Freddie was a priority for me.

Johnny arrived without having done any writing for the album. He wanted to cut real blues songs, which, as far as he was concerned, should be covers. He had some songs in mind. Dick and I had song ideas too. As we began to make choices about what to record, we had some interesting conversations about how to define blues. Johnny told me that he always thought that blues songs were simply songs that contained blue notes.[5] He defined blues musically. I tended to define blues by the stories the lyrics told as well as by the

---

5. Blue notes are notes in the musical scale that are played flatted, generally the third or seventh note of the major scale. The blues scale contains these notes rather than the major (nonflatted) notes of the standard European scale. Because of these flatted notes, it's sometimes difficult to determine if a blues song is in a major or minor key.

music's cathartic, soul-cleansing emotional effect on the audience through tension and release. He told me he had never thought of blues that way.

For Johnny's backup band, Dick and I recruited the top-notch rhythm section that was playing with Albert Collins—Johnny B. Gayden on bass and Casey Jones on drums. Ken Saydak, who played with Lonnie Brooks, was our choice for keyboards. These musicians were easygoing, friendly guys, and Dick and I thought their person-alities would work well with Johnny's. I had learned that Johnny's ego could be easily bruised, so one had to be as positive as possible around him. Johnny was a complex person. A former heroin user on methadone maintenance, he would sleep through much of the day, then wake up midday and take his methadone. We discovered in working with him that he would have a peak energy period, from around 9 p.m. until midnight. That was his productive time in the studio. Then he would begin to fade, partly because he was smok-ing pot and drinking screwdrivers. Without alcohol and marijuana, Johnny was impossibly wired. If his body chemistry was just right, he was energetic, fun, and focused. But he could easily become ir-ritable or unproductive.

Johnny liked to record at a fast and furious pace. He would often simply talk the band through the song, then cut it in a couple of takes while playing rhythm guitar, letting the band use their vast experi-ence to play their parts as they felt them. If we were happy with the track, we'd put it aside. He planned to come back and overdub solos and vocals later. I was used to recording as close to live as possible, so this layering of parts was a little different for me. But he knew what he wanted to hear. He didn't play busy rhythm guitar, and on some songs, he chose to delete the rhythm guitar part in the final mix. The songs seemed to be fully conceived in his mind. We recorded sixteen or seventeen songs in the course of four nights, mostly basic tracks but with a great feel. We were getting strong performances even though the sonic limitations of the studio frustrated me. It was hard to keep instruments from leaking into other instruments' mi-crophones in the small space. The low ceilings and carpeting meant that there was little natural reverberation; sounds that should have sustained died too quickly.

On our last night of band tracking, we were having a difficult session. Everyone was tense. Johnny Gayden had accidentally knocked over and slightly damaged Johnny Winter's custom-built Lazer guitar, which infuriated him. We had been battling to get a Magic Sam song in the can, but it wasn't working. I was getting edgy; I wanted that song. In the midst of this tension, Dick Meyer, the wealthy studio owner, appeared with a bottle of champagne and a tray of glasses. "It's the one-year anniversary of the opening of the studio," he announced, "and I thought we'd all have a glass of champagne together." Already on edge, I exploded with rage. "I'm renting this studio," I yelled. "Just because it's in your house doesn't mean you have the right to come in and interrupt my session!" Although he was politely insistent that he simply wanted to celebrate, he wouldn't leave. "This is ridiculous!" I yelled as I stomped around. "You're not treating me like a client! We're finding another studio!" I stormed out, taking Johnny Winter and the master tapes with me.

Freddie called me the next day. "Can't we make this all right?" he asked. But I refused to talk to Dick Meyer or reconsider my decision. Armed with the master tapes and good-sounding cassettes of Freddie's rough mixes, I set out to find a new studio and a new engineer. I first went to Chicago Recording Company, the biggest studio in Chicago, where I knew the studio manager. "I'm in trouble," I said. "I need your best engineer, somebody who can take these tapes and make them sound as good as this cassette." He gave me a well-respected engineer and a night of free studio time, but the engineer failed to create rough mixes that sounded as good as the cassettes. While Johnny fumed, trapped by himself in a suburban hotel room, I was becoming desperate. Still, I refused to go back to Red Label. Part of my brain was saying, "Are you handling this right or are you being foolishly stubborn because you refuse to give an inch and admit you might be wrong?" I kept ignoring that part of my brain, though I learned to listen to it later.

With great reluctance, I went to see the owner of Streeterville

Studios. I had a strong personal dislike for him, but it was one of the best studios in the city. After I explained the situation, he said, "I have a new, young engineer. He may be just the guy you want. His name is Justin Niebank." I spent an evening working with Justin at Streeterville, and not only did he duplicate the sounds on the cassettes, he made them better. "Hallelujah!," I thought.

We moved Johnny to a downtown hotel. To defuse the situation, I sat with him in his room and let him vent at me, but he was still mad. The first night at Streeterville Studios, we decided to try some guitar and vocal overdubs in a small studio just big enough for Johnny, his guitar, and amp. Justin, Dick, and I were in the control room. Johnny got roaring drunk and paced the tiny studio, repeating, "I'm gonna kill somebody, I'm gonna kill somebody" so loudly that we could hear it through the speakers in the control room. Between his rants, he tried to play some guitar solos, most of which were, not surprisingly, sloppy and unfocused. But Johnny got it all together for "Lights Out," a fast New Orleans rocker written by Dr. John. He played a slashing, killer solo instead of killing me. That's the solo that's on the record.

We finished the album at Streeterville Studios with Justin. When cutting the final vocals, Dick and I encouraged Johnny to use his signature growl sparingly and sing more melodically than he had on previous records. Johnny was famous for his fast, flashy, multi-note guitar style, but on some songs we convinced him to play more sparsely. As a result, he delivered some of the most moving and emotionally intense performances of his career. To add some sonic textures, we brought Billy Branch in to play harmonica for one overdub session and James Cotton for another. We all wanted horns on a couple of songs, so I called on one of my heroes, Gene "Daddy G" Barge. A venerated R&B tenor sax player, Gene had been the Chess Records horn arranger and coproducer of *Playing for Keeps*, Alligator's album by local R&B favorites Big Twist and the Mellow Fellows. Watching Gene working with the horn players reminded me immediately of Johnny Otis, with Gene acting simultaneously as the team captain, father figure, and ever-positive critic of the players.

Despite the tension between Johnny and me, we were all very happy with the record, which we titled *Guitar Slinger*. Paul Natkin, a famous Chicago rock and roll photographer, shot the cover photo and caught just the right spirit: Johnny as a confrontational hard-ass, cigarette dangling from his mouth and a Texas tattoo emblazoned on his arm.

In choosing the songs and sequence, I was thinking about rock radio. We needed airplay on those Album Oriented Rock stations, which didn't play much blues. But Johnny still had a lot of rock credibility, and we knew the programmers would at least give a listen to our record. We chose "Don't Take Advantage of Me," a Lonnie Brooks song written in his "voodoo blues" style, as the track to push to radio. Johnny had kept the essence of the original song, but his hyperaggressive playing and attack gave it a harder edge than Lonnie's version. We even manufactured a twelve-inch 45-rpm single, the accepted format for singles promoted to radio at the time.

We also decided that it was worthwhile to produce a Johnny Winter music video. MTV had recently come on air and was broadcasting music videos 24/7. We contacted Michael Dawson, who had directed a music video for Big Twist and the Mellow Fellows. Mindy Giles, my senior staffer, recruited actors from the Improv Olympic, an improvisational comedy theater company similar to Chicago's famous Second City.

Since Johnny was well known as a Texan and the album title, *Guitar Slinger*, was an obvious play on the words "gun slinger," we decided to film a western motif video. In the video, a couple of toughs are mistreating their girlfriends in a saloon when Johnny swaggers in like a skinny, white-haired John Wayne. Johnny proceeds to "beat up" the bad guys with the force of his music. Then, with a touch of his hand he brands each of the grateful girlfriends with a Texas tattoo, just like the one on his own arm.

So we launched *Guitar Slinger* just like the big labels did, with a twelve-inch single, a full-length album, and a music video. It all worked. Rock radio stations played the record, and the video got some rotation on MTV. By indie label standards it was a huge success. We made *Billboard*'s Top 200 chart. Johnny quickly became my biggest and fastest selling artist. He toured to support the album and delivered consistently strong shows. He was happy to be able to perform songs from a real blues record.

However, it was difficult to get Johnny's cooperation for promotional events like telephone interviews and backstage "meet and greets" with retailers and radio staffers; nevertheless, the record became a commercial landmark for Alligator, selling tens of thousands of copies. Johnny came back the next year to cut another album with essentially the same team, except that this time we moved to Streeterville Studios with Justin Niebank as the engineer. The album was called *Serious Business*, an appropriate name, because it was more strenuous to make than *Guitar Slinger*. Johnny brought a couple of newly written original songs for the album. For the most part, though, he wanted to record new versions of previously recorded tunes. Some of our choices weren't as inspired as those for *Guitar Slinger*. Johnny, annoyed by all the promotion that the label had asked him to do, no longer felt he was making a record for his friend Bruce; now he was making a record for a label owner with whom he had a business relationship. In the studio, there were struggles for control between us, with Dick Shurman trying desperately to mediate.

The big fights were about mixes. We just heard differently. Johnny wanted as little bass as possible, which to my ears made the mixes sound thin. Thinking about radio, I was asking Justin for a kind of commercial 1980s snare drum sound that Johnny didn't like at all (and now sounds very dated). Compromising was tough for each of us. By the end of the mixes, Johnny and I were barely on speaking terms. In the end, we made a strong record, but it wasn't quite as good as *Guitar Slinger*.

I had never had to handle an artist with such kid gloves, and I wasn't good at it. Johnny wanted to be catered to, and we both struggled for control. He no longer seemed like the unassuming friend and fellow blues fan that had pushed people's cars out of snowdrifts in 1978. He no longer saw me as a friend. By the time we finished with *Serious Business*, he was tired of me and I was tired of him.

Dick Shurman and Johnny produced *3rd Degree*, Johnny's last Alligator record. I acted as executive producer and wasn't involved in the day-to-day recording process. Without me, they made an excellent record, as good as *Guitar Slinger*. They brought in Dr. John, a friend of Johnny's, to play piano on a couple of tracks. Dick also had the brilliant idea of reassembling the trio that had cut Johnny's first album, *The Progressive Blues Experiment*, back in 1968. He flew in bassist Tommy Shannon and drummer Uncle John Turner to cut a few songs. Johnny was excited and stepped up with some intense performances. Johnny also broke out his National steel guitar for a couple of solo songs on which he overdubbed multiple guitar parts. One of them was cut in the studio's bathroom because the echo bouncing off the tile sounded so good. We were all happy with the record, though it was hard for me to admit how good a job Dick and Johnny had done without me. It was the final chapter of Alligator's relationship with Johnny. Teddy Slatus was determined to get him back on a major label, and Johnny was ready to go.

12

The excitement created by recording and releasing our first Johnny Winter album led Alligator to pursue other blues-rock guitar heroes. In the mid-1980s, I was still devoted to recording pure blues artists like Koko Taylor, Son Seals, Lonnie Brooks, Albert Collins, and James Cotton. But I was ready to reach beyond hard-core blues. After Johnny's success, we signed Lonnie Mack and Roy Buchanan, both of whom hadn't recorded for some time. We found that when we brought back a well-known musician who hadn't recorded for a while, the first record we released usually got a lot of media attention. Comeback stories are appealing, and established fans may be hungry for more of the artist's music. Often the artist is excited to be back in the studio and puts extra energy into the comeback record. That extra energy and commitment can be heard in albums like Johnny Winter's *Guitar Slinger*, Albert Collins's *Ice Pickin'*, Lonnie Mack's *Strike Like Lightning*, and Roy Buchanan's *When a Guitar Plays the Blues*.

Arguably, Lonnie Mack was the first blues-rock guitar hero. His music melded blues, country, and early rock and roll. His powerful guitar solos—including unexpected, soaring octave jumps, driving rhythm figures, and fast string bending using the tremolo bar on his signature Gibson Flying V guitar—were all his own. One of his favorite guitar players was Robert Ward, a black musician from Georgia, who had played with the Ohio Untouchables (later named the Ohio Players). Ward used a Magnatone amplifier that produced an unusual vibrato sound that Lonnie adopted as part of his sonic signature. Lonnie's other guitar hero was Merle Travis, the famed country finger picker who wrote "Sixteen Tons." Just as his guitar heroes came from both blues and country, Lonnie's favorite singers were Bobby "Blue" Bland, the R&B superstar, and George Jones, one of country music's immortal vocalists. For Lonnie, there were no lines separating blues, R&B, country, and rock and roll; he moved between the genres effortlessly.

Lonnie was a country guy with little education[1] who grew up in a poor farming family in southeastern Indiana, near Cincinnati. He rolled his own cigarettes, drank hard, talked with a drawl, and loved guns. He was a burly, bluff, plainspoken guy who could be full of laughter one minute and aggressive and short tempered the next. He got his start in first-generation rocker Troy Seals's band. One day in 1963, Troy failed to show up for a recording session for Cincinnati's Fraternity Records, and rather than canceling the studio time, the band decided to cut some instrumentals, including Lonnie's arrangement of Chuck Berry's "Memphis." Fraternity released it as a single, and before Lonnie knew it, "Memphis" became the number five rock and roll record in the country. He followed "Memphis" with "Wham!" a thrilling instrumental that was the first single bought by a young Stevie Ray Vaughan, who learned to play it note for note. "Wham!" supposedly inspired guitarists to call the tremolo bar that Lonnie used so well a "whammy bar."

Lonnie cut a series of singles for Fraternity. Most were instrumentals, but some were vocals, like the raw R&B ballad "Where There's a Will, There's a Way." He was such a convincing R&B singer that "Where There's a Will, There's a Way" was played on many black radio stations before the programmers found out that Lonnie was white. For half a decade, Lonnie barnstormed across the country in a Cadillac pulling a trailer, living, as he told me, on a diet of amphetamines and alcohol. His recordings from the mid-1960s are astounding. He sliced and diced every guitar player in rock and roll at that time.

---

1. He quit school after slugging his sixth-grade teacher.

After Fraternity folded, Lonnie went on to cut three albums for Elektra, which ranged from hard blues to schlocky pop-country. While working as an A&R (artists and repertoire) person for Elektra, he occasionally cropped up as a studio musician. He's on the Doors' fifth album, *Morrison Hotel*, playing bass and the guitar solo on "Roadhouse Blues." But none of his Elektra albums had ever sold well, and Lonnie had faded into obscurity in the 1970s.

Music journalist Ben Sandmel, the brother of a childhood friend of mine, first pitched Lonnie to me around 1980. I had seen Lonnie once or twice in Cincinnati, but by the 1980s he was off my radar. I was still ambivalent about recording white blues musicians, and I certainly wasn't interested in some forgotten middle-aged rock and roll guitar player. But Ben opened my eyes and ears, playing tracks of the blues side of Lonnie's music. They were so impressive that I went to see Lonnie perform at a dingy roadhouse outside of Hamilton, Ohio, while I was visiting my family in Cincinnati. Only about twenty people were there, but Lonnie was mesmerizing, playing with all the fire of his early recordings and singing with an immense amount of soul. I made it a point to see him on subsequent trips back home. On Sundays, he played a club called Coco's in Covington, Kentucky. I got to know him well enough to be invited to come out to the parking lot and snort cocaine with him from the blade of the big knife he carried. We talked about recording, but he seemed uninterested.

By this time, Lonnie had gotten to know Stevie Ray Vaughan, who idolized him. At Stevie's urging, Lonnie moved to the Austin area, where, in his typical laid-back fashion, he did almost nothing to get gigs for himself. In 1984, he called me and said, "Do you wanna do that album we talked about?" He was living near Spicewood, Texas, in a school bus outfitted with some bunks, parked at a fishing camp on the Colorado River. On the phone he seemed to have things together. "I've got this good studio down here where we can work," he told me assuredly, "and I'm gonna bring down Gene Lawson, my old engineer from Cincinnati. He can record the album and is also the perfect drummer for a few of these songs. He played drums on 'Memphis.' Tim Drummond [a veteran musician who had been the first white player in James Brown's band and had toured with Bob Dylan] is gonna play bass, and Stan Szelest is coming from Buffalo to play keyboards. My brother Billy will be on rhythm guitar." Lonnie went on to tell me, "I talked to Levon Helm [drummer, vocalist and songwriter with the Band], and he's gonna fly down and play drums on all the songs Gene doesn't play on." It sounded promising.

As the plans for the recording sessions firmed up, Mindy Giles, my right arm at Alligator during the 1980s, contacted Stevie Ray and asked him if he would be interested in helping out. Although he was becoming a rock superstar, Stevie didn't hesitate. He offered his services as producer. He lived in Austin, so he could come home off the road and go straight into the studio.

But when I arrived in Austin for the sessions, I found that things weren't as together as I had been told. The studio, Cedar Creek, was a funky, oddly wired place with rattlesnakes living in the tall grass around the building. Levon Helm was notably absent. "Oh, Levon got some movie role," Lonnie casually told me. "We don't have a drummer except for Gene, and he's not right for most of the songs." We tried out some local players, none of whom pleased Lonnie. We finally called Dennis O'Neal, Lonnie's old Cincinnati-based drummer, who flew down for the sessions.

Meanwhile, Lonnie's engineer friend Gene Lawson created a new problem. Confident and cocky, Gene thought he knew more about engineering a record than anyone else, and he immediately alienated the studio owner by denigrating the equipment and the studio setup. Tired of listening to Gene's grousing, the studio owner handed us the keys, wished us luck, and left us with only his inexperienced assistant. Without the help of the studio owner, Gene struggled to get the headphone mix working. Studio equipment frequently broke, and the session had to be stopped while it was fixed. After recording like this for a couple of days, including cutting a few songs with Gene on drums, we arrived at the studio one morning and found a note from Gene: "I went back to Cincinnati." Suddenly, we were without an engineer. Steve Mendell, the studio assistant, who was not yet a full-fledged engineer, stepped up and recorded the rest of the album.

Despite these challenges, Stevie and Lonnie were thrilled to be recording together. There wasn't any kind of preparation or rehearsal with Stevie; he just showed up at the studio and asked Lonnie, "What do you want me to do?" Clearly, Stevie was not going to be the real producer. He was lending his name value to Lonnie and happy to do it. He deferred to Lonnie in all matters.

Lonnie had written a slew of new blues and rock and roll songs for the album. I had heard most of them on cassettes in advance. But in the studio they were winging it much of the time. Lonnie had created a duet vocal for Stevie and himself called "If You Have to Know." Stevie learned the tune and cut it the same day. Although it wasn't planned in advance, Lonnie decided to record a new arrangement of "Watch Your Step," the old Bobby Parker song that had inspired the Beatles' groove on "Day Tripper." After cutting the instrumental track, he decided to write new words to the music. Lonnie, Stevie, Tim Drummond, and the famed songwriter Will Jennings created the lyrics in the course of thirty minutes. Then Lonnie immediately cut the vocal, singing so hard that he started spitting up blood. The song, "Strike Like Lightning," became the title of the album.

"Oreo Cookie Blues" was one of the tunes Lonnie had planned in advance. It featured Lonnie and his brother Billy on acoustic guitars and Stevie on a National steel guitar.[2] It's a song for Everyman and Everywoman:

> *Chocolate on my fingers, icing on my lips*
> *Sugar diabetes and blubber on my hips*
> *I keep the night light burning in the kitchen, babe, so I can go*
>   *downstairs and cruise*
> *I've got them Oreo crème sandwich, chocolate-covered, crème-filled*
>   *cookie blues.*

Toward the end of the sessions, Lonnie declared that the album needed a ballad. Rooting through his notebook of lyrics, he chose

---

2. Stevie was convinced his National steel guitar had once been owned by Blind Boy Fuller. It was definitely the same model as the one shown in a famous picture of Fuller, but, of course, National didn't make just one copy of that model. Nonetheless, Stevie was sure it was Fuller's guitar, and I wasn't going to argue with him.

"Falling Back in Love with You," a laid-back, romantic song he had written about his second wife. The song was later covered by Saffire—The Uppity Blues Women. When I married my beloved Jo Kolanda, in 1995, Saffire was one of the many groups who played at our wedding party. For our first dance together as a married couple, we danced to Saffire's version of Lonnie Mack's "Falling Back in Love with You."

Strike Like Lightning sold extremely well for Alligator. Stevie's involvement was crucial in boosting sales. Lonnie went on tour and delivered live shows every bit as fiery as the album. But he was constantly discontented with his bookings and kept changing managers in hopes of finding someone who could pull him up to another level of visibility. Even with the good sales and great reviews, plus a well-publicized jam with Keith Richards and Ron Wood at the Lone Star in New York, Lonnie was playing mostly clubs and blues festivals. The rock world wasn't paying as much attention as we had hoped for.

In 1986, we recorded a follow-up album called *Second Sight*, but it lacked the spontaneity and fire of *Strike Like Lightning*, and sales were disappointing. It was a great learning experience for me, resulting in my becoming even more of a control freak. Instead of recording live with the full band in the studio, which was the norm for Alligator and part of the reason *Strike Like Lightning* was so exciting, Lonnie decided to make *Second Sight* like a pop record. He layered one instrument at a time, beginning by playing rhythm guitar to a click track that he insisted on using.[3] After the rhythm guitar parts were laid, he brought in the bass player to play along to the guitar parts, then added drums, keyboards, lead guitar, and vocals one at

3. A click track creates a clicking sound that comes through the studio headphones and can be set to a certain number of beats per minute, depending on the speed the musician or producer wants. Like a metronome, it's used to keep the tempo of the song the same throughout. Ever since the disco era, the use of a click track has become standard practice for recording pop and rock songs. With no variation in the spaces between beats, the song is easier to dance to. The steady tempo also allows producers to more easily create remixed versions that add samples from other records. Playing to a click track is what I call machine time. If you listen to Hound Dog Taylor or B. B. King records, however, you'll notice that their songs tend to speed up as they go along, creating ever-increasing energy and intensity. Even if you don't hear it, you'll feel it, and it's exciting. It's what I call "human time."

a time. Even though the musicians were friends and were laughing and joking in the studio, the process was painstaking and soul killing.

Also, Lonnie's choice of songs was less inspired than those for *Strike Like Lightning*. I had given Lonnie creative control, and instead of relying on the spontaneity and risk taking that were an intrinsic part of his music, he had tried to duplicate what he thought was the hit-making process. It was contrary to the essence of Lonnie. There were still some good performances because Lonnie invested himself in the vocals and solos and he was a naturally soulful singer and kick-ass guitarist. But I saw the bad results that could happen if I gave an artist complete control over a recording.

This experience reinforced my belief that many musicians, no matter how talented, need guidance to help them focus on their greatest strengths. They may need to be told when they're playing it too safe, or when a song isn't up to what their standards should be. That's the job of a producer. Artists aren't always their own best producers. Since *Second Sight*, I've been cautious about letting a musician self-produce. For those who have recorded for other labels that simply allowed them to deliver their finished records, dealing with Bruce the Control Freak can create a lot of tension. Even though all Alligator contracts make my level of control specific (it may include mutual agreement on songs, producer, studio, mixes, sequence, or packaging), some artists have chosen not to sign with Alligator rather than allow me any control.[4]

Lonnie had signed a two-album contract with Alligator. After the release of *Second Sight* he was offered a major label deal with Epic. The resulting album, produced by veteran Muscle Shoals keyboard wizard Barry Beckett, failed to find an audience.[5] After his

---

4. These days, if they can raise the money, artists can record and release their own recordings. This can be a viable option. But it's rare for a self-released album to achieve even the modest success of being a "hit" in the blues world. Generally the support of a label, with its promotion and publicity skills and advertising budget, is necessary.

5. Although Lonnie didn't make a career for himself in Nashville, he insisted that Barry Beckett bring Justin Niebank, my favorite engineer, in for the sessions. Beckett loved Justin's work, and Justin moved to Nashville, where he has had a long and successful career as an engineer and producer.

disappointing Epic experience, a sadder but wiser Lonnie Mack returned to Alligator to cut a one-off live album at one of my favorite clubs, FitzGerald's Roadhouse, a well-established roots music venue in Berwyn, Illinois. It was a brilliant return to form, with Lonnie delivering all the guitar pyrotechnics and raw vocals that made him a musical giant. We called it *Live!—Attack of the Killer V*, a play on words mixing Gibson Flying V, the model of Lonnie's famous guitar, with the then-current publicity about killer bees.

Eventually, Lonnie tired of the road and toured less and less often. He moved into a log house near Nashville. Fortunately, he regained the publishing rights to some of his early songs just as Stevie Ray cut a new version of "Wham!" New royalties began to flow into his mailbox, so Lonnie had some regular income beyond his Alligator royalties. On his own, he issued CDs containing many of his early Fraternity label tracks and began selling them online. One day I called up Lonnie's wife, Carol, and asked her, "How are the online CD sales going?" "They were going fine," she replied, "until Lonnie shot the computer." I wasn't surprised. Lonnie was always his own worst enemy. After he and Carol divorced, he lived out the rest of his life in his log house, writing an occasional song. He died in the spring of 2016, his body worn out by years of hard living. He left a legacy of timeless American roots music that included two of the most compelling albums in the Alligator catalog.

Like thousands of other people, I was introduced to Roy Buchanan by an early 1970s public television documentary titled *The World's Greatest Unknown Guitar Player*. Roy's TV appearance launched his national reputation and made him an overnight sensation. In the TV show, he delivers inspired performances in multiple genres—blues with Johnny Otis and Linda Hopkins, country with Merle Haggard, and jazz with venerated guitarist Mundell Lowe. Roy more than holds his own in all these settings.

His colorful, somewhat mysterious life story added to his reputation as a secret guitar genius. When I met him, he was living in the Washington, DC, area. But he was born in Arkansas and spoke with a drawl; he called himself an "Arkansas gully-jumper." His parents were migrants who went to California during the Depression and grew cotton near Fresno. Roy grew up in an intensely religious family, which clearly had an effect on him. His father was a lay Pentecostal preacher. He told us more than once that he thought he was going to end up in hell, and he was serious.

Roy left home while still a teenager. He moved to Los Angeles and played for a while with Johnny Otis. He then toured and recorded with rocker Dale Hawkins (of "Susie-Q" fame), including recording "My Babe" with Hawkins for Chess Records. After that, he moved to Canada and joined the band of another Hawkins—Ronnie Hawkins, the expatriate Arkansas rock and roll singer. Roy quickly became known for his unparalleled technique and musical imagination, as well as his eccentric personality. This included turning his back on the audience so that they couldn't see what his hands were doing. One of the other members of Ronnie Hawkins's band was Robbie Robertson, later a founder of the Band. Clearly, Robbie learned a lot about guitar by watching Roy. After Canada, Roy moved to DC, where he was playing with local groups and his own band when the TV producers discovered him.

Roy was a true American roots musician. In his mind, blues, country, early rock and roll, and jazz weren't separate genres. Guitar players spoke in awe of his ability to move from wild string bending to thrilling speed picking, from sweet ballads to searing heavy rock. He was a master at the difficult technique of playing harmonics.[6] His signature tune was a soaring, melodic instrumental ballad called "The Messiah Will Surely Come Again," which had a dramatic spoken introduction that he delivered in an understated but effective way. His first album had been released on a tiny label in 1971. Packaged like a bootleg in a plain white sleeve in an LP-size burlap bag,

---

6. A guitar harmonic is a note played by preventing or amplifying vibration of the overtones of a string, often by touching the string very lightly with a fingertip of the fretting hand while picking it. Harmonic notes are often very high-pitched notes that are difficult or impossible to reach by normal fretting. Roy could execute a fast series of harmonic notes perfectly in pitch, which he did, for example, on "High Wire" from his *Hot Wires* album.

it was generally called the Burlap Album. After the TV show, he was pursued by the major labels. He cut three albums for Polydor before moving to Atlantic Records. But he was a musician's musician; he never sold many records.

My first meeting with Roy was quite unexpected and very embarrassing. While on a business trip to Toronto in 1983 to finalize a Canadian distribution deal with Warner Music, I went to dinner with Derek Andrews, a founder of the Toronto Blues Society. He had been booking my artists at various Toronto clubs for years. At that time Derek was booking a club called Albert's Hall, where Roy was playing. At dinner, I celebrated too much and got loaded before we went back to the club to see Roy perform. Too drunk to sit up, much less listen to music, I stretched out on the couch in the club's office and fell asleep. Derek soon rousted me and said, "Come down and meet Roy Buchanan." I stumbled downstairs to the music room and leaned against the wall, in danger of slithering down to the floor in a drunken heap. Roy's set ended, and Derek brought him over to meet me. Roy had abused a lot of substances in his life, but at that point, he was committed to staying sober. There I was, a record label president, hardly able to stand up, talking like my tongue was a mile thick, my eyes rolling around in my head. And there was Roy — cordial, shy, self-effacing, and completely sober. The next day I assumed that this musical legend had written me off.

Less than a week later my phone rang. It was Roy. He explained that he was unsigned and had no label and no manager, so he was shopping for a record deal on his own. In my drunken slurring at our first meeting, I had managed to say, "I make blues records." Over the phone, he said, "All I ever play, under everything else, is blues. I'd like to make a really good blues record."

Shortly after that, Roy was booked as the opener for Johnny Winter at Chicago's Aragon Ballroom, a rock and roll hall that held five thousand people. I greeted Roy backstage and we chatted before I went out into the audience. After playing some thrilling pyrotechnic guitar, Roy gave the drummer a solo. I saw Roy start to chord a rhythm figure behind the drummer, but there was no sound. Roy

looked at his guitar, looked at his amp and kept strumming, hoping the amp would come back to life. Realizing that something was
wrong, I ran backstage and came out on the stage behind the amps.
There were only two possible problems I knew how to fix: either
the amp had come unplugged or it had blown a fuse. I pulled a fuse
out of one of Johnny Winter's amps and swapped it for the fuse in
Roy's. Lo and behold, the amp lit up and Roy's guitar was audible
again. Roy saw me there and decided I had saved the day. After that,
we were friends.

We began talking about recording that night. I had brought Dick
Shurman with me. Dick is a likable guy, gentle and funny. He can
talk about obscure blues guitar players that I wouldn't even think
of. Plus, he knew more about Roy's older recordings than I did. That
night Roy and Dick bonded talking about Jimmy Nolen, one of Roy's
heroes.[7] After I signed Roy, Dick came on board as the coproducer.
He was a great asset to all three of Roy's Alligator albums.

Like Albert Collins, Roy was not much of a lyricist, but he had
no shortage of instrumental ideas. He told us he had trash bags full
of cassettes of instrumental snippets that he had recorded in his
basement. As we prepared for the recording session, we chose a
few of the snippets from his cassettes that we thought he could develop into full songs. We also discussed vocals. We hoped he would
do some of his signature talk-singing on the album. A perfect song
for that style was "When a Guitar Plays the Blues," a song we had
already recorded with Albert Collins on his *Don't Lose Your Cool*
album.[8] It seemed an obvious choice for a guitar hero making his
bluesiest record. Roy liked it and thought he could handle the vocals. But we knew we'd need other singers; Roy always had another

7. Jimmy Nolen played with Johnny Otis in the second half of the 1950s and then joined
James Brown's band. He was the inventor of those chopped, funky two- and three-note partial
chords that were rhythmically crucial to the James Brown sound. But Nolen could also play
beautiful, melodic blues. When we cut Roy's first Alligator album, *Guitar Player* magazine
asked us to record one of those floppy plastic singles that could be torn out of the magazine and played on a turntable. Roy cut an instrumental for them he called "Blues for Jimmy
Nolen," which Dick nicknamed "Stolen from Nolen."
8. It was an obscure tune by Roy Lee Johnson, who was perhaps most famous for writing
"Mister Moonlight," which the Beatles recorded. Dick Shurman had suggested it for Albert.

singer on his gigs and we knew his vocals weren't strong enough to carry a whole album.

Roy asked us to put together the studio band as we had done for Albert Collins and Johnny Winter. Because Roy's definition of blues was less traditional than Johnny's, we sought out a mix of seasoned, versatile musicians and guest vocalists who could provide the stylistic variety needed to go beyond traditional blues. We chose Morris Jennings, the former 1960s Chess Records studio drummer, who had recorded with everyone from Muddy Waters to Rotary Connection to Ramsey Lewis. Morris had the stylistic range we were looking for, as did the bass player, Larry Exum. For rhythm guitar, I recruited Criss Johnson, the brilliant gospel guitarist who had been a musical spark plug on our two previous Koko Taylor albums. As guest vocalists, we picked Otis Clay, the dean of Chicago soul singers, and Gloria Hardiman, a gospel-rooted vocalist who was part of a local group called Professor's Blues Revue.[9] With Otis, we decided to cut "A Nickel and a Nail," a soul classic originally recorded by O. V. Wright, the great Memphis soul singer. For Gloria, local songwriter Denise Osso penned a lovely ballad called "Why Don't You Want Me?" It was a testament to Roy's musical range and temperament that, although he was known for flashy guitar playing, he was happy to step into the background and create a melodic solo for a good ballad.

The instrumentals included "Hawaiian Punch," inspired by Elmore James's "Hawaiian Boogie," which Roy played using a nut extender. This device raised the strings of his guitar further off the neck so that he could play it like a lap steel guitar (his first instrument), using a heavy metal slider normally used by pedal steel guitar players. Roy also began using this slider to create some effects on his regular guitar. He began improvising a new song—a heavy, grind-

---

9. We continued to use guest vocalists to enhance Roy's albums. For *Dancing on the Edge*, Dick Shurman suggested veteran Texas roadhouse blues-rocker Delbert McClinton, who delivered a brilliant version of Aretha Franklin's "Baby, Baby, Baby." For Roy's last album, *Hot Wires*, we chose rough-voiced Chicago soul singer Johnny Sayles and a young female vocalist, Kanika Kress, who was just beginning to make waves on the Chicago scene. She died before reaching her full potential.

ing instrumental. At a certain point in the song, he got out the steel slider and hit the strings percussively to create weird, scary, spacey sounds. They reminded me of ray guns shooting at some monster in a bad sci-fi film, or perhaps fire shooting out of the monster's eyes. With these images in mind, we named the song "Sneaking Godzilla through the Alley," a play on the famous New Orleans R&B classic, "Sneaking Sally through the Alley."

The sessions went quite easily. We tried to give Roy as much freedom in the studio as we could. On almost every song, he wanted to use a delay pedal that created an echo effect. He was surprised when we let him, because many producers had told him how they wanted him to sound.[10] "Set your tone and delay the way you like them set," we told him. "We want this record to sound like you." Apparently no other producer had ever said that to him. He was pleased to be given that much control. He said he was getting a level of respect from Dick and me that he hadn't received in past recording experiences, and he felt that he was working with friends rather than bosses.

Roy was a sweet, emotionally vulnerable man who always seemed to be in a lot of emotional pain. His frequent talk of being doomed to hell seemed to reflect how little self-esteem he had, how little value he gave to his life. Perhaps he was protective or paranoid about revealing his playing techniques because he felt his musicianship was the only thing he had that made him a worthy person. It also seemed that the lines between truth and fiction were unclear to him. He told us a story about going to a fundamentalist church service in Danville, Virginia, and standing up during the sermon to argue religion with the preacher. He said that angry congregants beat him so brutally he awoke in the hospital without any memory of how to play guitar. He claimed to have taught himself to play all over again. I had no idea if there was any truth in this story, but he told it so convincingly and in such detail that it seemed believable.

10. Roy told us that the producer of one of his Atlantic albums insisted that Roy play only down strokes on his guitar because, in the producer's opinion, when Roy played up-and-down strokes, he played too fast. As far as Dick and I were concerned, these fast up-and-down strokes were an intrinsic part of Roy's style.

We heard another bizarre story when we were brainstorming possible names for an instrumental on Roy's second album, *Dancing on the Edge*. Dick Shurman and I both like wordplay, and we were trying to figure out an appropriate title for the feel of the song. I said, "That lick almost sounds like the wail of a banshee. Maybe we ought to give it a title with the word 'banshee' in it." Without hesitation and with a straight face, Roy said, "You know, we had a banshee on our farm in Virginia that would keep us awake nights, wailing over and over. It was just impossible to sleep. We finally gave up and sold the farm because we couldn't figure out how to get rid of the banshee." We ended up calling the song "Jungle Gym."

Roy's devils never stopped eating away at him. After a period of sobriety, he reverted to intermittent substance abuse. He attempted suicide after a gig in Cleveland. For someone who believed that he was doomed to hell, suicide would mean choosing to speed his journey to eternal punishment. Clearly, his battered self-image was sinking ever lower. In 1988, he was arrested for public intoxication after an argument with his wife. He was later found in his jail cell, supposedly hanged by his own shirt. His death was declared a suicide, but there was much speculation that he had been murdered by the local police. I had known Roy to be suicidal. He was also capable of provoking rage in others, the way he provoked the church congregation in Danville. So I believe that either explanation could be true.

Signing musicians like Johnny and Roy, who had been on major labels, forced me to learn to write more complex contracts than I had previously done. I didn't have the budget to hire a lawyer to do this for me, so I learned from textbooks and adapted language from other artist's contracts that I could find. In the early years, with musicians like Son Seals, Lonnie Brooks, and Koko Taylor, I made deals for one record at a time, figuring that if we were happy with each other, we'd cut another record. Each album was made under a separate contract. The artists weren't signed to exclusivity with Alligator, though we had an unspoken understanding that they would stick with the label.

Since the 1980s, I've usually signed musicians to exclusive multiple-record deals. Alligator guarantees one album and the label retains options for recording and releasing additional albums. There's a period of time after the release of each album during which I can decide about exercising our option for another record, usually twelve or fourteen months. During that time, the artist can't record for another label. If I exercise the option, the artist is bound to record exclusively on Alligator for another album. The label is also bound. Exercising the option means Alligator is making a financial commitment for funding and releasing the artist's next album. Every once in a while I make a single-record deal—called a "one-off"— with no option, as I did with our live Delbert McClinton album, which was the soundtrack from a performance on the *Austin City Limits* public television show.

In the old days, Alligator paid an advance to the artist and covered all the costs of recording and mixing (like paying the producer, sidemen, studio, and engineer). The label was responsible for controlling recording costs, and these often ended up going higher than anticipated. These days, Alligator's deals are generally structured so that there is a budget for each album; this allows us to calculate in advance what sales must be made before the label recoups its investment and before the artists receive royalties. If we don't spend the entire budget making the record, the remainder goes into the artist's pocket. Plus, if the artist wrote songs on the albums, there are separate royalties for the songwriting that the artist begins earning as soon as the album is released and begins selling.

But the larger the budget, the longer it may be before the artist receives royalties other than those for original songs. Recouping large budgets means making large sales. Ideally, the artist is benefiting from our investment with increased income from his or her gigs as a result of the publicity and airplay we create around a new release. Meanwhile we're earning back our investment. The label is shouldering all the financial risk. If the artist's albums sell well, he or she earns royalties. If the first album sells and the following albums don't, cross-collateralization protects Alligator from completely losing its shirt. Cross-collateralization means that all of the money spent making all of the records under any one contract, including money advanced to the artist, and all the royalties earned by all those multiple records, are comingled. This is why musicians often complain about record deals—they can release one record that sells well but they don't earn royalties because the other records produced under the same contract didn't sell as well. According to industry reports, the vast majority of albums never recoup their costs, and the artists never earn royalties from them. Most of Alligator's releases have recouped and are generating royalties for the artists. Royalties are Alligator's biggest single expense. I'm very proud of that.

13

Alligator's growth was helped by my making an early commitment to releasing our music on compact discs. CDs were still a new technology in 1985. I had read about them, and it seemed like a format that was going to stick around. I took a huge gamble, spending almost every penny Alligator had, to manufacture a dozen of our titles on CD. It was hard even to find a plant to manufacture them for us. The major labels were monopolizing the few CD fabricators. We found plants in Europe, California and even Korea. Those CDs were expensive; a bare, unpackaged CD cost us about five dollars. It was also impossible for us to find a pressing plant that would package the CDs. In the late spring of 1985, 37,000 CDs, packaged only in paper sleeves, arrived at our little building. They were packed in cartons the size of refrigerators; it took a full day to load them into the building. We had already printed booklets and back covers and the cardboard boxes that stores like them packaged in, and had bought thousands of plastic jewel cases, which arrived disassembled. Each CD had to be packaged by hand.

I assembled a crew made up of baggers from the local supermarket, women who changed beds at nursing homes, high school students, and some neighbors. We worked as a human assembly line from 6 p.m. until midnight every day and twelve hours a day on the weekends, putting the back covers in the plastic boxes, snapping in the trays, putting in the CD, snapping on the top cover, and inserting the booklets. In those days, CDs were sold in the stores in long cardboard "spaghetti boxes." Two would fit side by side in an existing LP bin. So Alligator had to print thousands of these boxes. Each assembled CD had to be inserted in its own box. I supervised the crew while running the shrink-wrap machine, pushing down the arm of the machine to seal the shrink-wrap for each of those 37,000 CDs. My right hand hurt for months afterward.

With their distinctive red-topped boxes, Alligator CDs stood out in the record store bins. The major labels hadn't yet manufactured many of their blues albums on CD. So, for a year or two, as we released more and more of our catalog on CD, Alligator discs dominated the blues CD sections of retail stores. My gamble had paid off; CDs became the dominant format of recordings for the next twenty-five years. LPs disappeared amazingly quickly; we stopped manufacturing them in 1991 but started up again in 2009 with a few albums in response to the renewed interest in vinyl. We've released more than a dozen titles on LP since then.

Starting in the mid-1980s, it seemed that high-quality newly finished records and worthy artists were finding me, even as I continued to seek out musicians who deserved to be on the label. Alligator was capitalizing on its reputation as a hardworking, artist-friendly label that valued the music and that could provide international distribution and strong promotion. Smaller labels and independent producers offered completed masters to us. Managers and agents began calling, touting both established and up-and-coming artists. The company kept growing through the 1990s; we often released ten or twelve new albums a year. With the success of our established musicians and continued sales of our earlier albums, we could afford to take risks releasing albums by unproven artists like West Coast jump blues band Little Charlie & The Nightcats, Chicago saxman and vocalist A. C. Reed, blues-funk-rock-reggae fusion band the Kinsey Report, Australian slide master Dave Hole, California roots rockers the Paladins, and Chicago guitar and sax player Maurice John Vaughn.

During the 1980s and 1990s, I matured as a producer and developed a clear sense of how I wanted an Alligator record to sound.

I had become much better at working with recording engineers as I learned how to speak their language. I had also become much pickier about audio quality and mixes, despite the fact that average listeners don't spend much time thinking about sonic quality. Some aspects of mixing a blues record seemed obvious to me. I wanted to hear the singing clearly and understand every lyric. I wanted to feel the groove, not just hear it. I wanted instrumental solos to be as loud as the vocals. I particularly wanted to feel like I was experiencing the music in a club, not a sterile studio, a concert hall, or a massive arena. I learned that you could shape the listener's aural perception of the band's performance space by applying digital delays and by microphone placement. I wanted to create the impression that the band was right in front of the listener, playing with normal live intensity and volume, with the music bouncing off the hard surfaces of the room. For me, the studio existed mostly as a tool to create a sense of live performance. I didn't try to instruct engineers how to create a live sound and feel. Instead, I found engineers I trusted and told them, "I don't want this to feel like it's recorded in a pristine studio or at the Auditorium Theatre. I want it to feel like we're in Pepper's Lounge or the Wise Fools Pub."[1]

During the recording of the first Hound Dog Taylor record, I wasn't thinking of developing an Alligator sound. I simply thought, "I want to make records that sound and feel like what I hear in the clubs." When Stu Black, who engineered the first six Alligator albums, asked if I wanted reverb (the echo effect you hear on most records) on Hound Dog's voice and guitar, I said no because I felt reverb would make the record sound too much like a studio recording. So Stu recorded the band completely dry, with no reverb. I wanted the raw club sound, but I wanted that rawness to be well recorded. If you listen to any of the Alligator records that Stu recorded, you will

1. Surprisingly, live records don't sell as well as studio records, even in the blues world, where live performance abilities are so important to the success of the artists. The exception is *Live from Chicago—Bayou Lightning Strikes*, Alligator's best-selling Lonnie Brooks album. For the most part, live records are considered by the public and the media to be filler by an artist who doesn't have new songs or ideas.

find that they are clear and crisp without sounding artificially brightened. You can hear some of the sounds of the instruments echoing
around the room, like in a club. I'm proud of the sonic quality of
those early Alligator recordings.[2]

When I mix, the first crucial decision for me is always the relationship of the vocal to the snare drum. To put it in spatial terms, I want
the snare drum to sound like it's about five feet behind the singer,
not ten feet behind, where it's not going to groove as well, and not
three feet behind, where it will begin encroaching on the audio space
that should be occupied by the vocals and lead instruments. Part of
the challenge is that the frequencies of the snare drum are close to
the frequencies of the human voice, so a snare drum is going to fight
for audio space with the vocal. Getting that voice-snare relationship
right is something I strive to do early on, but I may subtly readjust it
again at the end of a mix.

Putting the right mix of sounds together isn't the only job I set
for myself as a producer. I also spend a considerable amount of
time thinking about the right mix of musicians' personalities. Like
jazz, blues music is created as much by the interaction between the
musicians as by the individual parts that are played. Generally, the
musicians I record aren't studio musicians who read arrangements
written on sheet music. Most Alligator artists are gigging musicians
who are used to hearing and responding to one another in live performances. Even when I put together a band solely for a recording session, I choose musicians whose skills have been honed in the
clubs more than in the studio.

It's tricky to bring musicians into the studio who don't normally
play together. If the chemistry isn't right, everyone plays it safe and
the results can be mediocre. But with the right lineup, each player
can spur the others on to greater heights. The Grammy-winning al-

---

2. Not every record I produced sounds warm. Some of my mixes from the mid-1980s were
heavily influenced by the hyped-up, overly brightened dance-rock sounds that were prevalent
in pop music at the time. I listen back to my records from that period and find that the drum
sounds I initially thought were hip and contemporary now sound somewhat processed and
fake. Luckily, the performances are good enough to overshadow the dated mixes.

bum *Showdown!*, with Albert Collins, Johnny Copeland, and Robert Cray, is a perfect example. Cut in 1985, it was Alligator's first super session, bringing established bandleaders together in the studio. It was one of our most successful attempts to capture the dynamic spontaneity of musicians inspiring one another. The album grew out of the final set of the inaugural 1984 Chicago Blues Festival.[3] The festival closed with a Texas guitar showdown featuring Albert and Johnny playing with one of their key inspirations, Clarence "Gatemouth" Brown. They put on a terrific performance, and my frequent coproducer Dick Shurman and I were eager re-create their energy and enthusiasm in the studio.

Since the release of *Ice Pickin'*, Albert Collins had risen to blues stardom and become one of Alligator's best-selling and most popular artists. His close friend Johnny Copeland had begun his career sitting in with Albert's bands in Houston in the 1950s before going on to cut some regional black radio hit singles in the 1950s and 1960s. In 1972, when Johnny's Deep South career had petered out, he had moved to Harlem, where he played local clubs and house parties, living in relative obscurity. In 1981, he was sought out by Dan Doyle and Ken Vangel, who produced his comeback album, released on Rounder Records. With this album, Johnny attracted a new audience of white blues fans, and he became a solid draw at festivals and clubs, touring worldwide. Charismatic and good looking, Johnny was blessed with a big, gravelly, gospel-inflected voice that contrasted with Albert's lighter, conversational, storytelling vocals. Johnny also had boyishly

---

3. When Harold Washington was elected as the first black mayor of Chicago in 1983, he fulfilled his campaign promise to get rid of ChicagoFest, a weeklong musical event staged at Navy Pier on the Lake Michigan shoreline. ChicagoFest was operated by the same Milwaukee-based company that ran Milwaukee's popular Summerfest. Chicagoans were upset that the profits from ChicagoFest were going out of state. In late 1983, I was approached by Lois Weisberg, the new director of the Mayor's Office of Special Events. She told me that the city was preparing to launch a series of free music festivals in Grant Park and asked me to chair the Talent Committee for the first Chicago Blues Festival. I called on Gene Barge, Billy Branch, Jim and Amy O'Neal, Theresa Needham of Theresa's Lounge, Bill Gilmore of B.L.U.E.S. on Halsted, and others to help. The first festival was a huge success and the city has continued to present the Chicago Blues Festival annually ever since. It's now booked by a city staffer. I've continued to sit on the Advisory Committee. The Chicago Blues Festival is the largest blues festival in the world, and it's free to the public.

positive energy and attitude. Although not as distinctive a guitarist as Albert, he played with power and authority.

Gatemouth Brown was a more complicated personality. An immensely talented guitar player with a dry Texas vocal twang, he had cut classic singles for the Texas-based Peacock label in the 1940s and 1950s. In those years, if you wanted to call yourself a blues guitar player in that part of the country, you had to be able to play Gatemouth's hit instrumental, "Okie Dokie Stomp."[4] His career had fallen off in the 1960s, but he found an audience in Europe and then, like Johnny, made a comeback on Rounder in the early 1980s. He toured steadily, backed by a tight band that included a swinging horn section. Gatemouth could be a grumpy cuss. He was critical of fellow musicians, promoters, and producers alike.

When Dick and I approached Gatemouth's manager about the possible *Showdown!* recording project, the manager told us that Gatemouth was willing, but only if we agreed to record in Louisiana using his band. Gatemouth was known for controlling sessions and dictating arrangements. That was antithetical to a musician like Albert, for whom the arrangement was simply a starting point. We were afraid that if we agreed to those conditions, Albert and Johnny would merely be guests on a Gatemouth album. We dropped Gatemouth from our plans.[5]

It was probably Albert who suggested up-and-comer Robert Cray as an alternative. Robert idolized Albert. He had committed himself to being a bluesman after seeing Albert perform at a dance at his high school in Tacoma, Washington. By the second half of the 1970s, the Robert Cray Band had developed a following in the Pacific Northwest, and Albert often used them as his backup band when touring

---

4. In Chicago, the song that everybody had to know how to play was "Hide Away," the instrumental that Freddie King made into a hit. Freddie's song was actually based on an unnamed Hound Dog Taylor instrumental tune to which Freddie added musical quotes from Robert Junior Lockwood, the *Peter Gunn* TV show theme, and "The Walk" by Jimmy McCracklin. If you couldn't play "Hide Away," you couldn't get a gig in a Chicago blues club.

5. Although Gatemouth didn't appear on *Showdown!*, Alligator released three of his albums— *Pressure Cooker* (1986), which was composed of tracks he had recorded for the Black and Blue label in France, and *Standing My Ground* (1989) and *No Lookin' Back* (1992), both of which were produced in Louisiana by Gatemouth and his manager, Jim Bateman.

in that part of the country.[6] I had seen the Robert Cray Band perform in Los Angeles in 1978 and had gone to the show with my friend Bruce Bromberg, who was the sales manager for Tomato Records, another independent label. I liked the band, but their show confused me. Curtis Salgado, a very fine blue-eyed soul singer (a white musician performing in a vocal style inspired by the soul records of the mid- to late 1960s), delivered half the vocals.[7] The band played more R&B than blues. Robert was playing incisive, melodic lead guitar, and his polished, soul music–inflected vocals soared, but he seemed reluctant to be in the spotlight. I passed on signing the band. Bruce Bromberg produced the Robert Cray Band's debut record for Tomato, but it sank without a trace.

A few years later, Bruce produced another record with the Robert Cray Band (without Curtis but still with a lot of R&B) and offered it to Alligator. Like an idiot, I turned it down. It seemed to me that Robert was a work in progress, not quite ready for the national stage. Frustrated, Bromberg started the HighTone label in partnership with Larry Sloven, who managed a record distributorship in Oakland, California. HighTone released two records by Robert. It was around the time of the release of his second HighTone album, *False Accusations*, that Robert enthusiastically agreed to be part of the *Showdown!* project. Shortly after, he signed with Mercury Records and had an unexpected national FM rock radio hit with "Strong Persuader." He was hailed as the great blues hope of his generation just as we were releasing and promoting *Showdown!* Within months, rock fans knew Robert's name better than Albert's.

Because of the musicians' tour schedules, we had only four days for recording; Robert would be available for only the last two. Albert

6. Robert Cray told me a story about Albert's arriving late (as was often the case) for a club gig with the Robert Cray Band. After missing the first set, Albert snuck in the back entrance with his amplifier during the second set and joined the band on stage. Later, he tried to convince the club owner that he'd been there all night.

7. After leaving the Robert Cray Band, Curtis Salgado sang with Roomful of Blues and then went on to a solo career leading his own bands. He's won multiple Blues Music Awards as Soul Blues Male Artist and become a fixture on the Legendary Rhythm & Blues Cruises. He signed with Alligator in 2011.

was the best-known artist and the most familiar with the sidemen (bassist Johnny Gayden and drummer Casey Jones were members of his touring band, the Icebreakers, and keyboard player Allen Batts had recorded with Albert on three previous Alligator albums), so we decided that Albert would appear on every song. Johnny and Robert would join Albert as featured players either singly or together, depending on the arrangement. Both Johnny's and Robert's producers decided they wanted to be at the recording sessions; Dan Doyle and Ken Vangel came with Johnny and Bruce Bromberg came with Robert.

The first day of recording began inauspiciously. We had completed the painstaking task of arranging the guitar amps and vocal microphones to be completely isolated so that all three of the stars could sing and play simultaneously without sounds bleeding into the wrong mics, and we were eager to get started on the recording. But Allen Batts, the organ player, had an afternoon gig and was late getting to the studio. To kill time, Johnny Gayden began playing a funky bass line. Soon Casey Jones joined in on drums, playing just the right syncopated pattern.[8] Dick Shurman suggested that this groove might work for "Black Cat Bone," an old tune Johnny Copeland had wanted to include on the album. Johnny Copeland picked up on their new funky groove and began singing with it, *I believe / My baby's got a black cat bone.*[9] "No, no, no, it should be done as a shuffle," Copeland's producers insisted, but he refused to give in. "I can make it work this way," he told them. Then he proved it. First, he showed Johnny Gayden where the chord changes should go in this new arrangement. Then he improvised some introductory banter between Albert and himself. As soon as Allen arrived, they cut

---

8. Most blues songs are in 4/4 time, with the snare drum played on the second and fourth beats of each measure. For "Black Cat Bone," Casey intentionally left out the snare on the second beat and slightly delayed it on the fourth beat, creating an unusual tension and release in the song. This instinctive choice was part of Casey's genius.

9. The song had been a local hit in Houston in 1960 for "Poppa Hop" Wilson, a reclusive blues singer who played Hawaiian steel guitar and had cut a few 45s in the late 1950s and early 1960s. Hop had recorded the song as a shuffle with the title "My Woman Has a Black Cat Bone."

the song in one or two takes. It was an inspired performance, and, as it was being recorded, Dick turned to me and asked, "Is this as good as I think it is?" I could only answer, "Yes, yes."

We had a fair number of songs in the can by the end of the second night, when Robert Cray and Bruce Bromberg arrived in good spirits. Although we didn't record anything with Robert that night, he and Bruce went back to the run-down but conveniently located Heart 'O' Chicago motel, where we had booked rooms for them, and wrote a song together called "The Dream." We recorded it the next day. Although it had been written in a major key, Robert chose to cut it in A minor and gave Albert the first solo. As usual, Albert threw down the gauntlet with a fiery performance. Although he was typically a controlled artist who played with some reserve, Robert responded with some of the most passionate playing of his career. Despite having written "The Dream" only the night before, he sang the song with such feeling that his performance stands as one of his most soulful recordings. The *Showdown!* sessions were full of moments like that, with each bluesman challenging the others to deliver their best.

After the sessions were completed, Dick and I sat there with our mouths open. We had just produced a classic blues record, mostly by bringing together the right musicians and getting out of the way. Hailed as one the best blues records of the 1980s and winner of a Grammy Award, *Showdown!* continues to be one of the most popular records in the Alligator catalog. The record also earned Johnny, Albert, and Robert the accolades they so rightly deserved after many years of hard work and dedication to their music. Seeing these three dear friends holding their Grammys was a moment of great satisfaction for me.

Albert had become one of the top-drawing live artists in blues. With *Showdown!* having sold more than three hundred thousand copies, his royalty checks were substantial. But he must have felt he wasn't making as much money on Alligator as he thought he could be making. Soon after cutting his next album, *Cold Snap*, in 1987, he left the label. It was an Alligator employee who convinced him to leave. The employee resigned and took over Albert's management with the promise to Albert that he could do a better job of promoting Albert's career than we were doing. Alligator had been managing Albert since 1978 but, as his career blossomed, the job grew increasingly time consuming. I would have been happy if Albert had found an experienced, professional manager to advance his career, coordinate his tours, and take care of media opportunities.[10] But Albert, who hated confrontation, never came to me and said, "Bruce, there are some other opportunities I'd like to pursue." He just stopped being in touch with me. I was heartbroken.

Albert soon signed with Point Blank, a blues label that had recently been started by the large and well-established British-based label Virgin Records, which was distributed by the conglomerate EMI. It had been a long time since a major label had created a blues subsidiary, and Point Blank was getting some publicity with major signings like John Hammond, Charlie Musselwhite, and a promising newcomer named Larry McCray. I found out later that Point Blank's budget for Albert's new album was a good deal more than I had ever budgeted for one of his records. But it was an all-in deal to deliver the album. Albert's Alligator deals had guaranteed a separate advance to him as well as Alligator's paying the recording costs, although both the advance and recording costs were recoupable. Under the Point Blank deal, Albert would receive whatever money was left out of the budget after the album was recorded, mixed, and mastered.

Point Blank brought Albert and his band to England to record, and, true to form, Albert arrived with no songs.[11] This was a situation that Dick and I would have foreseen, and we would have worked out

---

10. The income that I earned managing Albert Collins was in the form of commissions from his live performances and from other opportunities that Alligator had helped make possible, like movie appearances and his recordings with David Bowie and with composer John Zorn. I never took a management commission on his Alligator royalties, as a manager typically would have done, because we were already making a profit on his recordings.

11. I am always amazed at how often artists who are thinking about recording ask whether the producer will bring some songs for the album. It makes me wonder why those artists want to record in the first place, if they don't have songs that move them. Making a record is not just something to do between tours; it represents a milestone in the artist's career. Many more people will hear the record than will ever hear the artist live.

a song list prior to recording. In contrast, Point Blank was paying expensive studio rates while Albert, the band, and the producer put songs and arrangements together. With much of the budget going toward studio time, hotels, and international flights, I imagine Albert pocketed little of that advance. He made three albums with Point Blank, including re-recording some of the songs he had cut for us. But even with Virgin's marketing machine, the releases didn't sell any better than his records on Alligator.

In 1993, Albert was diagnosed with inoperable cancer. In June of that year, Albert flew into Chicago to play two of his last gigs, in Peoria and Rockford, Illinois. Seven years had passed since we had last spoken, but when he called me, I went to see him at his hotel. Determined to fight the cancer, he told me that when he got well, he wanted to come back home to Alligator. He died before that could happen. His wife, Gwen, asked me to be a pallbearer at his funeral, and I was honored to do so. Albert had left the label, but he couldn't leave the family.

In 1990, five years after the release of *Showdown!*, I decided to record *Harp Attack!*, another super session, this time with harmonica players. This project would present an entirely different challenge from working with guitarists. Most blues harp players play harp as a lead instrument, playing individual notes. They have to bend the pitch with directed air pressure to create the notes of the blues scale and microtones between the notes. Each player bends a bit differently and plays with a different amount and speed of vibrato. Thus, it's hard for harmonica players to play perfectly in tune and perfectly in time with one another. As a result, playing multiple rhythm harmonicas behind a lead harmonica isn't commonly done, whereas playing multiple rhythm guitars behind a lead guitar is common. I thought we might be able to create a special harp album, using two or three harmonicas playing riffs, in a role similar to a horn section.

I recruited four of Chicago's most famous and accomplished harp players: James Cotton, Junior Wells, Carey Bell, and Billy Branch. James "Mr. Superharp" Cotton was a world-renowned master with a career spanning four decades. He had learned the instrument as a child in Mississippi, first playing with his mentor, Sonny Boy Williamson II, and then with Howlin' Wolf. In the early 1950s, while still a teenager, he cut a few vocal sides for the fabled Sun Records label in Memphis. When Muddy Waters recruited him in 1955 to replace George "Harmonica" Smith, Cotton moved to Chicago, where his huge sound and freight-train power became a signature of Muddy's band. It was Cotton who had suggested to Muddy that he cut "Got My Mojo Working." He played on the iconic version that appears on Muddy's album *At Newport 1960*.

After leaving Muddy in 1966, Cotton formed his own band and become one of the best known and most popular bluesmen playing for white rock audiences. He cut a series of albums with his own hard-charging groups and guested on albums by rockers like Johnny Winter and Steve Miller. Cotton had recorded two albums for Alligator in 1984 and 1986 but had then gone on to another label. A big, outgoing man who sang in a gravelly voice scarred by years of smoking, he was well known as both a take-no-prisoners harmonica player and a fearless party animal. I found Cotton to be a pleasure to work with. Full of boyish energy, he was a blues fan like I was. He told colorful stories about his years with Sonny Boy and Muddy, always with an ego-free attitude, as if to say, "How lucky was I, to have played with these blues giants and walked in their shadows?"

I had known Junior Wells since my early days working for Delmark, when he took me under his wing and made sure that no one bothered me at his gigs on the South Side. Junior and James were good friends, but they had different styles both personally and musically. Whereas Cotton almost always dressed casually in a T-shirt and jeans, Junior always looked dapper, usually dressed in a colorful suit with matching shoes and hat, his hands sparkling with jeweled rings. Like his personality, Cotton played loud, in-your-face harmonica. Junior's style was spare and percussive. If Cotton's sound hit you like a two-by-four to the head, Junior's was more like a switchblade between the ribs.

After years as an in-demand sideman, Carey Bell had begun his recording career as a bandleader on Delmark and later was part of Alligator's *Living Chicago Blues* series. I had befriended him when I was working at the Jazz Record Mart and seen him play many times on the West Side. A sweet guy with a prominent gap where he had lost a front tooth, Carey's laid-back demeanor showed his country roots. Even though he had been in Chicago since the 1950s, he still spoke with a thick Mississippi accent. He had toured with Earl Hooker, Muddy Waters, and Willie Dixon and had cut multiple albums of his own. Carey was a lyrical player in the mold of his mentor, Big Walter Horton. Carey knew exactly where to fit the harp in a song for maximum effect. His understanding of the blues was soul deep.

The fourth harmonica player for this project was Billy Branch, whom I had known since 1972. He had burst onto the Chicago scene by competing in the now-legendary harmonica contest that Little Mack Simmons, a fine harmonica player and singer, had put on at a South Side club called the Green Bunny. The prize was one hundred dollars, and all of us from the Blues Amalgamated gang of fans were there. Billy, a complete unknown in his early twenties, wearing overalls and sporting a large Afro haircut, became the audience's favorite. He was already a mature player with both technique and feel. Mack was a good harp man, but Billy sliced and diced him. Musically cornered, Mack suddenly declared that the ballad "Rainy Night in Georgia" (coincidentally one of Mack's showpieces) would serve as the contest-winning song. Clearly at a disadvantage, Billy nonetheless managed to hold his own through the song. Cheering, the audience yelled, "Give him the money; give him the money!" Mack promptly got on the microphone and announced that the police were towing cars out of the parking lot across the street. We all hurriedly left the club to rescue our cars, and when we returned, the door was locked. Little Mack kept his money, but Billy earned his reputation as Chicago's new young gun of blues harmonica. Billy went on to play in Willie Dixon's band starting in the mid-1970s, and he formed his own group, the Sons of Blues, in 1978.

Billy had spent years with Cotton, Junior, and Carey, working hard to absorb the techniques and styles of these blues harp giants. It was a tradition—Junior Wells had studied the style of Sonny Boy Williamson I; James Cotton had learned at the feet of Sonny Boy Williamson II; Carey Bell was taught by Big Walter Horton. And the most famous harp player of all, Little Walter, had influenced all three of them. Billy had learned from Cotton, Junior, and Carey just as they had learned from the past masters. A college-educated, modern young African American from California, Billy presented a contrast with his mentors. He hadn't grown up in the South or on the South Side, but he played with soul, energy, and passion.

I met with each harp player individually to finalize song choices. Carey, Junior, and Billy all had original tunes. Cotton had no originals, but his amazing memory for songs gave him a vast repertoire to choose from. All four musicians came to the first rehearsal. Junior took command as bandleader, calling out riffs and playing perfect background parts. But Junior didn't show up for the second rehearsal, and Carey was out of town. The rehearsal became useless and chaotic. I realized I had to go into the studio with my fingers crossed, hoping these experienced players and good friends would come through when the pressure was on.

I didn't plan to have all four harmonica players appear on every song. Instead, each song would highlight one of the musicians, usually backed by one or two others. Only one song would feature all four. We recorded Junior first. Rehearsed and professional, he cut his two numbers (both funky reworkings of familiar blues themes) quickly. Wanting a slow blues from Junior, I suggested he record the Sonny Boy Williamson II song "Keep Your Hands Out of My Pockets." Sonny Boy was one of his favorites, and Junior cut a memorable version in one or two takes, singing half of the original lyrics and making up others on the spot. Much to my relief, Junior didn't swear, as he often did in his improvised songs.

Cotton arrived near the end of Junior's session. Clearly under the influence of some substance, Cotton headed straight to the musicians' lounge, stretched out on the floor, and passed out. I was convinced he would be useless, but after we finished "Keep Your Hands Out of My Pockets," Cotton awoke from his stupor and cut two powerful takes of "Little Car Blues," which he had learned from pianist Willie Love's version on Trumpet Records. Before the first verse, Cotton added a spoken introduction with his raw voice and

Mississippi accent, requiring the listener to have a sharp ear to make out the words. When he was finished with the song, Cotton went back to the lounge and passed out again. Later on, he returned to cut a subtle, sensitive version of "Black Night" on the big chromatic harmonica.

That's how the *Harp Attack!* sessions unfolded. Much alcohol flowed, along with much banter and one-upmanship. Billy and Cotton tried to beat each other's solos on Little Walter's version of "Who." Carey cut two originals, with Junior interjecting comments with both his voice and his harp. When they weren't laughing, they were playing their asses off, backing one another up, and trading dueling solos, all with the spirit of their shared friendship. Despite the fact that their album was hardly rehearsed, they made a soulful, influential,[12] one-of-a-kind record that has stood the test of time. It succeeded because of their talent, their mutual understanding of the blues tradition and each other's music, and the love and rapport they shared.

---

12. When I met Dennis Gruenling, one of the best of the current generation of harmonica players, he told me that his first exposure to blues harp was hearing *Harp Attack!*

PART III

One snowy night in 1986, Lil' Ed & The Blues Imperials filed into the recording studio at eight o'clock, dressed in their winter clothes and huddled together like frightened cartoon characters. I had only seen the band play a couple of times before, at Blue Chicago and B.L.U.E.S. on Halsted, both on the North Side. Ed Williams was an animated entertainer and an energized, although not technically extraordinary, slide guitar player. He reminded me of his uncle, Chicago blues icon J. B. Hutto, whose music I loved and whom I had helped book in the early 1970s. With his short stature and toothy smile, Ed looked startlingly like J.B. The Blues Imperials were rough and ready, if somewhat sloppy, but they played with real blues feeling. Ed was to be the only slide player on The New Bluebloods, *an anthology album I was recording. As with nine other emerging blues bands that were to appear on that record, they would record two songs during a four-hour session. At the beginning of the night, I liked this band; by the end of the night, I loved them.*

With Ed were his bass-playing half-brother, James "Pookie" Young (who kept his rubber snow boots on throughout the session), a tough-looking West Side drummer named Walter Louis Henderson, and baby-faced rhythm guitar player Dave Weld, the only white guy in the band. I realized in talking with them that they had never seen a recording studio before. They checked it out nervously, looking as though at any moment they were going to flee from this confusing, unfamiliar place. "Don't think about the studio," I told them. "Set up your amps like you want them to sound at a gig. Play as loud as you want. Do what you know how to do."

Ed had come with two tunes: "Car Wash Blues," a song about his day job as a buffer at a car wash, and "Young Thing," a traditional Chicago shuffle in the style of J. B. Hutto and Elmore James. Because they didn't know anything about overdubbing or otherwise repairing their perfor- mances in the studio, the band performed everything live as though they were playing in a club. Thirty minutes after we began recording, the band had cut multiple takes of their two songs. That left three hours of reserved studio time with nothing to do. In one of the smartest moves of my career, I said, "Would you like to cut a few more and see how they come out?" "Sure," said Ed, grinning from ear to ear. Seeing that he had an audience on the other side of the control room glass—the engineer, a couple of Alligator staffers, my future wife, and me—he decided that this was a good opportunity to put on a live show.

Ed became not just a musician, but also an entertainer. He played on one foot, dropped to his knees and bent backward until his head touched the floor, duckwalked like Chuck Berry, and ran around the studio, playing all the while and rushing back to the microphone in time to sing each verse. The music was wildly infectious and full of energy— boogies and shuffles and the occasional slow blues. Almost all of the songs that he chose were unexpected. He did a few standards like Rufus Thomas's "Walking the Dog," but mostly he played either originals or J. B. Hutto tunes. At one point I asked him if he performed any Muddy Waters songs. Instead of one of Muddy's hits, he launched into the little- known "Soon Forgotten." I was more than impressed. This was exactly what a Chicago blues band was supposed to be, whether on stage or in the studio: spontaneous, raw, energetic, and musically telepathic. I was hooked.

After ten songs, I came into the studio from the control room and said, "Guys, this is wonderful. I want you on Alligator. I want to sign the band and do a full album with you—and I want to do it tonight. I can't negotiate a contract right now, so you're going to have to trust me." They eagerly agreed. "Is there anything that I can do to make things more comfortable for you?" I asked. "Well," said Ed shyly, "maybe we could each have a beer?" I sent for a six-pack. Between nine o'clock and midnight, Lil' Ed & The Blues Imperials recorded thirty songs, almost all in one take each. It was a magical night.

I chose the best performances for their debut album. I called the record Roughhousin' *because it was the closest thing I could think of to "Houserockin'." The title also evoked their kidlike enthusiasm for making music. The record had some rough spots, but you could feel how much these guys loved to make music together, and you could feel how long they had been doing it. Ed and Pookie had been playing together since they were children.*

Sometimes the best music is made when the producer gets out of the way. That was absolutely true that night. The only thing I could do to make them play better was to applaud and dance—exactly what I did. To paraphrase John Lee Hooker, it was in them and it had to come out.

14

By the mid-1980s, Alligator had reached a turning point. We were no longer a tiny label operating out of the owner's house, struggling just to get by. We had figured out how to survive, and we were getting better and better at promoting our artists and generating sales. Almost everything we released was selling at least well enough to break even. We had tapped into the resurgence of the blues market by recording well-known artists like Albert Collins and James Cotton and into the rock market with crossover musicians like Johnny Winter, Roy Buchanan, and Lonnie Mack. With the commercial success of Stevie Ray Vaughan, major labels were trying to reach Stevie's fans by jumping on the blues-rock bandwagon and signing blues-inflected guitar heroes like Mason Ruffner, Eric Johnson, and Omar and the Howlers. Chicago blues artists were finding steady work in the North Side clubs, where they were becoming better known not only to local blues fans but also to a growing audience—blues tourists. The blues market was so good that even the debut album by a relatively unknown local Chicago blues band like Lil' Ed & The Blues Imperials could sell more than ten thousand LPs in the first year of release.

I had recorded Lil' Ed in early 1986 as part of a project called *The New Bluebloods*, a single-album successor to the *Living Chicago Blues* series. Almost ten years had passed since that series had been released, and a new crop of younger musicians had emerged on the Chicago blues scene. I wanted both to document this new generation and to decide if any of them might be ready to become full-fledged Alligator artists. I approached ten bands or artists who were beginning to make noise locally; all were eager to be included. I booked Streeterville Studios for a series of twelve-hour sessions with the plan of recording three bands a day, four hours per band, two songs each. That would give me ten tracks for the album and ten tracks in the can, although I wouldn't have the rights to release the second batch. We discussed each one's song choices in advance; I didn't know most of the musicians well, but I had faith that they would arrive at the studio well rehearsed. Everyone saw this as a potential career booster and took it seriously.

The new bluebloods I had chosen included John Watkins, a promising young bluesman who was playing second guitar in Jimmy Johnson's band; guitarist and tenor saxman Maurice John Vaughn; pyrotechnic guitarist Dion Payton and his 43rd Street Band; funky guitarist Michael Coleman of James Cotton's band; six-string wizard Melvin Taylor; and big-voiced, sassy singer Valerie Wellington. Although Billy Branch had appeared with his Sons of Blues band on *Living Chicago Blues*, he had melded his band with the Chi-Town Hustlers, led by gravel-voiced bassist J. W. Williams. I decided they were essentially a new unit and worthy of being included. The album was rounded out by the Kinsey Report, a funky band from Gary, Indiana; keyboardist Professor Eddie Lusk and his Blues Review with featured vocalist Gloria Hardiman; and Lil' Ed & The Blues Imperials.

From this group of artists came not only *The New Bluebloods* but fourteen follow-up Alligator albums—nine by Lil' Ed, three by the Kinsey Report, and two by Maurice John Vaughn. As a result of his memorable session, Ed became a permanent member of the Alligator family; we not only recorded him but also managed him for many years. Shortly after Ed cut his debut album, Michael Wolancevich and Kelly Littleton became the band's permanent second guitarist and drummer. They've been with Ed for over thirty years; no other blues band I know has kept the same personnel that long. Lil' Ed & The Blues Imperials represent the heart and soul of Alligator's Genuine Houserockin' Music spirit. Whenever I'm asked who is the most authentic, most deeply rooted blues musician on the label, the answer is always Lil' Ed.

At that time, I believed that the Kinsey Report—composed of three brothers, lead guitarist and singer Donald Kinsey, drummer Ralph Kinsey, and bassist Kenneth Kinsey, and their friend guitarist Ron Prince—could be the next big thing out of Chicago. The Kinseys' father, Lester "Big Daddy" Kinsey, was a vocalist and guitarist in the style of Muddy Waters. He had encouraged the musical inclinations of his sons, and they became his backup band while still young teenagers. I was drawn to the edgy way they incorporated reggae, funk, and rock into their sound. I liked "Corner of the Blanket," the song they cut for *The New Bluebloods*, so much that I chose it as the lead track on the album. I brought them back into the studio the same year to cut their debut on Alligator, *Edge of the City*. They had a slew of original songs. Donald was an expressive singer, a creative, hard-rocking guitarist, and a passionate performer who had played in the touring bands of Albert King and Bob Marley and the Wailers. *Edge of the City* was well received, and the band began gaining a national profile.

In 1989, we recorded their second record, *Midnight Drive*. Both albums enjoyed airplay on Chicago's WXRT and some other loosely formatted rock stations around the country. But between Big Daddy's desire to control the band and Donald Kinsey's personal problems, tensions mounted and multiple band breakups ensued. Discouraged, I had to give up on them. Nine years later, after another band reunion, they convinced me to cut a third album, *Smoke and Steel*. It's a record I'm proud of, but the sessions were tense. After its release, the band did little touring to support the record. By this time, much of the public buzz around the Kinsey Report had passed. They were no longer a new story.

When I think of *The New Bluebloods*, I mostly think about what could have been. The careers of John Watkins and Dion Payton were sidetracked by drugs. Professor Eddie Lusk committed suicide. Valerie Wellington died young of a brain aneurysm after a lot of hard living. Even Lil' Ed left the label for a time after developing a drug problem that threatened to ruin both him and his career. During Alligator's twentieth anniversary tour in 1992, he would often pay the band after performances and then disappear. Thankfully, he always showed up the next morning. My experience with Ed helped me understand in a much more visceral way what drug addiction meant and how it could destroy a person's life. No one in the public realized that this boyish, smiling, full-of-energy guy could be an addict. With the help of his wife, Pamela, his friends, therapy, and religion, Ed finally got clean and stayed clean.

The New Bluebloods had been motivated by my original goal in creating Alligator—to document in the most dynamic way possible that real Chicago blues was alive and well. But it also signaled a readiness to go beyond my original focus on what I considered "authentic" blues. By the mid-1980s I had recorded many of the musicians whom I believed to be among the most important living African American blues artists. I had proven my commitment to the tradition and had even managed to make that commitment into a somewhat profitable business. I had also recorded Johnny Winter, Roy Buchanan, and Lonnie Mack, white blues-rock musicians whose national profiles placed them in a different commercial category than the authentic blues artists who formed the core of Alligator's roster. Now, I had the confidence to grow Alligator by releasing records that pushed the envelope of traditional blues. This included signing some white musicians who lacked established national profiles.

In 1987, I released *All the Way Crazy*, Alligator's first album by a group of terrific musicians from Sacramento called Little Charlie & The Nightcats. Their "jump blues" style combined jazzy, swinging grooves with virtuoso guitar and powerful Chicago-style harmonica, and they had a slew of streetwise songs written by harp player and vocalist Rick Estrin, some of which were hilarious. We released nine albums by this band as they gained national and then international stature. Little Charlie Baty, the bandleader and guitarist, was totally unpredictable, leaping between blues and jazz with wild imagination. Estrin, the harmonica player and front man, is one of the most memorable musical personalities in blues. He cut his musical teeth in the black clubs of San Francisco's East Bay, where he was accepted by the local blues community and performed with popular Bay Area bluesmen like Rodger Collins and Fillmore Slim (the latter immortalized in the documentary *American Pimp*). A world-class harp player and composer, Rick cuts a dashing figure. With his sharkskin suits, pompadour haircut, and pencil mustache, he seems a cross between a 1950s gangster and the world's hippest used car salesman. His witty songs tell slice-of-life stories with memorable hooks and sly humor. When Little Charlie retired from regular touring, Rick took over leadership of the band, and since then we've released four Rick Estrin & The Nightcats albums, full of hip lyrics and virtuoso musicianship.

One icy day early in 1988, I was driving down the alley behind my office when I almost hit a pedestrian—the well-known harmonica player and singer Corky Siegel. Corky's car had broken down, and since he lived in the neighborhood, he was walking home. Corky and his musical partner, guitarist Jim Schwall, had led the popular, lighthearted, semi-acoustic Siegel-Schwall Blues Band in the 1960s and 1970s. They still reunited for occasional shows. I had seen them a few times when I first came to the city, but they were too far from hard-edged, hard-core Chicago blues for my purist tastes. But by the mid-1980s, my ears were more open to less traditional sounds, and I could enjoy a band that didn't take themselves too seriously. As I gave Corky a ride home, he mentioned that the radio station WXRT had just recorded a Siegel-Schwall concert that might make a good Alligator record. I obtained the master from the station, remixed it, and released *The Siegel-Schwall Reunion Concert* later in 1988. The band's committed fans were eager for a new recording. We sold enough of it to make a modest profit, and Corky and I developed a lasting friendship.

Besides a second Siegel-Schwall record, Alligator also released two recordings by another Siegel-led band with a very different sound, Corky Siegel's Chamber Blues. This group plays a musically fascinating fusion of blues and classical chamber music, combining Corky's rollicking blues harmonica, keyboards, and humor-filled vocals with a string quartet and percussion. Corky's releases succeeded not only because of the quality of the music but also because Corky had developed a devoted fan following over many years. Signing musicians with established reputations meant we didn't have to go through the intense promotion, marketing, and advertising effort necessary to introduce a little-known artist or band like Lil' Ed & The Blues Imperials, the Kinsey Report, or Little Charlie & The Nightcats.

One of our important sources of good recordings during this period was King Snake Records, a Florida label started by Bob Greenlee, whom I met at a NAIRD conference. Bob had been the bassist for Root Boy Slim and the Sex Change Band, an outlandish 1970s rock group with a cult following. Bob had inherited a ramshackle mansion in central Florida from his wealthy uncle and had built a technically dubious recording studio in what had been the chauffeur's apartment over the three-car garage. He invited me for a visit, and when I arrived, I found a crude and dirty homemade studio, with low ceilings and a recording console that periodically buzzed until you hit it with your fist in just the right place. The space was so small that guitar amps were often placed in the bathroom for isolation. Bob played bass in the label's house band, the Midnight Creepers, and his studio (or "Bob's playhouse," as his wife, Sonja, called it) was as much a hobby as a business.

Shortly after I met Bob, he approached me with a Kenny Neal master called *Bio on the Bayou* that he had recently released on King Snake. I knew of Kenny both as Buddy Guy's bass player and the leader of his own band when he had lived in Toronto. In early 1988 Bob convinced me to fly down to Miami to see Kenny's live show. A handsome and confident young man of thirty-one, he played his battered old Fender Telecaster with a lot of attack, toughness, and swagger. Plus, he sang in an old-beyond-his-years voice and blew full-toned Louisiana-style harp much like his father, Baton Rouge harmonica legend Raful Neal. I arranged to remix, repackage, and release *Bio on the Bayou* under the title *Big News from Baton Rouge!!* Over the next few years Alligator released four more Kenny Neal albums, all of which were recorded in Bob's King Snake studio. Since then, Kenny has recorded for multiple labels and has become one of the most respected bluesmen of his generation.

My relationship with King Snake Records led to other releases that expanded the Alligator catalog. Among these records was Rufus Thomas's *That Woman Is Poison!* Another one of my musical heroes, Rufus was a musical Renaissance man. Intelligent and street smart, he had done many serious things without ever taking himself too seriously. He had been an essential part of the Memphis music scene since the 1930s, starting as a tap dancer on Beale Street with bottle caps attached to the soles of his shoes. He had worked as a DJ on WDIA, Memphis's groundbreaking black AM radio station. He had recorded hit novelty records like "Bear Cat" and "Do the Funky Chicken" for the Sun and Stax labels. He billed himself as the World's Oldest Teenager, and to prove it he performed in knee-high platform boots, hot pants, and a cape. Rufus came up to Chicago to participate in the mixes. He sat in the studio, eating cartons of vanilla ice cream and telling hilarious stories about the Memphis music scene.

Bob Greenlee also brought me a master by Lazy Lester, a harmonica player and singer from the bayou country outside Baton Rouge. Lester had been a popular artist on the Excello label in the late 1950s and early 1960s, recording classics like "I'm a Lover, Not a Fighter," later covered by the Kinks. Lester's relaxed harmonica and laid-back vocal style perfectly evoked a humid, 95-degree day in the South. We called the album *Harp and Soul*. Bob also licensed albums to Alligator by Raful Neal, saxman Noble "Thin Man" Watts, and two by the keyboard and guitar savant Lucky Peterson.

The same weekend that I flew to Florida to see Kenny Neal, I stopped in Atlanta to check out another promising bluesman who was on a smaller label. Tinsley Ellis had made his reputation in the Southeast as a rocking blues guitar hero. He had led the Heartfixers, a regionally popular blues band, and cut two albums for Atlanta's Landslide label. He wasn't yet a strong showman, but his guitar playing was on fire and his gruff vocals were a match for his high-powered playing. Tinsley had been working on a new album for Landslide, and I made a deal to acquire the master and sign him. Over the following decades he toured constantly, building a grassroots following that loved his high-energy shows. We ultimately released eight Tinsley Ellis albums filled with his original songs, high-octane guitar, and tough vocals. Plus, we reissued the Landslide albums *Cool On It* and *Tore Up*, the latter one with Tinsley and his band backing 1940s/1950s R&B shouter Nappy Brown. After leaving Alligator to release his own albums in 2011, he returned to the label in 2018 with his *Winning Hand* album. Even during his hiatuses from Alligator, Tinsley and I remained close friends, and he was always delighted to be introduced as an Alligator artist.

Blues had developed a worldwide audience beginning in the 1960s, and talented musicians playing blues or blues rock could be found in countries around the globe. In 1993, Jas Obrecht, who wrote for *Guitar Player* magazine, contacted us, raving about an Australian slide guitar player and singer named Dave Hole. Dave had self-released an album called *Short Fuse Blues* and sent a copy to Jas. Jas was so excited that he began a one-man crusade to find a US label for Dave. Listening to the album, I understood Jas's enthusiasm. As the title suggested, Dave played incendiary slide, combining the passion and signature guitar licks of Elmore James with the intensity and technique of Johnny Winter, as if Elmore had been exposed to some of Jimi Hendrix's sonic experimentation. To add to Dave's aura, unlike virtually every other slide player, he played slide over the top of the guitar neck, with the slide on his index finger rather than on his fourth or fifth finger. Many of his songs were originals, and he sang with power and passion (and a bit of an Australian accent). I liked his singing, but it was his guitar playing that fascinated me.

Times were good at Alligator in the early 1990s, so I decided to sign Dave as our first foreign-based artist and released *Short Fuse Blues* in the States. As we hoped, the guitar magazines loved the album. Dave came over for the first of ten US tours, determined to make a name for himself in the homeland of the blues. He drove thousands of miles and spent weeks traveling across the country, proving that he could be just as exciting and energized onstage as on

record. His technique fascinated the guitar heads, and his showman-
ship, including gravity-defying leaps, entertained club and festival
audiences. He continued to record in Australia, and we coproduced
one album in Chicago, but without steady appearances year-round
here, he was unable to build a loyal following that would come to
gig after gig and buy his new releases. We released seven Dave Hole
albums between 1993 and 2003, each filled with astounding, hard-
rocking slide guitar and tough vocals. But we couldn't get him in
front of enough audiences to create the sales we needed to continue
releasing his albums.

Although Alligator is often touted as a label for hot blues guitar players, I never thought of the label that way. I just wanted to sign the
best blues talent I could find. Two world-class harmonica players
joined the Alligator roster in 1990, both coming to us with finished
recordings. Charlie Musselwhite was already an established blues
star with a long recording career. Charlie was white, but he had a
background that was remarkably similar to those of black blues musicians. Born in Kosciusko, Mississippi, in 1944, he moved with his
family to Memphis at age three, and there he fell in love with the
blues. As a teenager, he sought out the local musicians of a bygone
era, including Will Shade of the Memphis Jug Band, who had performed and recorded in the 1920s and 1930s. Having recorded before
instruments were amplified, Shade played harmonica in a melodic
and folkie style and did not employ much of the pitch bending that
later became common.[1]

In Memphis, Charlie worked as a laborer pouring concrete and
played guitar and harmonica for fun, never thinking of becoming a
professional musician. Moving to Chicago in search of a better job,
he landed on the South Side, driving a truck for an exterminator.

1. Harmonicas can be played in multiple positions (using different holes on the harmonica to
play in different keys). Most blues harmonica players use primarily second position, creating
draw notes by inhaling. The pitches of draw notes are easier to bend than the pitches of blow
notes, which are played by exhaling. Bending the notes is necessary to create the flatted
"blue notes" of the blues scale.

He began to gain a local reputation as a harp player, sitting in with Muddy Waters and Junior Wells. Big Walter Horton became his mentor. They spent days together on the South Side, where Walter sometimes introduced Charlie as his younger brother. Walter liked to play in third position, and Charlie became an excellent third-position player. Using first, second, and third positions on the harmonica, he created unusual melodies and note choices by switching between harmonicas in the course of a single song. Only the best blues harp players play well enough in three positions to use this technique.

In 1965, when producer Sam Charters called Big Walter to appear with Johnny Shines and Johnny Young on volume 3 of the groundbreaking *Chicago/The Blues/Today!* series, Charters also cut one instrumental featuring Walter. Walter brought Charlie to the studio, and Charlie appeared as a guest second harmonica player on the track. Based on that appearance and his growing local reputation, Vanguard signed Charlie and released his first album in 1967, reaching white fans who had probably never heard of Little Walter or Sonny Boy Williamson. Charlie was ranked with Paul Butterfield as one of the best young blues harp players, and he deserved to be. Between 1967 and 1990, Charlie cut fourteen albums, bouncing from label to label.

Like his mentor, Big Walter, Charlie had been known to enjoy his alcohol, and fans grew to expect him to be well lubricated on stage. But at the end of the 1980s, after a very low period in his life, Charlie got himself clean and sober and assembled a fiery band featuring the Dallas guitarist Andrew "Junior Boy" Jones. Working with producer Pat Ford, Charlie cut an excellent album that was offered to Alligator; we happily released it under the title *Ace of Harps*. Charlie joined the Alligator family, cutting two more albums for us. The first of these, *Signature*, featured interplay between his harp and a jazzy horn section. For the second, *In My Time*, Charlie played beautifully subtle guitar on a couple of tracks, backed by the famed gospel group the Blind Boys of Alabama. The same album featured him (back on harp) with two different bands, one playing traditional Chicago-style blues and the other funky and modern. Charlie excelled in all these settings. He asked us to print T-shirts to promote the album. On the sleeve he had us print "Blues against Racism," a statement I could certainly support. As I had gotten to know Charlie, I found that beneath his low-key, quiet exterior was a man of wit, intellect, and wisdom, deeply committed to liberal causes and especially outspoken about racial equality. As a white southerner, he had grown up in segregation and seen blatant racism firsthand.

Charlie left Alligator in 1994. Like some other artists, he needed to find out whether the grass was greener with another label. He came back to us in 2011 with an extraordinary album called *The Well*, full of original autobiographical songs. It was nominated for a Grammy.

Another white harmonica giant, William Clarke, paid his dues much like Charlie Musselwhite did. Clarke came from a tough, working-class section of Los Angeles. Like Charlie, he began playing harmonica as a teenager, never thinking about a career as a musician. He dropped out of high school, married his longtime sweetheart, and got a job as a machinist.

William began hanging out at the black clubs in South Central LA, especially at bluesman Smokey Wilson's funky Pioneer Club. His mentor was George "Harmonica" Smith, a veteran player who, like Alligator artists James Cotton, Junior Wells, and Carey Bell, had played in the Muddy Waters band. Smith was a master of the big chromatic harmonica. His signature sound was created by playing octaves, which he achieved by blocking some of the holes of the harmonica with his tongue. The result was a massive, rich-toned sound, like a full horn section in a swing jazz big band. William absorbed Smith's techniques and put together bands with harmonica, jazzy guitar, swinging rhythms, and sometimes horns. This was the signature sound of the West Coast blues movement, whose artists included Little Charlie & The Nightcats, Rod Piazza and the Mighty Flyers, the Hollywood Fats Band, and Mark Hummel.

At the age of thirty-one, he quit his day job and became a full-time musician, releasing albums on a number of tiny labels. In 1990, my friend Dick Shurman alerted me that William had produced some outstanding new tracks at a modest Los Angeles–area studio. William sent a cassette to me. Impressed by the energy and creativity of his playing and surprised by the emotional depth of his vocals, I flew to Los Angeles to see him live. In person, he was overwhelming. Playing with great power and imagination, he stomped around the stage like a bull, soaked in sweat, throwing spontaneous cues to the band to accent certain notes and phrases, falling to his knees, playing on his back, and bringing the house down. It was the most physical harmonica playing I had seen since I first saw James Cotton. I was knocked out. We made an agreement to release the new album, which we called *Blowin' Like Hell*. He followed it with three more, each showing more creativity, with surprising, jazzy melody lines that most harp players wouldn't even attempt. His final release, 1996's *The Hard Way*, was the finest of his recording career.

William Clarke was a tough guy. He lived hard, drank hard, and toured hard. After suffering congestive heart failure in March 1996, he adopted a much healthier regimen, but the damage had been done. He died in November of that year from a bleeding ulcer, only forty-five years old and at the height of his powers.

The 1990s were not only good years for Alligator; they were good years for me personally. On August 5, 1995, I married the love of my life, Jo Kolanda, the woman who had first noticed me at a Hound Dog Taylor gig in Milwaukee twenty years earlier. We celebrated with a twelve-hour jam at Buddy Guy's Legends with a few hundred friends, some of whom flew in from Europe and Japan. It was one of the happiest days of my life. Jo and I danced to Lonnie Mack's "Falling Back in Love with You," performed by Saffire—The Uppity Blues Women. Lonnie Brooks's band, led by his son Ronnie Baker Brooks, backed dozens of special guests, including Koko Taylor, C. J. Chenier, Fenton Robinson, Carey Bell, Dave Hole, Vasti Jackson, the Mellow Fellows' horn section, Steady Rollin' Bob Margolin, Detroit Junior, Steve Jacobs, Mark Kazanoff, Dave Myers, Snapper Mitchum, Shirley Johnson, and Luther Allison, who had finally joined the label after all these years.

Luther and I had been estranged ever since that night in 1970 when he had jeopardized my job by refusing to stay with Delmark. He had gone on to sign with Gordy Records, part of the Motown label. It was Motown's first signing of a blues artist, and it was big news in the blues community. His first Gordy record, *Bad News Is Coming,* was released in 1972. It was a strong record that included all the production flourishes that Luther had wanted on his second Delmark album. But Motown failed to successfully promote it. There were two more Luther releases on Gordy, both with some strong tracks, but sales were disappointing. Disgusted with the stagnation of his career in the US, Luther moved to Paris and became a blues star in Europe, playing festivals and clubs there regularly from the late 1970s until the 1990s. He would occasionally come back to the States for a short tour, but he had become almost invisible here.

Early in 1993, Thomas Ruf, a young German who was managing Luther, came to Chicago to meet with me. Thomas was starting a label in Germany to release a Luther record, and he had hired the highly respected studio veteran Jim Gaines to produce it in Memphis. Thomas wanted Alligator to license the album outside of Europe. When I received the new tracks to check out, I was surprised to find that Luther, who had never been a prolific songwriter, had cut eight strong original songs, most of them cowritten with his old friend, Wisconsin-based guitarist Jim Solberg. The lyrics were intense, and the performances were full of energy; Jim Gaines had produced and mixed a thrilling record. It was a perfect fit for Alligator.

We released the record in June 1994 and named it after one of the catchiest songs, "Soul Fixin' Man."[2] Luther had been a shoeshine boy, so the title was a play on words. But I also liked the idea that this was an album of soul-healing music, which is just what the blues should be. Luther came back to the US right after the release, toured like a madman, and kicked butt everywhere he went. He would drive four hundred or five hundred miles and do a show that lasted for three hours without intermission. Then he'd come back for the encore and play for another hour and a half. After the show he would

2. Ruf Records released it in Europe as *Bad Love*. The albums are otherwise identical.

come out and greet everyone in the audience, shake hands, and sign autographs. He won an instant word-of-mouth reputation and quickly became our best-selling artist.

Almost immediately, Thomas Ruf had him back in the studio with Jim Gaines. Jim told me that the problem with recording Luther was that Jim couldn't get him to finish a song. Luther wanted to go on and on building the intensity, just like he did live. Onstage, Luther loved to wind up the audience tighter and tighter until the song ended and the audience exploded in applause. Jim's challenge in producing Luther was to compress the energy of Luther's ten-minute live song performances into shorter recorded versions.

We called his second Alligator album *Blue Streak*, a titled suggested by his life partner, Carolyn "Rocky" Brown. *Blue Streak* was a more stripped-down, harder-edged record than *Soul Fixin' Man*. "Cherry Red Wine" from *Blue Streak* received significant airplay on rock radio stations across the country, especially on stations that had adopted a new format called Adult Album Alternative (AAA), which allowed programmers more latitude than AOR stations did. Despite the conventional wisdom that positive, up-tempo tunes were more radio-friendly, "Cherry Red Wine" became Luther's most-requested song. With its ultra-intense lyrics about being in love with an alcoholic, it was a powerful, medium-slow blues, and Luther's performance was devastating.

It was clear that Luther had evolved into a master bluesman, both as a performer and as a songwriter. Most blues musicians sing about relationships and avoid songs about controversial subjects. Luther, to his credit, wrote and sang about injustice and civil rights. "Will It Ever Change?" was a passionate plea for racial harmony in a country still racially divided. "Move from the Hood" dealt with black-on-black crime. Luther could do it all. He could sing about racism, violence, drug addiction, and alcoholism, then turn around and sing a happy song like "Party Time in Memphis."

Luther returned to the States in 1995 for a summer tour. He flew directly from France to Chicago to headline the Friday night of the Chicago Blues Festival. Although he had been awake for twenty-four hours, Luther went on stage and just demolished the festival. It was an incredible performance, and every song was worthy of being on a record.[3]

In March 1997, we released Luther's third Alligator album, *Reckless*. Two months later, Luther went to Memphis to receive several W. C. Handy Awards. (Now called the Blues Music Awards, these are the highest honors in the blues world, presented annually by the Blues Foundation.) Afterward, he headed out for his summer tour. On July 10, 1997, my fiftieth birthday, I got a call from his manager, Miki Mulvehill. She said, "Luther's just come from the doctor, and he's been diagnosed with cancer in both his lung and his brain. He's going to play tonight in Madison, and he's going to play tomorrow night in Minneapolis, and then he's going to tell the band and go into the hospital." Shaken, I dropped everything and flew to Madison. I stood by the side of the stage and watched him perform. I saw that he wasn't able to give 100 percent, but he was still masterful. Afterward, he chatted with the fans, smiling the whole time. I said hello and asked him how he was, and he responded, "I'm okay." We never spoke about the cancer. That was the last time I saw him alive.

Luther died on August 12, 1997, after only a few weeks in the hospital. His death was a huge loss, not only to Alligator but also to the blues community and the future of the blues. Luther had all the talent, all the energy, and all the charisma that could have drawn new people to the blues. You could see in almost every photo just how much he enjoyed being onstage and how naturally he stepped into the spotlight. When Luther played, it was everything his bandmates and his audience could do to keep up with him. He was constantly pulling them forward, increasing the tempo, pushing his way through the chord changes, always attempting to create greater and greater momentum. (Luther told his band that if they couldn't play faster, play louder.) It was his nature to put every ounce of energy and soul into his music.

After his death, the immediate concern was his hospital bills. In

---

3. In 1999, Alligator released this festival set, along with highlights from a show at Buddy Guy's Legends, on Luther's album *Live in Chicago*. Ruf Records released the same album in Europe.

the course of a few days, we put together a benefit at House of Blues in Chicago with WXRT as the radio sponsor. The support from his fellow musicians was overwhelming — Buddy Guy, Jonny Lang, Otis Rush, Lonnie Brooks, Mighty Joe Young, and Jimmy Dawkins all performed in Luther's honor, and the place was packed with fans. The benefit raised more than forty thousand dollars. It was a spectacular success, both musically and emotionally, and a great outpouring from the community that recognized Luther as a true star.

15

Many people have gone into the record business dreaming that there was real money to be made, only to discover that it was a business of quarters, nickels, and dimes—a gamble for underfinanced entrepreneurs trying to create demand for something that a fickle public doesn't know it wants. Although the consumption of music is now primarily by download sales and on-demand streaming, sales through record stores, including online stores like Amazon, have always been a crucial part of Alligator's business. Since LPs and 45s replaced 78s, and continuing into the years of the dominance of CDs, the retail record business has almost always been a consignment business. Rather than selling directly to record stores, record labels sell to record distributors, who then sell to stores; the store pays the distributor, who pays the label. But the store can return unsold records to the distributor for credit, and the distributor can do the same to the label. In the end, the label takes all the risk; nothing is really sold until the customer buys it, takes it home, and doesn't return it to the store.[1]

This system has made it possible for record distributors to operate on very small margins—usually around 20 percent. The labels depend on timely payment from the distributors for cash flow.[2] In

---

1. The exception to the standard consignment policy has been the revival of vinyl LPs and singles starting in the early 2000s. Stores buy those "one way"; there is no right of return.
2. It wasn't easy for a record label to borrow money, as banks rightly considered the record business too speculative. Some hit-driven record labels in the 1950s and 1960s ended up

the old days, the distributors were reluctant to pay too quickly. They feared that they would be swamped with store returns and be "upside down" financially, which meant having a warehouse full of unsold records that they had already paid for. Alligator's first distributor, Summit Distributors in Chicago, went bankrupt for this very reason: it had tens of thousands of dollars' worth of returned records in its warehouse. Summit had paid the labels for them, and then the labels had gone belly up.

For our first three decades, Alligator was totally dependent on payment from distributors. We took a good cop–bad cop approach to dealing with them. I played bad cop. Around the twenty-fifth day of every month, I got on the phone with our distributors to press them into writing a check to us. Sometimes I had to threaten them with cutting off shipments. If their bills became more than 120 days past due, we usually put them on hold until they sent some money to us. Of course, this cutoff threat worked only if there was a consumer demand for Alligator albums. If we didn't have a strong new release, a distributor might wait 150 days or more to pay. I was constantly negotiating with our distributors for *some* payment, even if it wasn't the full amount.

The good cop in this drama was the Alligator sales manager. Starting in 1989, that was Kerry Peace. Kerry kept in touch with all of our distributors and the salespeople they employed to visit and call the stores. Kerry got them excited about our new releases, kept them informed about our artists' live appearances, and worked with them to set up in-store sales, promotions, and discounts. He talked with the salespeople about their individual store accounts and how Alligator and the distributor, as a team, could more effectively support them. We often offered discounts if the stores agreed to put up displays, put our records on the front racks where they were more visible, or give them a special sale price. Kerry, the good cop, was doing everything he could to motivate the distributor to sell more of our music, and I,

---

controlled by organized crime. Their owners, trying to finance their next possible hit, borrowed money from mobsters. When they couldn't pay, the mob took over control of the label.

the bad cop, was threatening to cut off the distributors if they didn't pay for the records they had already received.[3]

Although independent labels no longer have to struggle as hard to be paid, the record business, especially in the pop world, still depends on hype and borrowed money, sustained by the necessary belief that worthy records will be profitable, despite the fact that they usually aren't. Previous to the current domination of digital sales and streaming, it was easy for labels to believe their own hype, overinvest, overmanufacture, and lose a lot of money. It was also easy for distributors and stores to believe the hype and overorder. We did have some records whose return rate exceeded 40 percent of the number shipped (*Lone Star Shootout* is an example). But our mistakes were tiny compared to those of the major labels. They often offered new releases to stores with incentives for them to buy. If stores bought ten, they'd receive eleven ("one free on ten"). Big labels shoved millions of copies into the marketplace by making all kinds of deals, because the salespeople were trying to show big numbers to their bosses. All those CDs, even the free ones, were returnable to the distributors for full credit. The labels would announce that the release had been "shipped gold" (a gold record is defined as selling more than five hundred thousand copies). Six months later, huge numbers of those LPs or CDs would come back to the distributors. Often more were returned than were ever billed, so the distributors were issuing credit to the stores for returned records that the stores had never actually bought; they had received them free. The distributors in turn passed the loss on to the labels by deducting the credits issued to the stores from payment to the labels. Platinum records sold more than gold records (a platinum record is defined as selling more than one million copies), so a record that was returned in massive quantities was said to have been shipped gold and returned platinum.

---

3. These days there are only a handful of remaining record distributors and stores. Most of the distributors now pay the labels within seventy days after the end of the month following the sale of a record to a store. The "carrot and stick" collection techniques described here are less and less necessary.

Although we relied on distributors to get our releases into stores, that didn't keep us from working hard to build direct relationships with retailers. One of my first employees, Mindy Giles, said, "Records are sold in record stores. Don't count on your distributors; work the stores yourself." From Alligator's beginnings until the mid-1990s, the retail record business was full of people who loved music; they were our best friends. The independent stores and small chains (the so-called mom-and-pop stores) were often willing to accept more modest sales than the big retailers in exchange for the personal satisfaction of pleasing their customers by stocking good records of all genres. Of course, they had to stock the hits, but their passion was turning on their customers to high-quality music.

The indie retailers could connect emotionally with a label like Alligator, which was built on the love of one genre of music. So when someone from Alligator called a store (and we stayed in touch with thousands of stores), they were happy to talk with us. The equation was simple: the more goodwill we created with the stores, the more display space, in-store play, and sale pricing they gave us, and the more of our music they sold. With dozens of regional and national chains (including the Tower Records stores, famous for their large and varied inventories, which were referred to as "deep catalog" stores) and hundreds of independent stores, we had plenty of targets. Our personal outreach was meant to get store owners and managers to feel they were part of the Alligator family. We made sure they were invited to gigs and received personal copies of our releases. In turn, they gave us the kind of attention that they typically wouldn't give to a label our size.

The small-business economy of thousands of independent and small-chain record stores helped support dozens of regionally based, independent distributorships. By the late 1980s Alligator had seventeen distributors around the country, and we kept in touch regularly with all of them. The largest (M.S. Distributing in Chicago, California Record Distributing in Los Angeles, Big State Distributors in Dallas, Select-O-Hits in Memphis, Action Distributors in Cleveland, Landmark Distributors in Atlanta, Associated Distributors in

Phoenix, Music Craft Distributors in Hawaii) distributed hit albums and singles for the biggest independent labels. Other Alligator distributors (Rounder Distribution in the northeast, Passport Music Distribution in Denver, House Distributors in Kansas City, and Richman Brothers Records in Philadelphia) specialized in representing larger independent labels but few hit-driven labels. Small, sometimes one-person operations (Silo Inc. in Vermont, Record Depot in the Carolinas, Bayside Distribution in the Bay Area, and Tant Distribution and Old Fogey Distributors, both in Michigan) specialized in niche genres like blues, jazz, folk, bluegrass, and world music.

Sometimes, Alligator's commitment to fostering relationships between the label, the distributors, and the stores, could pay off in unexpected ways. That's what happened with *The Alligator Records 20th Anniversary Collection*. A double CD priced like a single disc, it was released in 1991 and sold an unbelievable three hundred thousand copies. It flew out the door and kept on flying.[4] By comparison, our best-selling single-artist albums at that time topped out at about thirty thousand or forty thousand records.

When the *20th Anniversary Collection* began to bring in money almost immediately, I decided to put together a 20th Anniversary tour of Alligator headliners—Chicago stalwarts Koko Taylor, Lonnie Brooks, and Lil' Ed & The Blues Imperials along with two more recently signed artists: two-fisted pianist Katie Webster and blues-rock guitarist Elvin Bishop. I was inspired by the touring R&B and rock and roll revues of the 1950s that crisscrossed the country by bus. Aiming for midsized venues that could hold audiences of one thousand to fifteen hundred, we put the tour on the road in 1992, traveling by rented bus, with the first gig at Chicago's Vic Theatre (where it was recorded and broadcast as a WXRT radio concert). From Chicago the tour headed out to Grand Rapids, Michigan, and from there into Canada and down the East Coast before running a West Coast leg from San Diego to Seattle. Attendance was good,

4. Of course, once you hit upon a successful formula in the record business, you repeat it. Alligator has released an anniversary collection every five years since 1991, although none has sold nearly as well as the first.

and the musicians loved playing to audiences larger than those at their club appearances. Documentary filmmaker Bob Mugge shot the concert at the Chestnut Cabaret in Philadelphia, added interview footage of the label's key artists and me, and created *Pride and Joy: The Story of Alligator Records*, which was recently rereleased on Blu-ray Disc.

Reluctantly (because the song is so overdone it verges on cliché), I decided to make "Sweet Home Chicago" our encore. We knew audiences would request it. During the encore, things could get chaotic with a half-dozen guitar players onstage together, but Lonnie's young guitar-playing son Ronnie Baker Brooks acted as trail boss, calling out the soloists and thanking the audience. The first night, he brought me on stage by saying, "Let's give a big round of applause to Alligator Records for keeping the blues alive!" Although I'm not fond of the phrase "keeping the blues alive" (because the blues isn't anywhere near death), hearing those fifteen hundred people clapping and cheering gave me a tremendous sense of achievement. My ego well fed, I left the stage feeling as though the struggles of the previous twenty-one years had been well worth it. For the musicians, the enthusiastic crowds were an affirmation that their careers had reached a new peak.

Given the tremendous commercial success of the *20th Anniversary Collection* and the positive experience of the supporting tour, we naturally released a midpriced live *Alligator Records 20th Anniversary Tour* double CD. It barely sold. We ended up with thousands of unsold copies in our warehouse. It's helpful to have a little dose of reality thrown in your face now and then.

From the moment of Alligator's founding, I've been conscious of the need to balance being an enthusiastic fan with being a realistic business owner. If I had any hope of building a label so that I could share the music I loved with the world, I had to think like an entrepreneur committed to the long-term success of his enterprise. That attitude was especially important in the label's impoverished early days. But as Alligator found its financial footing in the 1980s and 1990s, I could afford to do some gambling and make some decisions with my heart rather than my head. Financial security and a solid cash flow let me pursue some projects and artists who didn't fit Alligator's original mission. I had some success in stretching the definition of Genuine Houserockin' Music and signing some untried artists, but I also ran down a few dead-end streets.

In the first half of the 1980s, for example, Alligator stepped into the unpredictable world of reggae, releasing thirteen reggae albums. I liked the energy and directness of reggae as well as its deep roots in African Caribbean culture; it was sort of the Jamaican equivalent of blues. We didn't produce Alligator's reggae releases. Primarily we licensed masters from Jamaican record companies like Rockers and High Times that featured artists like instrumentalist Augustus Pablo, "dub poet" Mutabaruka (who recited his socially conscious lyrics backed by reggae instrumental tracks), and singer-songwriter Pablo Moses. Although the young white audiences for blues and reggae were quite similar, I found that dealing with reggae artists was much more difficult than dealing with blues artists. The marijuana-fueled world of reggae was too loose and laid-back for me. Arranging visas for Jamaican musicians to tour in the US was an endless problem. Plus, I could handle blues shows that lasted until 2 a.m., but reggae shows that began at midnight taxed my ability to stay awake. Beyond that, many of the artists, who were surrounded by adoring fans, had the impression that their potential album sales were huge, and we weren't able to meet their expectations. Alligator gave up on reggae in 1986. We released some memorable albums, but sales were never strong enough to earn back the costs in time and energy that it took to work with the artists. By that time the reggae business had exhausted me, and it ceased to be fun.

The search for world-class blues talent continued to be a priority. For the most part, I concentrated on urban electrified blues rather than on acoustic musicians. I felt that by the time I came on the scene, the best country blues artists had been discovered, either by the talent scouts of the 1920s and 1930s, by the Library of Congress's roving folklorist Alan Lomax, or by blues record men like Chris

Strachwitz, founder of the Arhoolie label. Like Lomax, Chris would visit rural areas and black neighborhoods, find somebody from the community and ask, "Who are the local musicians? Where do they play?" Eventually, after people figured out that he wasn't the police, he found many great musicians.[5]

Although Alligator's primary focus was electric, urban blues, we did release a few albums of acoustic country blues. In 1994, I received a call from Joe Wilson, head of the National Council of Traditional Arts, offering me a new recording by the Virginia-based acoustic duo Cephas and Wiggins. They were highly respected bluesmen playing mostly on the blues and folk festival circuit rather than in clubs. Their style, called Piedmont blues, was reminiscent of the beloved folk blues team of Sonny Terry and Brownie McGhee. Less gritty than its Delta counterpart, Piedmont blues is happy and lilting, gentle and flowing. It often incorporates ragtime chord changes, the so-called circle of fifths, as well as the standard three-chord structure that most blues is based on. The vocals tend to be relaxed and melodic, without the rawness or angst of the Delta or Chicago styles. Piedmont blues developed around the turn of the twentieth century in the southeastern United States. The giants of that music had been among the earliest male blues artists to record: Florida's Blind Blake, who was tremendously popular with black blues fans in the 1920s and 1930s; North Carolina's Blind Boy Fuller, who recorded throughout the 1930s; and Georgia's Blind Willie McTell, who recorded intermittently from the late 1920s into the 1950s. Piedmont blues didn't convert to electrification; it's a musical form intrinsically tied to the subtleties of acoustic instruments.

John Cephas was one of the best living practitioners of the Piedmont blues style. In live performance, he loved to expound on the Piedmont tradition and explain his guitar fingerpicking techniques

5. Chris searched for legendary Texas bluesman Lightnin' Hopkins in the Houston ghetto. He had heard Hopkins's earlier records and wanted to record him for Arhoolie. Chris was asking people everywhere, and they were saying, "Oh, he was here yesterday," or something else vague. Finally, Chris was stopped at a red light when another car pulled up next to him. A man rolled down the window and said, "I hear you're looking for Lightnin' Hopkins. That's me." So while Chris was stalking Lightnin', Lightnin' was stalking Chris.

to the audience. Formal and opinionated, he was not an easily approachable man. He did things his way, period. About twenty years younger than John, Phil Wiggins was a terrific acoustic harmonica player who thrilled audiences with his flashy soloing. He could play very fast but always melodically and with real feeling. As a duo, John projected wisdom and tradition; Phil was full of youthful energy. Their music brought a smile to my face.

Although Cephas and Wiggins didn't play a lot of club gigs because their style wasn't raucous bar music, I nonetheless decided to buy the master and release the album. I hoped they had established a fan base and the record would sell well enough to make a modest profit. I felt that having Piedmont blues on the label would deepen our catalog. To my pleasant surprise, we sold a few thousand units. We went on to release three more very fine Cephas and Wiggins albums before John's death in 2009.

The same year that I released Cephas and Wiggins, I was approached by Paul Kahn of Concerted Efforts, a booking agency that specialized in blues and world music artists. He was eager to convince me to sign his client, zydeco accordionist and singer C. J. Chenier. C.J. was the son of the famed King of the Bayous, Clifton Chenier, who had virtually invented modern zydeco. In zydeco, instead of guitar or harmonica, the accordion serves as lead instrument, accompanied by a rubboard (a sort of strap-on washboard played with spoons or bottle openers) along with a full electric band. Zydeco is often sung in French because of the intermingling of French, American, and African cultural traditions in Louisiana. Besides Clifton Chenier, famous zydeco musicians have included Beau Jocque, Buckwheat Zydeco (who later appeared on Alligator), Nathan and the Zydeco Cha-Chas, and Boozoo Chavis.

I liked zydeco. In 1982, Alligator had licensed a Clifton Chenier record, *I'm Here!*, from Sonet, and it won a Grammy. But I felt that most zydeco records didn't work as home listening experiences. Focused on grooves, rhythm, and energy, with lyrics including many repeated choruses and shouted phrases, zydeco songs were perfect for filling Louisiana dance halls, but they weren't so good for sitting in your living room listening closely to the lyrics. With C. J. Chenier's talent, I hoped there was an opportunity to create an album that worked both as a party experience and as an enjoyable home listening record, with well-written songs that had emotional depth.

C.J. was an exceptional player of the big piano accordion and a fine singer, with a deep, raspy blues voice. He was touring a lot and his live shows were drawing well, so I agreed to a contract with a significant budget per album. I thought that producing C.J. would be a fun project for me, and that, with his busy tour schedule, we would be able to sell enough copies to justify the large budget. It was indeed a fun project, but it turned out to be a very bad financial decision.

C.J. had plenty of talent. His big problem was repertoire. He performed his father's songs and lots of zydeco and R&B standards. That worked fine in live performance, but I was determined to make a zydeco album full of memorable songs, both originals and carefully chosen covers. I met with C.J. in Houston to listen to his songs and present some song ideas of my own to him. A smart, funny man with a ready smile, C.J. was easy to like. He was living in a boarded-up house; he had to pry plywood off the window to get in. The yard was full of fire ants. He had a few original song ideas, but they weren't finished compositions. I decided to send him to Nashville to write with my friends, professional songwriters Fred James and Mary-Ann Brandon. They had written tunes for the Kinsey Report, Koko Taylor, and Katie Webster. C.J., Fred, and Mary-Ann hit it off right away, and together they wrote three catchy songs for the album, including the title track, "Too Much Fun."

I decided to record C.J. in Memphis at the world-class Ardent Studios. C.J. insisted on recording with his own band, and although the rhythm section was tight, I was worried about whether his three guitar players were going to be able to create record-worthy parts to play. Live, they tended to improvise without much regard for what each other was playing. I decided to bring in Vasti Jackson to help out on guitars. Vasti is one of those musicians who can listen to a song and create a rhythm part that locks the whole song together.

C.J. himself was a terrific musician who could learn a new song in a flash and then sing and play it as though he had been performing it his whole life. He was a pleasure to work with because of his spark and energy as well as the quality of his playing and singing. He could sing a serious song like "Richest Man," a ballad by Austin songwriter Bill Carter that I had found for him, and infuse the song with anguish.

> *If teardrops were diamonds*
> *From the African mines*
> *If heartaches were silver*
> *My whole life would shine*
> *Yeah, I'd be the richest man, yeah, the richest man*
> *In the world.*

Not every song on the album was so serious. Most of the songs were fun, as zydeco songs should be. But they had memorable melodies and lyrics as well as danceable grooves.[6]

I had what I thought was a brilliant commercial idea for this album. At that time, Z. Z. Hill's "Down Home Blues" was being played on every southern black radio station that still aired blues records. I thought we should cut the song in Cajun French for airplay on zydeco radio shows in Louisiana and east Texas. Unfortunately, C.J. didn't speak any French. John Frederick, his bass player, translated the lyrics into French, and C.J. sang the whole song in convincing Cajun French while reading the lyrics. Unfortunately, not a single zydeco radio show ever played it.

We made two more albums with C.J., in 1996 and 2001, both cut at Dockside Studios in Maurice, Louisiana, which is one of my favorite studios. But no matter what songs we chose and how good the per-

---

6. During the recording, I found myself in the unenviable position of having to argue about arrangements with the Memphis Horns, one of the best R&B horn sections in the world. After listening to their first take of a horn section part for one of the songs, I told them, "That's too stock. I need something less familiar." "They're all stock," trumpeter Wayne Jackson replied. I answered, "Then just play something stock but less familiar."

formances and production, I could never sell enough C. J. Chenier records to recover those big advances I had agreed to. Eventually I had to let him go. None of his albums ever turned a profit, but I'm sure proud of them.

In late 2000, I was again contacted by Paul Kahn, the Boston-based booking agent who had brought C.J. to me six years prior. This time he offered me a new Holmes Brothers recording. The Holmes Brothers were guitarist and keyboardist Wendell Holmes, his bass-playing brother Sherman Holmes, and their honorary brother, drummer Popsy Dixon. Musicians with an intentionally rough-edged, improvisational instrumental style, they were above all wonderful singers. Their repertoire ranged from blues to old-school R&B to early rock and roll to pure gospel and even some country music. The most thrilling moments in their songs came when they sang in three-part gospel harmonies. They were just as likely to harmonize on secular songs as on straight gospel tunes. No one else in the blues world sang that way. They had honed their sound while playing in their small hometown in Virginia, gigging in both local juke joints and at church services. As Wendell said, "We'd rock 'em on Saturday and save 'em on Sunday." Prior to Alligator, they had released a number of very good records on the Rounder label, although Rounder didn't seem to promote them well. Wendell, the most verbal and outgoing of the Holmes Brothers, said they were in Rounder's "artist protection program"—not to be seen or heard of by anyone.

The new record Paul offered to me had been produced by Joan Osborne, famous for her mammoth 1995 pop hit "One of Us." Some tracks employed percussion loops (where a percussion or drum track is set up to play repeatedly) and samples (sounds or beats from other sources that are edited into the performance). These techniques are often used on hip-hop records but rarely in blues. Loops and samples were normally antithetical to Alligator, but it was a sonically intriguing record, with a raw vibe. Still, I was reluctant to release a Holmes Brothers record. Although they were an established group in the blues and roots music world, they didn't sell well. Besides that, it was a gospel record, or at least an inspirational record. Alligator was all about secular music, not religious music. But the record kept calling out to me. Between the performances and the production, I realized it was something special. My brain said no but my gut said yes. My gut won.

Alligator went on to release four more Holmes Brothers records. We built a close, familial relationship with the three of them. Despite positive press and even an appearance on *Late Night with David Letterman*, it was difficult to get them the attention and sales they deserved. One of their later records, *Simple Truths*, did well for us, but the others had disappointing sales. Still, I'm proud to have had them on the label. Both Wendell and Popsy died in 2015. They toured until just a few weeks before Popsy's sudden death. Like most Alligator artists, they were true road dogs, and the thought of retiring was the furthest thing from their minds.

16

For a long time, the blues world has been primarily a world of male artists, despite the fact that the earliest recorded blues artists and biggest stars were women. Most of those early female blues stars came out of black vaudeville shows and boasted larger-than-life personas and uninhibited lifestyles that became stereotypes for many blueswomen. Blues singers like Ma Rainey and Bessie Smith were famous for double-entendre blues songs like "Kitchen Man," "One Hour Mama," and "I Need a Little Sugar in My Bowl." Lucille Bogan is the perfect example of a wild, wild woman. Primarily a singer who also played some piano, she is most famous for "Shave 'Em Dry," a song containing vivid sexual imagery. The stereotype of the highly sexed female blues singer has been carried on by a host of blueswomen, whether they lived the role or not. In our double-standard world, good-loving bluesmen were admired for their sexuality whereas pleasure-seeking blueswomen had the image of being easy.

In addition, most female blues artists were featured vocalists who didn't get the same respect as singers who also played an instrument. Top-echelon female blues instrumentalists were rare. Memphis Minnie was famous for playing guitar as well as any man. Sister Rosetta Tharpe, who performed both blues and gospel, was a much-admired guitarist. But the list of famous female instrumentalists playing blues is very short.

The blueswomen signed by Alligator refused to be stereotyped. Koko Taylor, known as the Queen of the Blues, abhorred the "wild woman" image of the female blues artist. She was a committed non-drinker who was devoted to her husband and daughter. She never shook her hips, and she rarely sang directly about sex (unless it was about being cheated on). But she certainly had a "don't mess with me" personality. She felt it was necessary. She constantly talked about having to be as tough as the male artists; for that reason she felt she had to be very much in command of her band, often chewing them out after a show if she didn't feel their performance was tight enough. She believed she always had to exert control, or it would be wrested from her and she would become the cardboard singer in front of the band.

Katie Webster, known as the Swamp Boogie Queen, was the second blues woman signed by Alligator. She also broke the stereotype. A world-class pianist, Katie could be playfully flirtatious on stage, but she was also a family woman and devoted mother. In the 1970s, Katie wasn't on my radar because she was based in California and not performing much. In 1988, Ice Cube Slim, one of the most colorful nonmusicians in the blues world, talked me into flying to San Jose to see her perform. Slim, whose real name was Dan Untermyer, was a DJ, occasional music journalist, and artist manager who spoke with a New Orleans accent despite being a California native. He was a self-appointed cheerleader for Louisiana music.

A two-fisted piano player and gospel-influenced singer, Katie started her career in the late 1950s. Growing up in Houston, she was barred by her strict religious family from playing anything but gospel music. But Katie loved blues and boogie-woogie piano, which she launched into whenever her parents left the house. While still a teenager, she rebelled, left home, and moved to southern Louisiana, where record producers quickly discovered her talents. At the age of sixteen, she began cutting sessions in Crowley, Louisiana, for Jay Miller, a producer for the Nashville-based Excello label who had discovered and signed bayou blues stars like Slim Harpo, Lightning Slim, Lonesome Sundown, and Lazy Lester. Katie also recorded regularly for the Goldband label in Lake Charles, Louisiana. Goldband's roster included zydeco musicians like Rockin' Sidney and Boozoo Chavis, country singers like the teenaged Dolly Parton, and swamp pop artists like Freddy Fender and Phil Phillips.

The young Katie's playing epitomized the medium-slow, loping swamp pop style of southern Louisiana, which included lots of right-hand triplets, like those she played on the original recording of "Sea of Love" by Phil Phillips. She recorded some 45s on her own at that time, though none was very successful; most of her recording was as an accompanist. She also played solo lounge gigs around south Louisiana. Besides swamp pop songs, she played early rock and roll, soul music, ballads, and anything else on the jukebox. Otis Redding caught one of her solo gigs and immediately hired her for his road band; she appears on his album *In Person at the Whiskey-a-Go-Go*. Katie was pregnant and off the road at the time of Redding's death in a plane crash in 1967. She was so heartbroken that she ceased performing and moved to California to care for her parents. There she met Ice Cube Slim, who convinced her to relaunch her career and became her manager.

Like many musicians who had established their reputations in the United States when blues was still being played on black radio, Katie was remembered by hard-core blues fans in Europe. She began to tour there as a soloist, sometimes appearing with European bands. Katie recorded a few solo albums for small European labels and one for Chris Strachwitz's California-based Arhoolie label. I loved the blues and boogie-woogie on her records, but her repertoire of pop standards by artists like Stevie Wonder, Diana Ross, and the Rolling Stones was too far away from the blues for my tastes. Nonetheless, when Ice Cube Slim invited me to come out to San Jose and see Katie perform at a big club, I decided to go.[1]

1. On the same trip I also attended a performance by Elvin Bishop, who had been a member of the Paul Butterfield Blues Band. Although I had never taken Elvin very seriously because of his comic country-boy persona, I knew that he was a good slide player and entertainer. So when his road manager, Whit Lehnberg, called to say that Elvin had recorded an album's worth of new tracks and wondered if Alligator might be interested, I decided to catch Elvin's live show while in San Francisco. It was an exhilarating, blues-soaked performance, and I ended up signing him. Over the years, Alligator has released seven albums by Elvin, and he's become a good friend of mine.

Katie began her set with some bland pop songs before turning up the heat and delivering legitimate, tough blues and boogie-woogie with a soulful voice straight out of church. She clearly loved the spotlight and was a natural onstage, bantering and flirting with the audience, teasing her band members, and then bearing down into each song with great intensity. She was a hard-pounding, real deal blues piano player. I didn't have any piano players on the label at the time. Katie had talent, personality, and the unique qualification of being a female blues pianist of the first rank.

Her performance sold me. I brought her to Chicago to record, and between 1988 and 1991, we cut three albums. Constantly in high spirits, Katie was a bundle of energy in the studio. Together she and I wrote "Two-Fisted Mama," which became her theme song and the title of her second Alligator album. Katie became one of our best-loved artists, playing clubs and festivals and joining the Alligator Records 20th Anniversary Tour in 1992. Sadly, in 1993 she suffered a stroke while on tour in Greece. She continued to perform with the help of Ice Cube Slim and her loyal guitarist Vasti Jackson, but her health deteriorated. She eventually came off the road and died at her daughter's home in 1999, only sixty-three years old.

Of all the female artists who recorded for Alligator, the most unlikely success story was that of Saffire—The Uppity Blues Women. They had so much going against them. They were females in a male-dominated music. They were one of a handful of acoustic acts on a label known for electric blues. And the three members were already middle aged when they formed the group. When I became aware of them, they had earned a loyal following in the mid-Atlantic states but were hardly known elsewhere. I signed them because I liked their warm, relaxed music and their rollicking live performances. I never thought they would bring us much commercial success. Instead, they turned out to be among the most popular and best-selling artists in Alligator history.

The founders of Saffire were Ann Rabson and Gaye Adegbalola. Ann was a feisty New Yorker who had fallen in love with the blues as a teen and mastered the fingerpicked acoustic guitar styles of Big Bill Broonzy and Brownie McGhee. She undertook a solo career, performing primarily the songs of her folk blues inspirations. After the birth of her daughter, she moved to Fredericksburg, Virginia, where she held day jobs while continuing to perform at night in area clubs. One night she was approached for guitar lessons by Gaye, an award-winning local high school science teacher with a background in theater and a history of civil rights activism. As Gaye molded herself into a blues artist, she was drawn to the blues of the 1920s, especially the bawdy tunes by Bessie Smith, Ida Cox, and Alberta Hunter. At the same time, Ann began teaching herself blues piano. They started performing together, with Ann on piano and Gaye on guitar.

The pair was soon joined by Earlene Lewis, a secretary who moonlighted as a bluegrass upright-bass player and sang with a country twang. Earlene added songs by Patsy Cline and Bonnie Raitt to the group's repertoire. Ann and Gaye were both *very* direct women: Ann was smart and smart mouthed, with a wicked sense of humor and strong left-wing political views, while Gaye held passionate convictions about everything, including civil rights, women's rights, and gay rights. When they named the group, they adopted the word *uppity*, which had been used to describe black people who didn't "know their place" and were unwilling to accept segregation. Visually, they were a study in contrast. Ann was a plus-size white woman with round glasses and a head full of curls. Gaye was a slender African American with gray hair styled in a triangular Mohawk. Earlene, more conservative and traditional in her politics and personal style, was the rosy-cheeked country girl who could have been a relative of Tammy Wynette.

I vaguely remember receiving a self-produced tape from the group around 1987. I try to respond to every demo I receive, and I'm told I responded to theirs as being pleasant but containing too many well-known songs. But they intrigued me. Unusual for blues, the group featured multiple singers. Some songs even employed vocal harmonies, not often heard in blues. After rejecting their tape, I began hearing about them from a friend, a female blues fan who was enthralled with the group. In November 1988, I attended the Blues Foundation's W. C. Handy Awards (now the Blues Music Awards) ceremony. Saffire played at the pre-awards dinner, and I was charmed. Ann sang some serious blues and played strong, two-fisted piano. Gaye's flirtatious stage presence and big-voiced vocals were in the spirit of Bessie Smith. The highlight of their set was a bawdy Gaye composition called "The Middle Aged Blues Boogie." The audience loved them, and so did I.

Shortly after, Earlene contacted my friend Bob Greenlee, who invited them down to his funky studio in Florida to record. When I next saw Bob, he gave a cassette of their sessions to me. I listened casually; Alligator was an electric blues label, and Saffire's acoustic music wasn't what I had in mind. But I kept coming back to the cassette, listening to Ann's hard-hitting boogie piano and subtle acoustic guitar and to Gaye's smile-inducing and sometimes ribald songs. I figured that, if I enjoyed it, other people would too. Alligator was doing well, and I thought that if I could make a good deal for the master and release it at little expense, Alligator would either make or lose a small amount of money. We released *Saffire—The Uppity Blues Women* in February 1990.

We sent the album to our regular blues DJs and press, as well as to some programmers of radio shows that featured acoustic music or female musicians. Our publicity efforts yielded a feature in *People* magazine and some radio play. But the album started selling on its own, primarily by word of mouth, without our spending many advertising or promotional dollars. As I attended Saffire's gigs, I found that they were reaching a whole different audience—primarily middle-aged women, including a fair number of lesbians at a time when demonstrative same-sex couples were a very rare sight at blues shows. (It was a while before Gaye chose to publicly come out as a lesbian, although she was living happily and openly with a woman.) Saffire's audiences were loyal, appearing at gig after gig. To date, Alligator has sold more than eighty thousand copies of their debut album, making it among the top twenty releases in the label's history.

I had become close to the whole group, especially to Ann Rabson, who became a good friend. We agreed that I should work with the group in the studio as their producer, and over the next few years, they came to Chicago to record four more albums. I brought in Sam Fishkin, a fine recording engineer, for the Saffire albums because I felt his gentle personality would create a positive vibe in the studio. Some of the more macho engineers I worked with would have had a hard time with these "uppity" women.

When we were planning their third Alligator album, tensions that had arisen in the group began to boil over. Ann and Earlene were hardly speaking. And it seemed Earlene was uncomfortable with some of Gaye's public stances. Gaye wasn't just writing outspokenly humorous relationship songs like "(No Need) Pissin' on a Skunk" and "Two in the Bush Is Better Than One in the Hand." She was also writing strong social commentary, including songs about underpaid laborers and the drug epidemic. For this album, Gaye wrote a song about the Los Angeles police beating of Rodney King, an unarmed black man, which had become a national news story. Gaye's song "If It Had Been a Dog" was an angry outcry for justice. Earlene quit the band in the middle of the recording sessions. We decided to release the album, *Broadcasting*, as a duo record. Andra Faye, a friend of the band's from Indianapolis, came into the studio to play fiddle and mandolin on a few songs. Within months, she became a full-fledged member of Saffire, moved to Virginia, and learned upright bass to fill Earlene's slot. Andra was a true blues fan and a strong vocalist, so with her joining the band, there were now two excellent soloists (Gaye stuck pretty much to rhythm guitar) and three featured singers with very different personalities. Earlene had always been the junior member. Now all three women were equals onstage and equally featured, as well as being fast friends. Until we signed the Holmes Brothers, Saffire was Alligator's only group with multiple equally featured artists; all our other bands were leaders and sidemen.

Saffire stayed together for twenty-five years and remained one of the most popular groups on the label, gigging as much as they wanted. They each pursued side projects and cut solo albums. Ann was embraced by blues veterans who loved to jam with her, including three venerated former members of the Muddy Waters band—guitarist Steady Rollin' Bob Margolin (who recorded three albums for Alligator in the 1990s), drummer Willie "Big Eyes" Smith, and piano legend Pinetop Perkins. Gaye worked on LGBT issues, including coproducing a film. She was still writing songs for Saffire from her take-no-guff woman's viewpoint, including classics like "Bitch with a Bad Attitude" and the not-too-subtle "Silver Beaver," an ode to the powerful allure of mature women. Her "uppity" songs were among the most requested, and she gloried in describing herself as a bitch, which she defined as an acronym for "Being in Total Control of Herself." Saffire fans loved these songs. I was proud when Gaye told me that her songwriter's royalties helped put her son through college.

After Ann won two bouts with cancer and endured a lengthy hospitalization stay for sepsis, Saffire came into the studio to cut what they decided would be their final album, 2009's *Havin' the Last Word*. Ann was not long out of the hospital. Every day in the studio was a struggle for her, but listening to the album you couldn't tell. Her indomitable spirit and the love shared by the three of them triumphed. They officially disbanded later that year but remained close friends. Ann wasn't as fortunate with her third cancer, which was incurable. Refusing to give up, she continued to gig until weeks before her death in 2013. Gaye and Andra continue to pursue musical careers and have cut multiple albums in the past few years. Every female artist on Alligator has been her own version of uppity, but none has worn the label more proudly than the members of Saffire. As the child of another uppity woman, I was glad they found a home at Alligator.

Marcia Ball has become one of Alligator's most popular and best-selling artists, as well as one of our most prolific songwriters. Like Katie Webster, Marcia is a world-class blues and boogie-woogie piano player. Born in a Texas-Louisiana border town, she went to college in Baton Rouge and then moved to Austin, where she began making a name for herself in the late 1970s. I first met Marcia in 1980 when she was gigging in Chicago for the first time, playing at the Wise Fools Pub. Six feet tall and with striking red hair, she sat cross-legged at the piano and sang in a voice that sounded like Irma Thomas with a Texas twang. I was pleasantly surprised to find that her piano playing showed the influence of Professor Longhair, whose music was a challenge for the best of players. I liked Marcia, but her up-tempo party music seemed too far away from the kind of hard, authentic blues that I wanted to be the focus of Alligator at that time. Plus, I was still a few years away from bringing white blues musicians to the label.

Marcia signed with Rounder and began developing a large, devoted fan base with her year-round touring. Bill FitzGerald, owner of FitzGerald's nightclub, became her Chicago-area patron and brought her back again and again. Each time I saw her I was more impressed. Although I had initially questioned her seriousness, she had matured as an artist; as I got to know her as a person, the depth of her emotion and intellect became more and more apparent. She was starting to include more slow blues and ballads in her show, balancing the party tunes with soul-baring songs of love and loss. Sometime in the early 1990s, I took her out to dinner. Aware that she was between contracts with Rounder, I made a hard pitch to her about how much more Alligator could do to promote her career and visibility. She listened politely, then re-signed with Rounder and continued to release top-quality albums. Nine years later she was ready for a change and finally signed a deal with Alligator.

It was clear that I was not the right producer for Marcia. With Rounder, she had been used to choosing her own producers, studios, and songs and delivering her finished records to her label. A strong-willed woman, she was prepared to fight for any song she believed in. She cut her Alligator debut, *Presumed Innocent*, in Austin in 2000 with Doyle Bramhall Sr. producing. We battled over the photograph for the album cover. Marcia had chosen the picture she wanted to use, and it was the *only* one she was going to accept. I felt that, while it was an interesting photo, it was subdued and didn't capture the essence of the record, which was full of energy, passion, and humor.

She was adamant, and I eventually gave in. It wouldn't be the last battle we fought over packaging.[2] The record did very well. The best marketing tools that any Alligator artist gives to us are great live performances. Marcia won fan after fan from the stage. She toured endlessly and did everything we asked of her—she would do any interview, anywhere, anytime. She understood what she needed to do to help us to sell records.

Marcia has done a hundred or more gigs per year since signing with us. She is consistently an exhilarating, spontaneous live performer with well-rehearsed bands and a warm, personal stage presence and energy that reaches every audience member. Marcia Ball is a woman of intelligence, generosity, and resolve. At festivals, I have seen her sit at the autograph table until the last drunk fan stumbles up and requests an autograph on his arm because he doesn't have the money for a CD. She will treat that fan with the same respect that she treats every polite, sober one. She also plays many benefit shows every year, and she has occasionally alienated some fans by being outspoken about her liberal politics (which agree with mine). If you ask people what Alligator Records is, many will say, "It's the label Marcia Ball is on." I'm very proud of that.

It was in early spring of 1997 that I first experienced the power and soulfulness of Shemekia Copeland, the finest female blues singer of her generation. I was in New York for a meeting, and a blues fan friend told me it was imperative that I catch Shemekia's performance

2. Packaging has always been a major headache for Alligator. I constantly say to artists, "Let's plan the packaging in advance of recording. Let's make sure that the photo shoot happens in plenty of time so that photos can be re-done if they don't turn out well." Nonetheless, packaging always seems to happen at the last possible minute, and this sometimes results in cover photography and design that is not as powerful as it could be. (Release dates are often announced before the album is completed.) Marcia Ball and I have clashed over packaging numerous times. I feel that cover photos and design are a sales tool that should communicate the contents of the record. Marcia feels that the photos are ultimately her image, and she should control it. At one point, when Marcia insisted on using a photo I didn't feel was going to help sell the album at all, I said, "Our contract calls for mutual agreement on photos. This isn't by mutual agreement." I refused to pay the photographer. She paid for the photos. I eventually reimbursed her as a gesture of goodwill, but the situation caused a rift between us that took a long time to heal. For one of her most recent albums, we used a drawing instead of a photo. We were both happy.

at Chicago Blues, a club in the West Village. I knew Shemekia was Johnny Copeland's daughter, so she had the blues in her gene pool. But I wasn't prepared for what I heard that night. Only seventeen years old, she was working the relatively small audience like she was headlining a major auditorium. She didn't seem like a teenager; she carried herself like an adult. Her voice, emanating from her Rubenesque five-foot-one body, was huge. Had she been alive in the 1920s, when blues women like Bessie Smith were singing without microphones, she could have competed with any of them.

Shemekia's vocal style was different from Koko's rough growl and edgy attack; instead, she incorporated the big vocal bends and vibrato used by the best gospel singers. She sang with power, intensity, and maturity, and above all, she sang the meaning of the lyrics. There were no vocal gymnastics to show off what she could do; her gigantic voice was always in the service of the song. The most charismatic performance she gave that evening was of her father's song "Ghetto Child," sung from the point of view of a poverty-stricken child "in this so-called free land." I was flabbergasted to find a talent this mature in a teenager. I chatted with Shemekia and her manager, John Hahn, between sets. I found her to be a charming mix of high school girl and adult woman. She was poised, outgoing, and slightly flirtatious in an "I'm just having fun" way.

Sometimes I've been fooled by a strong live performance, thinking that it would translate to a record. When I left New York the next day, I still doubted myself, unsure if Shemekia was as impressive as I had thought. Within a few weeks, I suggested that we do a four-song demo session to see how she would sound in the studio. Backed by a group led by Jimmy Vivino, the guitarist for the house band on *Late Night with Conan O'Brien*. Shemekia delivered everything I had hoped for. A first- or second-take singer, her pitch and vocal bends were perfect. But more important, she had the soulfulness and honesty of the best blues singers. After the session, I said to John and Shemekia, "OK, I believe it. I didn't know if it would work in the studio, but you've proven yourself to me. Let's make a record." She was just turning eighteen, old enough to sign a contract.

To record the rest of the album, we went into a little New York studio in Chinatown called Sorcerer Sound. To add credibility to her debut, we brought in some friends of Shemekia's who were better-established artists. Joe Louis Walker, one of the most soulful bluesmen of his generation (who later cut two albums for Alligator), joined Shemekia for "My Turn, Baby," and Michael Hill, who had just finished his second album for Alligator and was well known on the New York blues scene, contributed some dynamic soloing with his signature bending of the blues rules. On "Ghetto Child," teenage guitar prodigy Monster Mike Welch delivered a subtle, passionate solo, with beautiful tone and dynamics. I knew we were making a terrific record, and I felt certain that Shemekia was going to be heralded as one of the most talented new blues artists.

We released the album, titled *Turn the Heat Up*, in late 1997. The title track, a catchy, hook-laden song with a Memphis soul groove written by John Hahn and Jimmy Vivino, earned some significant airplay on album rock stations that rarely played blues. Programmers liked the idea of a new, *young* female blues singer. In the blues world, the album was a sensation. The fresh, new songs, some filled with sassy attitude and humor, were well received. Hahn helped assemble a solid touring band for her, and Shemekia hit the road hard, easily earning slots at all the major blues festivals. Sales of Shemekia's debut were as good as those of our established female stars, Koko Taylor and Saffire—The Uppity Blues Women. They went far beyond my wildest expectations. It was a memorable beginning.

We had a four-record deal with Shemekia. Hahn, Vivino, and I produced the first two albums, *Turn the Heat Up* and *Wicked*. The third, *Talking to Strangers*, was produced by New Orleans icon Dr. John, and the fourth, *The Soul Truth*, by Memphis soul legend Steve Cropper. For all of their strengths, these last two didn't sell as well as her earlier albums. I felt that some of the songs were simply too cute. At eighteen, an artist can get away with a few lightweight or funny songs. When she is twenty-seven, it's time to be taken more seriously. We believed it was time that she recorded weightier material with greater emotional depth. I was also worried that Shemekia's records were becoming a bit formulaic—the funky song, a couple of funny songs, the slow blues, the rocker, and the soul ballad. She-mekia had never invested herself much in songwriting, preferring to personalize other people's songs through her interpretations. The team at Alligator presented her with many songs that we believed in, but she wasn't hearing herself singing them.

After the fourth album, Shemekia and her manager decided to leave Alligator for the Telarc label. There they recast her as a more serious artist who combined blues and R&B with Americana, the country-influenced genre that melds rootsy songwriting with raw, edgy production and sometimes a bit of twang. Telarc didn't seem to do much to promote Shemekia, and in the summer of 2015 she re-signed with Alligator. That year we released *Outskirts of Love*, an emotionally mature, multilayered album produced by Oliver Wood, who had also produced her Telarc albums. During her years away from Alligator, Shemekia and I had remained on good terms, and the whole Alligator staff saw her often, especially after she moved to Chicago. As I told her, "You can leave the label, but you can't leave the family." She toured for months promoting *Outskirts of Love*, play-ing at upscale venues like City Winery, but sales were nowhere near those of her earlier Alligator releases.

Shemekia's image has matured, but her voice has the same power and soulfulness that I heard when she was seventeen. Unlike some of the current hard-edged female pop singers, she's not somebody's cartoon tough girl. She's the real thing. She's lived it—growing up in Harlem, learning the blues from her father, and playing a thousand one-nighters around the world. I can imagine her recording a song that could become a staple on the same radio stations that would have been playing Bonnie Raitt a few years ago. I think she's one song (the right song with the right promotion) away from breaking into a whole new audience. The peaks of her career and popularity may still be ahead of her. She deserves to be a household name.

Another uppity woman was a vital part of the Alligator story. She wasn't a musician; she was an inspiration and a mentor—Lillian Shedd McMurry, the founder and owner of Trumpet Records. From

1950 through 1955, Lillian recorded and released some of the finest blues and gospel records of the era. Based in Jackson, Mississippi, in the days of racial segregation and few female-operated businesses, this southern white woman ran a successful label with a roster made up almost entirely of African American artists. At a time when record labels often took advantage of black musicians desperate to record, Lillian was scrupulously honest. She proudly paid royalties to both artists and songwriters.

Lillian first encountered the blues after moving to Jackson from a small town in Mississippi and marrying her beloved sweetheart, Willard. In 1949, Willard, who was in the furniture business, purchased a bankrupt store in a black neighborhood. While cleaning out the store, Lillian found a cache of unsold records. One was "All She Wants to Do Is Rock" by blues shouter Wynonie Harris. It was love at first listen. She recalled, "It was the most unusual, sincere, and solid sound I'd ever heard. I'd never heard a black record before."[3] Within months, she reopened the store as the Record Mart. Soon she was making regular runs to New Orleans to buy blues and R&B 78s, sponsoring a radio show, and selling records by mail order.

In 1950, she founded Trumpet Records after realizing that she could be making records herself rather than selling records produced by other labels. The next year, she tracked down Sonny Boy Williamson II, who was broadcasting on KFFA in Helena, Arkansas, and playing in Delta juke joints but had never recorded. With his vibrato-laden voice and warbling harmonica, he became Trumpet's most frequently recorded and most popular artist. His Trumpet sides, including "Eyesight to the Blind," "Pontiac Blues,"[4] "Mighty Long Time," "Too Close Together," and "Nine Below Zero," rank among the best blues recordings ever made. Lillian not only produced the sessions, she also took on Sonny Boy's management and

3. Marc W. Ryan, *Trumpet Records: Diamonds on Farish Street* (Jackson: University Press of Mississippi, 2004), 8.

4. Lillian told me that the Pontiac in the song was her car. She would lend it to Sonny Boy to go to gigs, but only if his wife, Mattie, was driving. Lillian didn't trust that he would be in a condition to drive by the end of the night.

booking; he even sang her office and home phone numbers in "309," one of his Trumpet singles. Lillian also produced Elmore James's first and most famous recording, "Dust My Broom." A blues hit, it made it to number 9 on *Billboard* magazine's R&B chart. Lillian's other star was Greenville's Willie Love, a wild pianist famed for "V-8 Ford," "Nelson Street Blues," and "Little Car Blues."

For five years, Trumpet successfully competed for radio play and distribution with powerhouse labels like Chess, Atlantic, and Modern, all run by tough, big-city businessmen. Eventually the labels with bigger budgets and more clout won. Lillian closed Trumpet in 1955. Refusing to go bankrupt, she worked two jobs to pay off her debts. Then she faded into obscurity.

In 1988, I was searching for the publisher of "V-8 Ford Blues," which had just been recorded by Little Charlie & The Nightcats. I found a phone number for Globe Music. When I called, I was amazed that Lillian answered the phone. Impressed that I was trying to find the right royalty recipient, she decided that I was her kind of record man, and eventually we became friends. She wrote to me in great detail about the legal problems she had encountered trying to maintain ownership of her masters and publishing. A few years later, Alligator had a chance to release a series of seven Trumpet re-issue CDs. Lillian had leased the rights to Marc Ryan, a fan who had released some of the material on CD but didn't have the money to continue the project. I was thrilled to have Alligator be the vehicle to bring Trumpet's music back to the public, packaged with Ryan's detailed liner notes and archival photos.

In 1994, my future wife, Jo, and I took the train to Jackson to visit Lillian. We spent a delightful afternoon at her home, hearing stories about Trumpet and Sonny Boy, as well as being told in no uncertain terms what crooks she thought most of her competitors had been. I knew Lillian was a tough woman, but I didn't know how tough. She recounted that she had found out one of her contracted artists had agreed to record a session "on the sly" for the Bihari brothers' Modern label. "I walked into the session with the sheriff, holding their contract in one hand and my pistol in the other hand, and took the tapes," she told us. After showing us a room full of file cabinets, she explained that she calculated the royalties owed to every Trumpet artist and every Globe Music songwriter, even if they had disappeared decades before. If their heirs ever appeared, she would know exactly what they were owed. I told her we did the same thing at Alligator. At her urging, I helped to get Sonny Boy's royalties flowing from Universal Music to his widow, Mattie. Over the next few years, I led a successful crusade to have Lillian inducted into the Blues Foundation's Hall of Fame.

In the late 1990s, a controversial blues entrepreneur named Steve LaVere claimed to have acquired the Trumpet masters from the fan who had licensed them to us. Alligator's rights were terminated, and we had to take the CDs out of print. Lillian was outraged; she believed that she had legal rights to many of them. Others she had given to the University of Mississippi. She battled to get them back but was unable to do so before her death in 1999.

In her will, Lillian left the remaining songs in the Globe Music catalog to me, trusting that I would continue to pay the songwriters and keep up the royalty accounting. It was one of the greatest honors of my life. There's a picture of Lillian above my desk, and every day I wear a silver bracelet made for me by Lillian's daughter, Vitrice. That way Lillian is always with me. I feel the same about Lillian as I do about Bob Koester—I walk in their giant shadows.

17

Of all my decisions to let my heart lead my head, the most disastrous came in 1997, when I agreed to take on the distribution of Black Top Records. Black Top was a first-class New Orleans–based blues and R&B label founded in 1981 and operated by Hammond Scott with the help of his brother Nauman. Black Top had started modestly with a record by an up-and-coming Dallas-based band called Anson Funderburgh and the Rockets. Hammond built the catalog, recording world-class roots artists like Earl King, Buckwheat Zydeco, the Neville Brothers, Snooks Eaglin, Solomon Burke, and Hubert Sumlin, plus younger musicians like Mike Morgan and the Crawl, Ronnie Earl, Bobby Radcliff, and a number of bands from Louisiana and central southern states.

As a blues fan, I looked forward to every new Black Top release. As a label owner, I felt that the quality of Black Top's albums made them one of my best competitors. Many of their releases were cut at Ultrasonic Studios in New Orleans and produced with great care by Hammond. Early on, Black Top made a production and distribution deal with Rounder Records. Black Top created the masters, designed the covers, and ran the song publishing while Rounder did the manufacturing and sold the releases through Rounder's distributors. Rounder recouped their manufacturing costs, kept a percentage of the wholesale price, and paid the rest to Black Top.

In the late 1990s, Black Top pulled the label from Rounder Records, convinced that they were getting a bad deal. A distribution agreement with a Denver company called Encore Distributing didn't go well. Hammond, who had been a friend of mine for a long time, asked Alligator to take over distribution. Black Top was low on funds, so the agreement would require us to provide a significant financial advance. Without looking at the label's books or talking with its accountant, I agreed. I was convinced that there was no way the Black Top label could survive without Alligator's help. I didn't want to see this wonderful label with quality music and so many worthy artists go under. Alligator was doing well financially, so I decided to take the risk. As a business move, it was probably the dumbest thing I ever did.

Almost instantly after we announced that we were taking over Black Top's distribution, our distributors were flooded with requests from retailers to return unsold CDs. We issued credit after credit while our warehouse filled up with returned CDs that the Scott brothers thought had already been sold. Then Black Top released some less distinguished records to create short-term cash flow at the expense of long-term planning and sound bookkeeping. We spent significant amounts of money manufacturing these releases, mailing out promotional copies, and buying advertising, only to be stuck with low sales and big returns. Ultimately, Black Top was generating so little income that it wasn't coming close to recouping our costs. Some of the advance we had given the label had been earned back, but we were still swimming in red ink.

Then, while attending the 2000 National Association of Recording Merchandisers Conference in San Antonio, I got an unexpected phone call from an executive of E Music, a new company that was getting into the digital distribution business. He informed me that E Music had just purchased the Black Top catalog and was eager to get the masters and print materials from me. I was stunned. Hammond had given no indication to us that he was selling the label. "That's in violation of our contract," I said. "And not only that, I've had no opportunity to announce this sale, to solicit returns, or to make any kind of financial settlement with Hammond." "We don't know anything about that," the E Music exec replied. "We just want to get the masters and offer these titles digitally." I called Black Top. "We're completely broke," I was told, matter-of-factly. "We had this opportunity and we had to take it." My only choice at that point was to either sue a friend or to swallow hard and walk away. I took the latter course. It's hard to know how much Alligator lost trying to save Black Top. My best guess would be about one hundred thousand dollars. As Earl King sang on one of his Black Top records, "It all went down the drain for you and I." Or in this case, for I alone.

Even with the Black Top debacle, for the sixteen years between 1984 and 2000, things went well for Alligator more often than not. Despite a slowly shrinking blues audience, the company kept growing. We were helped by a supportive new commercial radio format, Adult Album Alternative (AAA), which emerged in 1992. Looser than AOR, the AAA format centered on singer-songwriters but also found a place for a little blues and other roots music. At the format's peak, about 120 stations around the country called themselves AAA.

But there were signs of impending trouble through the second half of the 1990s. The distribution and sales networks that had remained relatively stable over most of Alligator's existence began to unravel. Over the course of the 1990s, many of our longtime distributors were acquired, went bankrupt, or simply folded. Some distributors were honest dealers who paid their labels too readily and went bankrupt with warehouses full of unsold records that they were unable to return to defunct labels. Some distributors were not so honest. Perhaps there was a mysterious warehouse fire, or questionable investment scheme, or the distributor's coffers were drained by the owners until the company went bankrupt. One night the owner of our New York distributor loaded a diesel truck with every CD and cassette in his warehouse, drove to Texas, and sold them all for cash to people who peddled music at swap meets and flea markets. He disappeared owing thousands of dollars to many labels, including Alligator.

Changes in the record business also made the situation harder for independent distributors. The independent labels they distributed were starting to be acquired by the majors, which sold to the stores directly through their in-house distribution arms. Giants like Sony (formerly Columbia), WMG (Warner Music Group), Polygram, Universal (originally Decca, then MCA and EMI), and BMG (formerly RCA) acquired valuable independent labels like A&M, Motown, Priority, Island, Def Jam, and Tommy Boy. Many of the major labels had set up their own distributorships decades earlier. Capitol founded its own distributorship in the 1940s, followed by Columbia in the 1960s, and then RCA, MCA, and WEA (Warner/Elektra/Atlantic). By the end of the 1990s, all the major labels handled their own distribution.

Since 2010, following gigantic corporate acquisitions, only three majors remain—Sony, Universal, and WEA. Sony and Universal are parts of international media conglomerates. Each one operates a distributorship to sell records on the labels they own. Each also operates a separate distributorship to sell records by independent labels. Sony operates The Orchard, Universal has Caroline Distribution, and WEA runs ADA (Alternative Distribution Alliance). A few years ago ADA acquired Ryko Distribution, an independent that had started distributing Alligator nationwide in 2000. So Alligator, while remaining independently owned, is now distributed in the United States by an arm of WEA.

The record industry could be a dog-eat-dog business, and in the 1990s it became even more so. In that decade, many mom-and-pop record stores disappeared, and national chains grew and consolidated. The trend seemed to signal victory for the people who called CDs *product*, those who saw recorded music as just another commodity with a barcode. (Of course this view had always been true of the largest chains, but local stores had continued to be music centered.) In 1995, the consumer electronics big-box chain Best Buy jumped into the record business. Initially, every label thought Best Buy was its new savior. It was a massive chain, with more than five hundred stores stocking deep catalog selections and promoting a broad range of music. Soon, however, Best Buy began using music as a loss leader (a retail strategy for luring customers into a store) by selling CDs for less than the CDs cost them. By pricing CDs at $9.99, Best Buy convinced consumers nationwide that paying $15 or more for a CD at an established record store was a rip-off.

When Alligator first got into the CD business, we set $19.98 as our suggested list price (the price at which we wanted retailers to sell our CD to the public) because we were paying $5 for an unpackaged disc. With packaging and royalties, CDs were costing us close to $8.50. If a store sold them for $19.98, after the store markup and the distributor's margin, we were making about $12 per CD, a $3.50 profit margin. As manufacturing costs dropped dramatically, we lowered our suggested retail price to $14.98. With inflation, our price started creeping back up, ending at $17.98. But if the price of music recordings, whether on CDs or LPs, had kept up with inflation since the mid-1960s, they'd be selling for nearly $40 in a store—the equivalent of $5 in 1965.

Normally, distributors agreed to reimburse stores for the cost of advertising, often based on how much the stores bought. (The independent distributors would then charge back that cost to the labels and deduct it from what they paid to the labels.) When Best Buy insisted on pricing CDs under cost, the major label–owned distributors refused to credit Best Buy for advertising low-priced loss leader CDs. The largest distributors, speaking for the conglomerates that owned them, insisted that any ads for which Best Buy was to be reimbursed needed to advertise prices above wholesale—what was called the Minimum Advertised Price (MAP). The case went to federal court. Under Fair Trade regulations, Best Buy won. That's because retailers were allowed to sell at whatever price they wished; their suppliers couldn't dictate the price. The labels were forced to continue to provide advertising dollars to Best Buy, because the law required them to offer the same terms to all retailers. Unable to compete with Best Buy's ridiculously low prices, record stores quickly began dying. After hundreds closed, Best Buy backed out of the record business, first raising their prices and stocking only big hits, and finally ceasing to stock CDs at all.

In the late 1990s, with a declining number of customers for Alligator's six remaining distributors, I was feeling increasing pressure to move the label to a single national distributor. One option was INDI, a company created by a conglomerate called Alliance Entertainment. Alliance had bought up independent distributors, including some that distributed Alligator, like Big State Distributors in Dallas, California Record Distributing in Los Angeles, and Passport Music Distribution in Denver. Alliance had also bought some major one-stops—wholesalers that stocked CDs from many distributors and labels and sold to smaller, independently owned record stores. Alliance was effectively trying to corner the wholesale independent record business. But in doing so, Alliance overleveraged its financing, and there were rumors that it was in financial trouble. In 1997, two of Alligator's key staffers and I met with a group of Alliance executives at a Chicago restaurant. They had come to convince us to dump our other distributors and commit to INDI for national distribution. When we arrived, the first words out of the Alliance spokesman's mouth were, "Who have we fucked? We've never fucked anybody." I immediately thought, "Perhaps I should be worried that Alligator is about to get fucked." Throughout dinner, the executives told us why INDI should be Alligator's exclusive national distributor. But they also told us that current hits were the only thing that mattered, a comment that denigrated deep catalog sales to a deep catalog label. It wasn't a very effective sales pitch. We decided the time was coming for Alligator to leave INDI.

Before we had time to pull Alligator out of INDI's network of distributors, Alliance went bankrupt. Because Alligator had good friends working at the distributors that Alliance had absorbed, we suffered less financial pain from that bankruptcy than almost any other label. Our friends made sure that the unsold Alligator inventory in their warehouses was returned to us before it could be seized in the bankruptcy proceedings. In each case, this happened at the last possible moment. Just before he was forced to padlock the warehouse, the former owner of Big State (which had been sold to Alliance) personally loaded pallets of Alligator CDs and cassettes onto a truck to be returned to us. The manager of Passport in Denver called and said, "Fax me a blank return authorization *right now*. I'm going to return every Alligator CD and cassette we've got in the warehouse today." The warehouse manager at California Record Distributing called and said, "You need to get your inventory out of here right now." We did. INDI later threatened to sue us for receiving preferential treatment just before they declared bankruptcy. We reached a settlement to avoid being sued, but we still escaped with less loss than many other labels.

The final straw came in 1999 with the demise of M.S. Distributing, the oldest independent distributor in the country. Founded by Milt Salstone in the 1940s and based in a Chicago suburb, M.S. was one of Alligator's biggest distributors. Though we sometimes had to beg them to send us money, they always paid their bills eventually. Then, during the internet boom, the owners of M.S. suddenly sold their operation to a startup company founded by a wealthy twenty-eight-year-old music business novice. He had the crazy idea of turning M.S. into an Amazon-like retailer, selling records by mail order. M.S. sold in bulk to retail stores; it wasn't set up to fulfill individual mail orders. The new owner believed that the real value of this enterprise wasn't going to be in profits from mail order sales, but rather in selling its consumer data to other online businesses. The old owners of M.S. saw an opportunity to cash out, and they took it.

Although the new owner intended to transform the company into a mail order house, initially he needed to keep the distribution business (and its cash flow) going. M.S.'s biggest distributed label was the Fantasy Group, which owned the extremely lucrative Creedence Clearwater Revival catalog as well as the gigantic Prestige and Milestone jazz catalogs. I called Fantasy's national sales manager, Phil Jones, after hearing about the sale of M.S. "Our deal with M.S.," Phil told me, "is that they pay us every thirty days. The new owner of M.S. is already behind on our payment schedule." I began calling Phil almost daily to see whether he had received a check from M.S. yet. His answer was always no. One day he said, "If we don't get our check in ten days, we're pulling out of M.S." I knew that losing Fantasy would destroy M.S. Ten days later, I called Phil. No check had

266 BITTEN BY THE BLUES

arrived, and Fantasy was leaving M.S. We instantly rented a truck, and I headed to M.S. with Kerry Peace, our national sales manager. We left that day with every Alligator CD and cassette in their warehouse. Twenty-four hours later, the warehouse was padlocked, and M.S. was in bankruptcy. They owed us thousands of dollars that we would never receive, but at least we had recovered our CDs and cassettes.

The collapse of M.S. finally convinced me to seek a national distribution deal. With easy-to-ship CDs and cassettes as our formats and with the growth of national chains that purchased centrally, Alligator no longer needed a distributor in every city. Instead, we needed a well-run, well-financed national distributor that could service all the major retail accounts. The smaller stores could buy our music from the one-stop wholesalers. After much research, many meetings, and visits to various national distributors with two of my most trusted employees—national sales manager Kerry Peace and retail promotion director Chris Young—we chose Ryko Distribution. Run by the capable and experienced Jim Cuomo, Ryko didn't have too many labels. Its orientation was catalog sales, not hits. Ryko paid its bills and had good relationships with retailers. Polygram Distributing, which was owned by one of the major multinationals, did all the warehousing, shipping, billing, and collections for Ryko Distribution, though Ryko had its own sales and marketing staff. As part of their agreement, Polygram guaranteed Ryko Distribution's receivables. If Polygram was willing to give credit to a retailer or one-stop, then it would guarantee that if that account didn't pay its bills to Polygram (if, for example, the retailer or one-stop went bankrupt), Polygram would cover the loss, and Ryko and its distributed labels, including Alligator, would be paid. After our experiences with Alliance and M.S., we wanted that bankruptcy protection.[1]

---

1. We didn't realize how soon we would need that bankruptcy protection. One of Polygram's accounts was Valley Media, the largest one-stop wholesaler in the country, which also owned DNA, a well-respected independent distributor. In 2001, Valley Media went bankrupt. Many indie labels lost tens of thousands of dollars. Polygram absorbed the loss for Ryko-distributed labels like Alligator, so we lost nothing.

When I made the distribution deal with Ryko in 2000 I called up our six remaining distributors to tell them personally. Almost everybody wished me well and said, "If it doesn't work, come back." The exception was Mark Viducich, the president of Bayside Distribution, which had been acquired by Tower Records. Mark told me to go fuck myself. Four years later, Tower and Bayside declared bankruptcy.

In the late 1990s, our blues CD sales were slowing down, and we were having a hard time establishing fan bases and sales for our lesser-known artists. Increasingly anxious about taking a chance on unproven talent, we concentrated on recording new albums by our proven sellers. We felt we had to play it safer. We didn't know that even more difficult days were just around the corner.

Perhaps one of the strongest indications that the marketplace was beginning to change was the complete failure of one of our best records. Released in 1999, *Lone Star Shootout* was Alligator's third super session. It featured three string-squeezing guitar players who were also old friends: Lonnie Brooks, Long John Hunter, and Phillip Walker. All three had started their careers in the Beaumont–Port Arthur area of east Texas, which had been a blues mecca in the 1950s and 1960s.[2] With their similar musical styles and their longtime personal relationships (as both rivals and friends), I felt they could create an album as exciting and fun as *Showdown!* or *Harp Attack!*

Lonnie had been with the label since 1978, when we chose him from among Chicago's finest talent for the *Living Chicago Blues* series. By 1999 we had released six Lonnie Brooks albums. All of them featured his roaring, soul-tinged vocals and his "voodoo blues" guitar. Although his record sales never seemed to match his potential, he was a charter member of the Alligator family. Lonnie was more widely known than either Long John or Phillip.

Long John, the oldest of the three, was also already signed to

2. After World War II, Port Arthur and Beaumont were major oil ports where large numbers of black people worked as laborers. The countryside around Port Arthur was dotted with roadhouses and juke joints that catered to black customers. According to Phillip Walker, some clubs had tent roofs with open sides and no indoor plumbing. It was a wild and woolly scene.

Alligator. With a swinging single-string guitar style inspired by B. B. King, T-Bone Walker, and Gatemouth Brown, Long John had begun his career in the Port Arthur juke joints in the 1950s and cut his first single for Houston's famous Duke label. By the end of the decade, he had moved to El Paso and was performing in a rowdy joint called the Lobby Bar, where he was famous for hanging from the rafters with one hand while playing the guitar with the other (which inspired the title of his second Alligator release, *Swinging from the Rafters*). He became a word-of-mouth legend in west Texas. In the early 1990s he recorded a comeback album for the Spindletop label called *Ride with Me* (which we reissued in 1998). True blues fans were excited by the reemergence of this raw, authentic Texas bluesman. We had signed him in 1996 and released new albums by him that year and in 1997.

Phillip Walker had made his reputation in California as a stinging, jazz-inflected blues guitarist and a dry, slightly nasal vocalist. Before he left Texas, Phillip, like Lonnie Brooks, had been a member of zydeco king Clifton Chenier's band. After moving to California in the late 1950s, he had recorded for various West Coast labels, including the short-lived Playboy label. I knew Phillip because my friend Bruce Bromberg had produced Phillip's album *Someday You'll Have These Blues* and released it on his Joliet label. When Joliet closed up in the late 1970s, Bruce had licensed it to Alligator. Phillip had gone on to cut a number of albums, including two for Black Top.

We recorded *Lone Star Shootout* at the top-notch Arlyn Studios in Austin. Just as they had tried to steal one another's gigs (and women) in Port Arthur in the 1950s, each guitarist wanted to outdo the other. But because they were friends, each wanted the other to shine. Phillip even showed some alternative chords to Long John that enhanced the arrangement of one of Long John's songs. Each one came to the sessions with a few new songs, but we also chose tunes from quintessential Texas and Louisiana musicians like T-Bone Walker, Gatemouth Brown, Lightnin' Slim, Clarence Garlow, and Lonesome Sundown. We even rearranged one of Lonnie's 1950s Gulf Coast hits, "Roll, Roll, Roll." We cut as much as we could live in the studio, with three live vocal microphones, just like *Showdown!* Each guitarist delivered solos with the kind of sparks that can only come when musicians are jamming together in real time.

Throughout the sessions, the three of them laughed and joked with one another and recounted stories of the Texas clubs of their youth. But we had a limited amount of studio time booked, so the recording days and nights were long. I had to think creatively to keep up the energy level of these three older musicians through some late-night sessions. One night we cut a slightly risqué Lightnin' Slim song called "It's Mighty Crazy." Needing to get these three tired men in their sixties to sing like they were wide awake, smiling, and having a good time, I went out into the studio while they were recording, dropped my pants, and mooned them. I got the result I wanted; they recorded for another hour because they were laughing too hard to feel tired.

I believed that *Lone Star Shootout* was a classic Alligator release, in the same musical league as *Showdown!* and *Harp Attack!* But it bombed, despite receiving good reviews and decent airplay on blues radio shows (though virtually none on commercial stations). We even presented the three guitarists as a package at some blues festivals. But for whatever reason, the combination of these three talented musicians didn't even create as many sales as their individual albums. The record was returned to us in droves.

It was increasingly clear to me that the social and musical culture that gave birth to Hound Dog Taylor, Koko Taylor, Son Seals, and Fenton Robinson, and to newer Alligator artists like Lil' Ed, was disappearing. From the mid-1980s on, it became harder and harder for me to find younger African American blues musicians who were rooted in the tradition but had something of their own to say. More and more, the best artists I was hearing had discovered the blues from records or a live concert or club performance by an older musician. They hadn't been born into a world where the blues was part of everyday life.

In the mid-1990s, I signed two visionary young black blues musicians who hadn't grown up in the tradition. Both cut groundbreaking albums for us that failed to find a wide audience. Corey Harris and Michael Hill both came from big-city, middle-class homes with educated parents. They had chosen the blues rather than the blues having chosen them.

Corey came to Alligator as a young street busker performing mostly traditional, acoustic blues. He had grown up in Denver, far from the Delta, sported long dreadlocks, and had studied African culture in Mali. But he had a deep understanding of the Delta blues tradition and his interpretations of Delta blues were intensely moving. There are a number of musicians who are very good at playing in the styles of Son House and Bukka White. Corey played fine guitar, but it was his haunting vocals that seemed to channel the essence of those long-gone Mississippi bluesmen without imitating them. His singing was full of brilliant pitch bending, with vocal swoops, vibrato, and falsetto. But Corey didn't stick with the acoustic blues that led to my signing him. Over his five years with Alligator, he evolved into an exploratory musician whose vision of the blues included all the music of the African diaspora. His most wide-ranging Alligator album, 1996's *Greens from the Garden*, included everything from acoustic blues to hip-hop and reggae.

After cutting four albums for Alligator (only one that I produced—a duet recording with New Orleans jazz-blues pianist and vocalist Henry Butler), Corey left us for the Rounder label and then moved to Telarc Records. He embraced reggae and cut a couple of strongly reggae-influenced albums. He lost much of his blues audience without winning other fans, and his record sales declined. These days, Corey is living in Europe. Recently, he has self-released albums that reflect his wide-ranging vision. He's still a thrilling performer of country blues.

Michael Hill, a native New Yorker, was pulled into the blues by his love of Jimi Hendrix (the same path that future Alligator artists Selwyn Birchwood and Toronzo Cannon would follow). He's a brilliant guitarist, alternatively hard-edged and lyrical, in addition to being a rule-breaking, socially conscious songwriter. His original songs range from outcries about urban violence and police brutality to odes to beautiful women. Michael cut three albums for Alligator that I coproduced with him, and music critics hailed all three as cutting-edge new blues.

Michael is a gentle, intellectual, and jovial man. But with his dreadlocks and African-inspired stage garb, he was somehow pegged as a spokesman for Black Power. Even while singing lighthearted songs like "Women Make the World Go Round" and "Lost in the Sauce," he failed to find an audience in the blues clubs and at festivals. He was stereotyped by songs like "Evil in the Air" and "Soul Emergency." The blues audience didn't know what to do with him, and his booking agent struggled to find gigs for him. Eventually, Michael gave up the road and returned to New York to teach and raise his son.

Both Corey and Michael deserved wider audiences. Our inability to find those audiences for them was a clear message to me that much of the existing blues audience wanted its new blues to sound just like its old blues, or like its old blues rock. Many blues fans had come to the blues after hearing British blues-rock bands, Johnny Winter, or Stevie Ray Vaughan. They were fine with screaming guitar solos. But when they heard a socially conscious lyric, or a nontraditional chord progression or rhythm, some just tuned out. It seemed that a lot of fans enjoyed blues simply as party music. They didn't want to hear the serious side of the music, the side that deals with healing emotional pain. These fans paid lip service to the heritage of the blues but avoided dealing with the historic (and contemporary) oppression for which the blues was an antidote.

18

In 1999, after more than a decade and a half of steady growth and catalog expansion, Alligator began to lose sales. Digital technology changed everything. The public began to realize (as I certainly hadn't) that a CD could be ripped in a home computer and each song converted into an MP3 file. Those files could then be emailed or uploaded and shared with the rest of the world with no compensation for the label or artist. A relative of mine proudly told me that he was sharing his favorite albums by copying and burning CDs for everyone in his office. When I pointed out that he was ripping off exactly the artists whose music he purported to love, he was completely shocked. He had never thought of it that way.

Websites suddenly appeared where anyone could, in exchange for viewing some online advertising, find and download almost any song free of charge. No one was getting paid—not the labels, not the song publishers, not the songwriters, and, of course, not the recording artists. The new mantra (especially among teens and college students) was that music should be free. The biggest of these free download sites was Napster. These sites disrupted the record industry business models like nothing before. Music sales plummeted. Until the introduction of legal download stores like iTunes and its competitors a few years later, the pirate sites ran rampant. Record stores that had survived the consolidation of the 1990s went out of business as their sales disappeared. This was especially true of stores near college campuses. The value of owning a physical recording seemed to become a thing of the past.

Since then, the recording industry, especially the independent industry, has struggled to figure out how to create enough income from commercial recordings to continue to make any kind of profit. It took me a while to see the writing on the wall. Although most local and regional independent distributors had folded, and the independent stores and small chains were fast disappearing, it didn't cross my mind that people would want to stop owning music in a physical form. But many of our adult customers never converted to buying from online stores like Amazon or purchasing digital files from iTunes and other download stores. They simply stopped buying music.

For a brief while, we took refuge in the belief that older fans would continue to buy CDs when Borders Books & Music stepped up to replace the faltering Tower Records. Our biggest account from the early 2000s until 2009, Borders ran very good deep catalog CD departments that appealed to adult customers, and its stores stocked a large part of the Alligator catalog. My retail promotion coordinator periodically went to Ann Arbor, Michigan, to visit Borders' national headquarters, where a few buyers bought centrally for the whole chain. We always participated in its retail programs; for two thousand dollars in credit, Borders would bring in two thousand copies of almost any new Alligator release and give it a top-shelf position in more than five hundred stores. Returns from Borders were relatively small; most of the Alligator CDs in its stores sold through to consumers. Alligator was in Borders' sweet spot: our adult customers were its core demographic.

Unfortunately, there was a trade-off. Borders' success was killing off even more independent record stores, many of whom were our friends. But we had no choice. Soon, Borders was virtually the only deep catalog retailer in the country. By 2008, Borders was falling on hard times as the book business began moving to online sales. The chain cut back on music, which was a huge mistake. As its music selection became poorer, Borders lost its loyal music customers. Once that happened, sales dropped, and Borders reduced its selection further, creating a downward spiral of diminishing sales and diminishing selection. The chain went bankrupt in 2011 and with it went Alligator's last major nationwide retail outlet. Barnes & Noble has many stores with music departments, some of which stock selected Alligator titles. As a chain, however, it has much less commitment to music than Borders did.

Fortunately, Alligator started the transition to online sales early. We launched our website, alligator.com, in 1995, long before most indie labels had an internet presence. Selling CDs, label-branded clothing, and other merchandise online became a small but important part of our business. The website also gave us a place for artist bios, an online jukebox, tour calendars, and news, and we constantly update it to make it more user-friendly. Taking advantage of technology, we also began sending out our thousands of press releases by email rather than physical mail. We've built a fan email list of almost forty thousand. More recently, we began providing foreign radio stations and DJs with downloadable digital files of our new releases rather than mailing CDs to them.

It was harder to move some of our musicians into the new digital reality than it was to make our music available digitally. In the past, artists had private lives. Between gigs they could go home, enjoy their families, and create new music. Now they are expected to launch, maintain, and update websites, then to create a social media presence on multiple platforms, where they are constantly posting new information, photos, and responses to their fans, creating podcasts and playlists, and using whatever is the latest digital social networking fad. Fans who had previously been happy to meet the artists at a gig and have a CD signed and a picture taken now expect them to respond to their online messages and be available twenty-four hours a day. Fans also expect to be allowed to shoot videos of live performances on their phones and post them online without artist approval. Musicians who balk at all this online activity are considered standoffish or arrogant, and their online invisibility hurts their careers. Elvin Bishop perfectly summarizes some artists' anti-technology stance in his song "Old School":

[I] don't fool with no Facebook, Twitters and tweets
Call me on the phone if you want to talk with me.
Now don't send me no email. Send me a female!
I'm old school.

Some Alligator artists have limited computer skills, limited formal education, and simply not enough time for this new digital world. Yet they must post something online about how much they enjoyed meeting fans last night in Pittsburgh (plus a selfie taken with those fans) and how much they are looking forward to tonight's gig in Cleveland. Otherwise they aren't following the new promotional norm and aren't competing effectively with other, newer artists. Of course, a musician might not have had time to do that because he's driving his own van to the Cleveland gig rather than being online. Sometimes older musicians playing for older fan bases can get away with little online presence, but for our younger artists with younger fans, it has become essential.

We finally insisted on access to our artists' social media pages and websites, just so that we could post news of their careers and keep their tour calendars up to date. Sometimes we had to battle with musicians to convince them to invest time in their online presence. Eventually I asked one of our staffers, Josh Lindner, to head our one-man New Media department and devote himself to helping both the label's and the artists' digital outreach and visibility. Ironically, Josh had originally been hired to do retail promotion, which involved staying in constant contact with record stores and chain buyers and persuading them to give Alligator more in-store presence. The implosion of retail record stores freed him up to devote his time to digital promotion.

As record stores began closing in 1999, I decided that we had to change our focus. For years, we had developed close relationships with retailers. Even though we didn't sell to them directly, we had staffers calling retailers constantly to grease the relationships, to solicit in-store displays, in-store play, sale pricing, and front-rack positioning. We ran annual display contests with cash prizes; often close to two hundred stores participated. We created sampler CDs for in-store play. Our store relationships were part of our secret of success. At one time we had two employees on the phone with retailers all day. By the early 2000s, those two employees were reduced to one. By 2010, calling retail stores was at best half of one staffer's day. Now it is a couple hours a week.

We realized that CD sales by the artists at their shows would have to make up for lost in-store sales because many of our customers were not going to buy our music online. I decided that we needed to publicize and promote every gig by every Alligator artist, whether or not the artist had a new release. With two full-time publicists (Marc Lipkin and Chris Levick) and two full-time radio promoters (Tim Kolleth and Matt LaFollette) plus Josh acting as New Media specialist for online promotion, we were well equipped to pursue media coverage from major media like National Public Radio and *USA Today* down to the smallest community radio station and weekly newspaper. The strategy worked. Gig sales increased, with some of our artists selling thousands of copies of each of their CDs at their shows. The most outgoing of them, like Tommy Castro, Marcia Ball, and Selwyn Birchwood, sit at their merchandise tables for an hour after each show, signing CDs and building personal fan loyalty in a way that could never be done online. (Selwyn and his band sing "We've got CDs for sale" in four-part harmony at the end of every performance.) I continue to believe that if we can help to attract good-sized audiences to every gig and if the artists sell CDs effectively, we can survive the virtual death of record stores.

The proliferation of blues festivals in the 1990s and early 2000s helped bring large groups of blues fans together, allowing artists to sell more than one hundred CDs at a time instead of just twenty or thirty in a club. In 1993, a Kansas City club owner named Roger Naber founded the popular Legendary Rhythm & Blues Cruise. It's a sort of floating weeklong festival that sails from both Florida and California, featuring dozens of musicians and performances. On each cruise a few thousand fans have the chance to socialize with their favorite artists and experience both rehearsed sets and impromptu jams. Tommy Castro, the Bay Area blues-rock guitarist and vocalist whose career has spanned almost forty years, has become the unofficial captain of these cruises, leading the jams and performing with his own band, the Painkillers. With his energized music and warm, accessible personality, Tommy has won a following of blues cruisers, who also support his year-round touring. Each cruise ship houses a store where the musicians have a chance to sell not only their recordings but also merchandise such as T-shirts, hats, and videos. Festival and cruise sales are an essential part of marketing success for any blues or other niche music artist or label.

As hip-hop and rap became dominant pop genres in the 1990s and early 2000s, hit-oriented indie labels arose to exploit those genres. Most of these labels had never felt at home in the niche music, catalog-oriented world of NAIRD/AFIM. There was one exception. Tommy Silverman, the visionary founder of the Tommy Boy label (which had giant hits with Queen Latifah, De La Soul, Coolio, and many more), sat on the board of NAIRD for years. In 2005, after NAIRD/AFIM had folded, he and the heads of some of the big indie labels, like Beggars Group, Roadrunner, TVT, Bar/None, and Lookout, founded a new organization—the American Association of Independent Music, or A2IM. These labels financed A2IM well enough for a small professional staff to be hired. A2IM's first major battle in behalf of fairness for indie labels was with iTunes.

The digitalization of the record industry that had begun with illegal sites like Napster was followed by the growth of legal download stores, especially iTunes. The iTunes model was brilliant in its simplicity. At this writing, iTunes pays the labels a flat rate of seven dollars per album sold and seventy cents per track. These rates aren't mandated by the government, but they have become the industry standard. However, that wasn't always the case. When it launched iTunes, Apple presented its terms to labels as nonnegotiable—take it or leave it. At first, the deal iTunes offered to independent labels called for paying five cents less per downloaded song and fifty cents less per downloaded album than what iTunes was paying to the giant multinational conglomerates, which controlled about 70 percent of the music sold in the United States. When the big independent labels, now organized under A2IM, threatened to publicize this disparity, Apple quickly revised its policy so that all labels, indie and major alike, were paid the same amount per download.[1]

Under the iTunes model, it's always been up to the labels to pay the artists and the song publishers,[2] just as it is for the sale of a CD. The difference for the label between the sale of a CD and the sale of a download is that with the latter, the label doesn't have the cost of manufacturing a physical product to sell. Although the label makes less per sale of a downloaded album or track, the lower retail price also means that the label generally pays lower royalties to the musicians for download sales than for CD or LP sales.

Digital broadcasts online and satellite and online radio were also new concepts for exposing listeners to music. After Sirius and XM, the two competing satellite services, merged to form Sirius XM, they acquired millions of listeners. Unlike terrestrial radio, satellite and internet radio pay royalties to the copyright owners and artists for the tracks they broadcast. That royalty rate is set by the Copy-

1. Impressed by this success, I ponied up a couple thousand dollars in dues and joined A2IM. I was quickly recruited to run for the organization's board of directors and served for six turbulent years (2007–2013), during which we saw the launch of streaming services, the consolidation of the multinational conglomerates into three giant companies, and battles to persuade digital services to pay rates that would allow independent labels to survive. In 2014, A2IM's membership voted to present its third Lifetime Achievement Award to me. Coming from my peers, it was one of the greatest honors I've received. A2IM continues to be a vital organization for America's independent music industry, though the high cost of membership makes it tough for the smallest labels to afford to join.
2. Song publishers pay the songwriters. The royalty that labels pay to song publishers is set by the Copyright Royalty Board, which is under the auspices of the Library of Congress. Labels pay the same amount to the song publishers for the sale of a downloaded track as they do for the sale of that track on a CD or LP. For a number of years, the rate for a song under five minutes has been .091 cents per sale, with additional amounts for each minute over five. The label and publisher, however, may negotiate a lower rate, which is called a controlled composition rate.

right Royalty Board. These royalties are paid to a nonprofit called Sound Exchange, which was founded to handle digital performance royalties for sound recordings. Sound Exchange splits the money between the labels and the musicians. For an independent label like Alligator, income from digital royalties can be substantial. Alligator receives more than one hundred and thirty thousand dollars a year from Sound Exchange. Like terrestrial broadcasters, the satellite and internet radio stations also pay a separate royalty for musical compositions to the three performance rights organizations—known by their abbreviations BMI, ASCAP, and SESAC—which in turn distribute these payments to song publishers and songwriters.[3]

Pandora is a different kind of digital music service—a music discovery service. It assumes that people want to hear music they haven't heard before. Pandora employees listen to music and decide which tracks from submitted albums to incorporate into their music database. Songs are categorized and coded so that they can be plugged into the algorithms (for example, "R&B with horns," "R&B without horns," "up-tempo R&B," "female vocal R&B," "group vocal R&B"). Listeners cannot choose which specific songs they will hear, but they can create so-called online radio stations named after their favorite artists. Pandora's algorithms find similar songs by other artists that Pandora thinks will match the listener's musical tastes. Like Sirius XM, Pandora is governed by the Digital Millennium Copyright Act. Its royalty rates are set by the Copyright Royalty Board. Pandora must pay a large portion of its income to copyright owners (usually labels) and to publishers. Like Sirius XM, Pandora pays royalties to Sound Exchange for artists and labels, and royalties to the performance rights organizations for song publishers and songwriters. Both Sirius XM and Pandora have been on a crusade for lower statutory rates so that they can pay less to the artists and labels. I've

---

3. Traditional broadcast radio stations do pay the performance rights organizations for the compositions they air. But in America, unlike almost every other country in the world, terrestrial radio is not required to pay the labels or the artists. Decades ago, the broadcasters convinced Congress that radio play was promotional for the artists and labels. The only other countries that don't require traditional broadcasters to pay artists and copyright holders for music are Iran and North Korea.

testified before the Copyright Royalty Board about the economics of running a small label when the board has periodically reconsidered Sirius XM's statutory royalty rate. The income received from digital broadcasters and discovery services is crucial to the future of labels like Alligator.[4]

In 2014, download sales through iTunes and other services began to flatten out. Sales have continued to shrink with the rise of on-demand streaming services like Spotify and Apple Music, which have become dominant forces in the digitized music industry. These streaming services have dramatically reduced the possibility for record labels and musicians alike to make a decent profit from their music.

Unlike Pandora's discovery service, on-demand streaming services assume that people want to hear music that they already know. Users can choose whatever songs or artists they want from these services' libraries. There are two levels of Spotify use: free, which forces the listener to listen to commercials, and subscription, which is commercial free. Apple Music operates on paid subscriptions only. Because users of Spotify and Apple Music can choose what songs they want to listen to and when the songs will be performed, those companies are not bound by any statutory royalty rate for the use of the recordings; no law covers this type of service. All their rates are negotiated. Spotify pays the record labels a percentage of both advertising and subscription income, while Apple Music pays a percentage of subscription income. The payment for each time a song is streamed, however, is tiny—typically between .002 and .008 cents per stream. From our perspective, they're simply too small to enable labels without mega-hits to survive. By a rough estimate, if one of our songs is streamed on Spotify 233 times, Alligator makes seventy cents, as much as if the same individual song is sold once on iTunes.

There is only one way that on-demand streaming services can generate enough money to pay labels an amount that covers the cost of

4. In 2018, in a major victory for the labels and artists, the Copyright Royalty Board raised Sirius XM's rate to be paid to Sound Exchange by about 40 percent. I'm hopeful that my testimony had some influence in this decision.

recording and promoting new music—by growing their subscriber base from millions to hundreds of millions. Income from streaming is growing for labels, but in Alligator's case, not nearly quickly enough to make up for the plummeting income from decreased physical and download sales. No one in the record business knows if the economics of streaming will succeed or fail for the labels. But one thing is certain: the labels' traditional practice of paying for the recording, paying the musicians, distributing the music, promoting the music, and selling the music, and then paying royalties to the artists and song publishers, is going to end.

It's also clear to me that physical and digital sales are ultimately doomed. At Alligator, we're being forced by declining CD sales to take a number of older titles out of print (that is, to cease manufacturing them), particularly those by musicians who are deceased or not touring, because without sales at live performances, it isn't economically viable to pay the higher prices for manufacturing small quantities of those recordings. It's emotionally painful for me, but it seems inevitable that sometime in the future we will have no more physical releases. But digital sales are falling too. Since 2011 Alligator's digital sales income declined by almost half as the public abandoned buying downloads and migrated to streaming services. The good news is that, ever since the advent of digital download sales and streaming services, our recordings can never go out of print. In the digital realm, with no manufacturing necessary, our music can remain available forever.

19

With the business instability, financial uncertainty, and flat sales that Alligator began facing early in the twenty-first century, we stepped up our efforts to support our artists and expand the audience for blues music. We were steadily releasing albums by our established stars, including Koko Taylor, Saffire — The Uppity Blues Women, Lil' Ed & The Blues Imperials, Little Charlie & The Nightcats, and Shemekia Copeland. We signed musicians who had established loyal fan bases while recording for other labels, like Texas roadhouse piano queen Marcia Ball, the gloriously gospel-tinged R&B trio the Holmes Brothers, and Albert Collins's protégé Coco Montoya, a soulful vocalist and the most elegantly lyrical of blues-rock guitar heroes. Loyal fans continued to buy them, and the label, though not growing, was holding steady. But I knew that there were not going to be many new artists who were as immersed in the tradition as those I had already recorded. With Corey Harris and Michael Hill, I had found that the mainstream blues audience, which was aging right along with me, was not always ready to embrace artists who pushed the boundaries of the genre.

It was time for me to find some artists who were carrying on the spirit of the blues, but who could excite an audience outside of the hard-core blues fans that Alligator was already reaching. I knew this could be tricky. I didn't want to lose the integrity of the Alligator brand. But I needed musicians who were creating fresh blues-based music and were reaching a new (and younger) audience.

Alligator's best-selling albums of the 2000s have been by JJ Grey & Mofro, presenting the songs of JJ, a singer, guitarist, and harmonica player from rural Florida. I had seen an early incarnation of the band, then just called Mofro, at the Springing the Blues Festival in Jacksonville Beach, Florida, sometime in the 1990s. JJ was a young white man who sang with so much grit and intensity that he forced me to pay attention. Almost all his songs were originals, some about the backwoods of Florida where he had grown up, some about country cooking, busted marriages, and politics, and some about songs of love and loss. JJ's vocal style could be called blue-eyed soul, but his voice also had a country twang. Some of the rhythms had the laid-back swampiness of Tony Joe White (famed for his 1968 hit "Polk Salad Annie"). But JJ was no mere imitator of songs or styles. His writing was his own, and the angst of his vocals and lyrics spoke to me. I asked my friend Sam Veal, the festival's producer, to introduce us.

JJ told me he had begun singing in soul cover bands in joints so rowdy that chicken wire had been stretched across the front of the stage to deflect flying bottles. While working in a lumberyard, he had begun to write his own songs, eventually putting together a band to perform them. He was a proudly blue-collar guy from a family that had been farming in Florida since before the Civil War. I liked him immediately.

But after that meeting, I didn't hear his name again for some years. I was unaware that he had cut two albums for a small Bay Area label, Fog City Records, owned by Dan Prothero, a meticulous producer. I didn't know that he had won a young (by Alligator standards, anyway) audience and that he could fill clubs and small theaters across the South. In late 2006, I got a call from JJ's manager, Jesse Aratow, asking if I'd be interested in releasing a new album JJ was working on. Remembering how I'd been struck by him in Florida, I said that I wanted to hear it as soon as possible. Meanwhile, JJ and his band were booked at a street fair in Chicago. I wanted to see his current band and also see how a northern big-city audience responded to his music. I went down to catch JJ's show along with some Alligator staff members.

My first surprise was the big camper parked behind the stage. Most of Alligator's artists travel by van, sometimes pulling a trailer. As the vans age, the artists themselves often improvise jerry-rigged repairs. (I remember Michael Burks doing a radio interview on his cell phone while he replaced the wheel bearings on his trailer by the side of the road.) JJ Grey seemed to be doing well for himself. When I saw him onstage, I understood why. He had the audience in the palm of his hand, playing biting lead guitar and funky keyboards and harmonica, singing in that drawling, raspy voice, and telling stories to set up each song. The band responded to his every nuance, building up driving soul beats, then bringing the volume down for an intimate ballad. I was amazed that the audience of around four hundred was singing along and calling requests. JJ's label was obscure, and he had never played a major Chicago venue or gotten radio play in the city. Yet many in the audience knew the lyrics, especially "Lochloosa," a song in praise of a lake near his home in the swampy backwoods near Jacksonville:

> *Every mosquito, every rattlesnake*
> *Every cane break, everything*
> *Every alligator, every blackwater swamp*
> *Every freshwater spring, everything*
> *All we need is one more damn developer*
> *Tearing her heart out . . .*
> *Homesick but it's all right*
> *Lochloosa, she's on my mind*
> *On my mind*

The songs for his new album knocked me out. They ranged from raucous rockers to beautifully produced, whispering ballads. The funky band was augmented with horns and, on a few tracks, strings. There was enough blues feel for Alligator, but it also seemed accessible to a wider audience. Taking a leap of faith—and based on the fact that his small-label albums had sold almost twenty thousand copies each without much distribution, marketing, or advertising—I made an offer that I felt confident he and his manager would accept. It was a lot of money, but this was an artist who had built a devoted fan base with little media attention. He had done it the Alligator way—cutting memorable, soulful records and delivering killer performances night after night.

We released JJ Grey & Mofro's Alligator debut, *Country Ghetto*, in February 2007. A cross-country tour followed, with radio station visits and in-store performances. Our publicity team of Marc Lipkin and Chris Levick set up dozens of interviews, and JJ did them all. We brought on an independent radio promoter to augment the work of Alligator's radio promotion staffers Tim Kolleth and Matt LaFollette. Rather than trying to market JJ as a bluesman, we cast him more as a southern singer-songwriter/rocker. By the 2000s, blues had been pegged by the media as the music of older generations, but JJ Grey & Mofro didn't have that onus. Just as Johnny Winter had brought Alligator to the rock audience in the 1980s, JJ brought Alligator to a younger rock–jam band audience.

Country Ghetto sold better than any Alligator release in some years, eventually approaching ninety thousand copies. Over the next seven years, we released four more JJ Grey & Mofro albums (and reissued his first two Mofro releases) as JJ continued to build a larger and larger audience through relentless touring both in the United States and overseas. None of the other releases sold quite as well as *Country Ghetto*. But without them, it would have been much tougher to weather the years when thousands of record stores worldwide were closing their doors.

The success of JJ Grey & Mofro created credibility for us outside the blues world. I found two other roots musicians who reached much the same audience and had some real success on Alligator. Eric Lindell is a singer-songwriter who grew up in northern California and honed his songwriting style in New Orleans. He blends blues, roots rock, a bit of country, and old-school New Orleans R&B into a laid-back, loose sound. His best songs are instantly memorable, and with his relaxed, off-the-cuff "slacker" stage personality and ever-changing repertoire, fans (I'm one of them) have fallen in love with both the music and the man. In 2006, we released his Alligator debut, made up of the best tracks he had produced for his previous self-released albums. We also hooked him up with a booking agent, who helped get Eric in front of a national audience, where he won a whole new fan base.

Anders Osborne also came out of New Orleans. He had recorded on various labels in the past and was a hero in his hometown. But he was also a troubled soul whose well-known battles with substance abuse had nearly destroyed his career. When Anders came out of rehab in 2009, his manager convinced me to fly to New Orleans to see him at the famous Tipitina's club. Anders was a mesmerizing musician, playing white-hot electric guitar (which I found out later was in open D tuning, most commonly used by Delta blues musicians) while almost hurling himself around the stage. Accompanied only by drums and a tuba playing bass lines, he sang as though the songs were being wrenched out of him. Many of his songs were about his addiction and recovery. I signed Anders, and we released an album he had been working on called *American Patchwork* that included songs like "Darkness at the Bottom" and "Echoes of My Sins," both intensely emotional outcries that I found very moving.

We released five albums by JJ Grey & Mofro and three albums each by Eric Lindell and Anders Osborne, and then parted company with each for reasons that had nothing to do with their music. JJ was looking for a label with stronger distribution in Europe; he signed with the Belgian-based Mascot/Provogue label but cut only one album for them. Eric found us too demanding. Anders chose to release albums on his own. Though JJ and Anders are no longer with the label, we have maintained friendly relations with them. I hope they might return to Alligator someday. Eric Lindell re-signed with Alligator in 2018, after self-releasing five albums. I'm proud of JJ's, Eric's, and Anders's Alligator releases. Their blues-inspired roots rock fits the spirit of the label.

All the time that I had been adapting to major changes in the industry, I had also been scouting for talent. Roots rock artists brought Alligator a new audience. But I didn't want to miss out on emerging blues talent or miss hearing about an established or developing blues musician whose contract with another label had expired. Since 1990, we've signed a number of established artists who were produced by someone other than me or who acted as their own producers. But, being a control freak, I've supervised or watched over every Alligator album that I didn't personally produce, making sure I'm satisfied with the choices of songs, studios, engineers, and producers.

We signed the long-established and much-recorded "little big band" Roomful of Blues, who, like the Holmes Brothers and Marcia Ball, had recorded extensively for Rounder. Coco Montoya and Tommy Castro joined Alligator after cutting multiple successful albums for Blind Pig Records. Guitar Shorty, a six-string legend, had recorded for a number of labels, including Black Top. W. C. Clark, known as the Godfather of Austin Blues, cut two albums for us after recording for Black Top. Soul and blues vocalist and harmonica player Curtis Salgado, an original member of the Robert Cray Band, had recorded for Shanachie. Passionate blues and soul singer Janiva Magness came to us after recording for Northern Blues. San Francisco–born blues guitar and vocal giant Joe Louis Walker cut two Alligator albums after a long career recording for HighTone, Universal, and Stony Plain. James Cotton returned to Alligator after a twenty-five-year hiatus, during which he had recorded for Verve and Telarc. Tinsley Ellis rejoined the Alligator roster after cutting albums for both Capricorn and Telarc. Elvin Bishop re-signed with Alligator after spending fifteen years with other labels. We reignited the career of Mavis Staples, the gospel and R&B legend, with a single-album release in 2004. We even released two fine roots rockabilly albums by former Stray Cats bassist Lee Rocker. Of all the signings of established artists who had been on other labels, there was only one act that I produced—the Dallas-based team of pyrotechnic guitar hero Smokin' Joe Kubek and singer-guitarist Bnois King, who had previously recorded for Blind Pig.

Not all of these artists stayed with Alligator. It's normal for musicians to think that another label will offer a better deal or raise their career to new heights. And sometimes the personalities of the musicians and the culture of the label just don't mesh. Some of the artists who came to Alligator during the 2000s left us later on, but only Mavis Staples earned significantly greater acclaim and sales with another label. Shemekia Copeland, Coco Montoya, Elvin Bishop, Eric Lindell, and Tinsley Ellis each cut multiple successful albums for Alligator, then released albums on other labels, and returned to Alligator after the grass on the other side of the fence turned out to be not so green. Even while they were recording for our competitors, we all remained friendly, and we went to see them whenever they played in Chicago.

20

Having so many well-established and popular blues and roots musicians on Alligator has kept both our musical quality and visibility high. It's given me great satisfaction that these artists have trusted us and felt we were giving them the support they deserved. But the most fulfilling projects for me are those where I see great promise in a musician and feel that Alligator could help realize his or her potential. Four of these developing artists became personal missions for me in the 2000s—Michael "Iron Man" Burks, Selwyn Birchwood, Jarekus Singleton, and Toronzo Cannon. All of them played guitar, but the paths that led them to the blues were vastly different.

Michael Burks grew up in a blues family. His grandfather was a Delta blues guitarist. His father and teacher, Frederick Burks, had played bass with Sonny Boy Williamson II when the family was living in Milwaukee, Michael's birthplace. A child prodigy, Michael began playing guitar at the age of four. His father had challenged Michael to learn new songs by offering a dollar reward for each one, but soon he was going broke paying his precocious son. Eventually the family returned to Frederick's hometown of Camden, Arkansas, where Frederick and his sons built a three-hundred-seat concrete-block roadhouse at the edge of town, calling it the Bradley Ferry Country Club. Camden, though small, was a regular stop on the chitlin' circuit, where popular touring blues and R&B acts would play one-nighters. As a teenager, Michael led the house band at the club and had to be prepared to play virtually every type of popular black music, from down-home blues to James Brown–style funk to sweet ballads. He didn't sing much, but he became a killer guitar player.

Then, in his early twenties, Michael married and became a father. Devoted to his daughter Brittney, he put his guitar under the bed for thirteen years and got a factory job. It was only after his daughter was almost an adult and Michael was almost forty that he returned to music. He began gigging locally and then, as the buzz grew, played small clubs across the South. In 1994, while still holding down his day job, Michael competed in the International Blues Challenge, the contest organized and promoted by the Blues Foundation in Memphis. I vaguely remember seeing him there, but at the time dismissed him as being too much under the influence of Albert King.[1]

In 2000, Michael was booked on one of the smaller stages of the Chicago Blues Festival. His manager begged me to come to the show. I told him that I'd be there but that I wasn't signing anyone new because Alligator's roster was full. That afternoon, I saw a musician transformed. A big, burly man, Michael tore into the strings of his Gibson Flying V guitar, playing and singing with undeniable passion and grit. He was soaked in sweat. His band could hardly keep up with him. His energy and intensity reminded me of the late Freddie King, one of the most powerful bluesmen ever. Although I was hesitant to sign an artist with a low national profile, my gut overruled my head. I went backstage to meet Michael and his manager. Michael deferred to the manager, speaking little and framing his words carefully and slowly in the manner of so many people from small southern towns. I could tell that he was a no-bullshit straight shooter. But he showed almost no emotion, even when I complimented his performance. It seemed like he didn't know how to smile. It took a long time for me to earn his trust and for him to open up to me.

Over the next few weeks, we negotiated a recording deal. I knew Michael didn't have many original songs, but by this time I had col-

1. Because of his ability to combine signature string bending with funky, danceable Memphis soul grooves and storytelling vocals, Albert King remained popular with black audiences longer than B. B. King did. In the 1990s, black blues guitarists were more likely to perform songs by Albert King than by any other artist.

lected more than two thousand songs that I thought worthy of re-cording. I gathered about seventy of these and sent them to Michael to see if any of them resonated with him. A few weeks later, I traveled to Arkansas and we hashed out a song list for his Alligator debut. He had three original songs—one was a soulful ballad; another had lyrics written by Shemekia Copeland's manager, John Hahn; and the third was a raw, down-home blues Michael had written with his father. The other nine tunes were ones he had chosen from the songs I had sent to him.

We recorded in Memphis at Ardent Studios, where I had cut C. J. Chenier. We agreed that the touring band Michael had at that time wasn't really studio quality, so I recruited three Memphis musicians who had recorded with Luther Allison—David Smith on bass, Steve Potts on drums, and Ernest "Blues Bear" Williamson on keys. I also asked my old friend Vasti Jackson to come up from Mississippi and play rhythm guitar. To complete the Luther Allison connection, I called on Jim Gaines, who had produced both Luther and Coco Montoya, to help us in the studio. A laid-back, affable southerner, Jim had started as an engineer and musician and later earned his reputation as the producer of Steve Miller, Santana, and Stevie Ray Vaughan. He had also produced some of the best contemporary blues records. I was in awe of him, though he carried himself like a regular guy.

Michael's guitar playing in the studio was consistently searing, but he was clearly less comfortable as a singer. As he explained, he had been a guitarist since he was a child but a singer for only a few years. Jim patiently coaxed and coached Michael, offering constant encour-agement even as Michael struggled nervously, his voice sometimes cracking. Jim probably showed more patience with Michael's vocals than I would have, and his positive attitude paid off (a good learning experience for me). We rehearsed and recorded *Make It Rain*, one of the strongest Alligator debut albums ever, in just a few days. The potential I heard in Michael had become reality. *Guitar Edge* maga-zine declared it one of the one hundred best guitar albums of all time. I quickly connected Michael with a good booking agent who specialized in blues, and his career as a national and international touring artist was launched.

Like every blues musician, Michael had to prove himself in the crucible of live performance. He played clubs across the country, insisting on driving the van himself, often for hundreds of miles without a break. He'd load in his own gear and, like Luther Allison, play shows so long that he left audiences exhausted. Night after night, gig after gig, he built his own confidence onstage and won a loyal following. He became a headliner at the annual King Biscuit Blues Festival, presented on the levee of the Mississippi River in Helena, Arkansas, and began touring Europe regularly.

In 2003, I traveled down to Camden, where Michael was taking care of his dying father, Frederick, to help plan Michael's second Alligator album, *I Smell Smoke*. Michael adored his father, who had mentored him so well. I got a chance to tell Frederick how Michael's fan base was growing, and about the great future I saw for him. I wanted to be sure that he knew that his son was proudly carrying on his legacy. During that weeklong visit, I felt that Michael was beginning to trust me. While Michael and I worked together on writing and choosing songs, he drove me around Camden and told tales of his childhood that revealed his sentimental, vulnerable side. He showed me where a tough bootlegger named Miss Mercy[2] had lived, and he recalled the cab driver who would deliver Miss Mercy's moonshine in the trunk of his car. Laughing, he told me that as boys, he and his cousin found a stash of corn liquor in his grandmother's home and drank themselves sick. He also told me about his gun-toting Cajun grandfather, who scared everyone around, white as well as black. When the songs were ready, I called on Jim Gaines to help us in the studio again, and we hired the same top-flight Memphis musicians who had done such a terrific job on *Make It Rain*.

While in Chicago in 2007, Michael landed in jail for an offense for which he could have been released with only a warning. I spent four-

---

2. Michael cowrote a song about Miss Mercy with John Hahn, and we included it on the album.

teen hours of my sixtieth birthday bailing him out of Cook County Jail, then feeding him at an all-night diner and bringing him back to my home to recover. This was Michael's first time behind bars, and he was deeply shaken by the experience; I had never before seen him so scared. I hired a good lawyer for him (former Alligator employee Richard McLeese), who over many months extricated Michael from his legal problems and made sure he had no criminal record that would bar him from touring overseas. Michael finally understood that being part of the Alligator family meant a lot more than just having a friendly business relationship. We had bonded.

As we got closer personally, Michael and I felt ready to coproduce his third album on our own in Chicago, without the help of Jim Gaines or studio musicians. I found a gap in Michael's touring schedule in November 2007 and brought his road-tested band (Jerome "Popcorn" Louden on drums, Wayne Sharp on keys, and Don Garrett on bass) to Chicago. With only four days in the studio, we cut twelve songs. The very experienced engineer Blaise Barton and I were determined to capture the feel of Michael's shows, recording and mixing his guitar super-hot, just like he played it live. About this time, a blues society publication in Buffalo ran a feature on Michael. The writer dubbed him "The Iron Man from Arkansas" because he was famous for playing hours-long sets (festivals learned to put him on last, as he would often play for three hours without a break) and then driving all night to his next gig. The nickname stuck. We released *Iron Man* in April 2008 to universal acclaim. With three of Michael's original compositions and four that he had cowritten, the album represented his most personal statement yet. Working as a team, he and I felt we had created his best recording.

It took another three years to get him back in the studio for his fourth Alligator album; he was constantly on the road. We again had to record during a short break in his relentless touring schedule, with rehearsals in the Alligator warehouse. We cut the whole album in six intense twelve-hour studio days. A few weeks later, Michael returned with a pair of hot new amplifiers, insisting on redoing every rhythm guitar part and re-recording three or four takes of every solo, as well as re-recording half the vocals on the album. It was a grueling test for him, but his playing and singing actually got better each day. Trusting my judgment after three albums, he left me to supervise the mixes and drove 650 miles straight back to Arkansas. I spent long nights in the studio sifting through his solos, sometimes combining parts of different takes to feature his most electrifying playing. The results were stunning; he had exceeded his already high standards. As mixes were finished, I emailed them to him for approval.

In April 2012, Michael and the band headed to Europe for a three-week tour. I had been worrying about his health for a long time; he had gained a huge amount of weight, mostly by eating to stay awake on his all-night drives from gig to gig, and he suffered from sleep apnea, which he refused to have treated. Michael left for the tour exhausted and sick. As it went on, he felt so bad that he had to perform sitting down, which was totally against his nature. On May 6, 2012, while changing planes in Atlanta, he collapsed and died. The official cause of death was heart attack, but the likely cause was deep vein thrombosis, a blood clot from sitting too long in one position on the plane. He was only fifty-four, and his most creative and successful years were still ahead of him. I finished the mixes, and we released his final album, *Show of Strength*, in August 2012. Ironically, the last song recorded for the album was "Feel Like Going Home," Charlie Rich's classic song sung from the point of view of a man weary with life. Michael thought it was the best thing he had ever recorded.

That October, at the King Biscuit Blues Festival's campground, where Michael had loved to come with his camper and spend the week hosting and cooking for friends and fans, we had a gathering to pay tribute. His wife, Bobbie, whom he had met at the festival, buried some of his ashes there. It seemed like he really was home. I miss him every day.

Michael Burks was the last blues artist on Alligator to have grown up immersed in the blues culture, just like Hound Dog Taylor, Son Seals, and Fenton Robinson had before him. Michael hadn't learned just from records; he had learned from listening to real African American blues artists playing in their own communities, carrying on the tradition that had started hundreds of years before. I doubt that another musician will come to the label so deeply rooted in the traditional blues way of life.

The Blues Foundation's International Blues Challenge,[3] held in Memphis each year in late January, was where I found two of the most promising younger-generation bluesmen—Selwyn Birchwood and Jarekus Singleton.

I first saw Selwyn when he made the finals of the 2012 Challenge at the Orpheum Theatre. A very tall, slender, baby-faced young man in his twenties with a giant Afro, he was backed by three older musicians with the unusual lineup of bass, drums, and baritone sax. He performed all original songs with immense energy and confidence, alternating between fiery electric guitar (showing the influence of Albert Collins and Buddy Guy) and slide-propelled lap steel guitar. He sang in a slightly gravelly voice older than his years, and he clearly knew how to tell a story with his lyrics. I bought his self-produced CD in the lobby and sought him out for a conversation. I found him earnest, outgoing, straightforward, intelligent, and very much driven to succeed.

Selwyn grew up in central Florida, taking up guitar as a young teenager and playing the music of rock bands like Metallica, the Red Hot Chili Peppers, and Alice in Chains until the simplicity of the music bored him. Then he discovered the transformative music of Jimi Hendrix. His exploration of Hendrix's influences led him to the blues and musicians like Elmore James, Muddy Waters, Buddy Guy, and Howlin' Wolf. "Once I heard the blues guys," he told me, "it was like I finally found the sound that I was searching for, and a music

3. Founded in 1980, the Blues Foundation is an organization of blues fans and blues societies, with more than four thousand members. The foundation presents two major events: the International Blues Challenge, which takes place at multiple clubs in the Beale Street area of Memphis, usually in January, with the finals at the Orpheum Theatre; and the Blues Music Awards, which are presented at the Memphis Convention Center in May. A four-hour event, the BMAs include more than twenty mini-sets by nominated musicians. In addition, the Blues Foundation created and operates the Blues Hall of Fame in Memphis. Alligator artists and albums have received more than one hundred Blues Music Awards.

that I could truly relate to." His live blues baptism was a Buddy Guy concert that he attended when he was eighteen. Then and there he committed to becoming a blues musician.

Shortly after, Selwyn heard about an old bluesman who was rehearsing with friends in a neighbor's garage. The "old bluesman" turned out to be Sonny Rhodes (born Clarence Smith), a Texas blues journeyman only in his sixties. Sonny took a liking to the serious young Selwyn and invited him to spend the summer in his road band. From Sonny, Selwyn learned the ins and outs of leading a band and how to survive on the road playing for minimal money. He also got his first lessons in how to play the lap steel guitar, an instrument not often heard in blues music. While in college and graduate school (he holds a master's degree in business administration), Selwyn spent almost every summer on the road as Sonny's right arm. Selwyn started his own band in his early twenties, recruiting veteran players to support him. He quickly built a local touring circuit in Florida and began writing his own material. When I met him he was already working on songs for his second self-released CD.

Throughout the following year Selwyn sent his new songs to me for my input. Some of them were in rough demo form, but others were professionally recorded. I suggested some places where I felt he could improve his lyrics, and he responded by writing new and better ones. By the time I returned for the International Blues Challenge in 2013, I was seriously considering signing him. Even better than the year before, he beat 150 other groups to win both the band competition and the Gibson Guitar Award. Shortly after, I flew down to Florida to hear a full evening's performance. He not only played and sang with real authority, but his unassuming, casual stage personality won over the audience. He made us feel like we were in his living room. Halfway through the performance, he kicked off his shoes and performed the rest of the night barefoot. At the end of the show, in the tradition of Lil' Ed and J. B. Hutto, he climbed onto the bar while playing and walked its length without disturbing a single glass. The audience went wild.

We kept in touch, and over the next few months he sent more

visionary and well-crafted songs to me. They ranged from tall tales of voodoo men in the swamps and scenes in raucous juke joints to serious compositions about alcoholism and suicide. I brought him to Chicago to meet the Alligator staff, and we hashed out a record deal. He went back to Florida with enough financing from Alligator to professionally record the rest of his songs, then brought the tracks up to Chicago where we mixed them together with engineer Blaise Barton. Alligator released Selwyn's Alligator debut, *Don't Call No Ambulance*, in June 2014. By then, he had a good booking agent and was crisscrossing the country, playing anywhere and everywhere, winning fans both in the United States and in Europe.

In 2017, we released his second album, *Pick Your Poison*. It was a giant artistic step forward, full of striking original songs that ranged from raw rockers to solo acoustic tunes. He sang about serious topics like police brutality and soul-killing jobs, then turned around and delivered a hilarious song about drunken texting, followed by a gospel-styled rave-up about religious hypocrisy called "Even the Saved Need Saving." He took more chances than before with his music, pushing the blues envelope with songs that didn't follow traditional blues structures or lyrics but still *felt* like the blues. Selwyn Birchwood is fulfilling all the promise I first heard in him. It's clear that he will emerge as one of the crucial blues musicians of his generation.

At the same 2013 International Blues Challenge that Selwyn won, I spotted another young talent. Though he didn't make the finals, Jarekus Singleton revealed himself as a bluesman of real potential. If Selwyn's onstage persona made you feel like you were in his living room, Jarekus's presence was almost threatening. Standing six-foot-three with an athlete's build, he worked the stage like a stalking lion, performing a set of audacious originals that blended blues, soul, rock, and funk. His vocals, although not as good as his guitar playing and songwriting, definitely had authority. I wanted to hear more.

A few weeks later I flew down to his hometown of Jackson, Mississippi, to get to know him and see him perform in a club. I found him to be an intense, serious young man who spoke quietly and modestly but carried himself with a bit of streetwise swagger. I learned that he had started out playing bass in church at age nine and learned quickly by playing three services a week. At the same time, he began playing basketball and quickly became a high school star. He fell in love with rap and began writing his own rap lyrics. He told me later that many of his raps expressed anger at his distant, judgmental father.

When Jarekus was fifteen, his uncle took him to a Jackson nightspot where he heard a local bluesman performing Albert King's "I'll Play the Blues for You." Jarekus was instantly hooked. He had already switched from bass to guitar. He began learning blues tunes on the sly because his religious family considered blues to be the devil's music. But basketball was the center of his life and his potential career. He was recruited by the University of Southern Mississippi, where he became a star point guard. He had tryouts with two NBA teams but was never drafted. Then a bad jump shot shattered the bones in his ankle. He returned home, his dreams destroyed, and slept on his mother's couch for weeks while his ankle healed. It was then that he picked up his guitar again, and the first song that he chose to play was "I'll Play the Blues for You."

Jarekus soon began writing his own blues tunes, often combining rap-style rhyming with funk rhythms and rock energy, all punctuated with blues string bending. Because he had never learned standard blues tunes and chord progressions, he created melodies that were influenced by blues but took unusual twists. He put together a band whose core members had played with him in church and began promoting his own shows in Jackson. He was clearly smart, driven, and determined to make his own musical statements.

At the club gig I attended, he commanded the room, delivering a mix of originals along with familiar soul, rock, and reggae tunes. But his vocals didn't match his musicianship. He had a strong voice but couldn't sustain his notes long enough. Sometimes, when he bent his vocal pitches—a crucial part of blues singing—he didn't quite hit the notes he was reaching for. When we talked after the show, I told him his singing had to improve. I suggested he find a vocal coach to teach him breath control and improve his pitches.

Within weeks I began receiving demos from Jarekus that showed me he had taken me seriously. His singing was dramatically improved. He began sending more original songs. His images were fresh, but he had a tendency to cram a lot of words into a verse. Some of his rap-style songs were startling because the rhymes fell in the middle of the line rather than at the end.

I brought him to Chicago, where we holed up in a motel room, honed his songs, and got to know each other. I encouraged him to write some new verses, simplify some of his lyrics, and fit the words more closely to the meter of the songs. But he told me that the main revelation my coaching gave him was that rap songs focused primarily on how cool the rapper was, what he owned, and whom he had sex with, and how often. Blues lyrics, on the other hand, were about how the life experiences, troubles, and triumphs of the singer were like those of the audience. His songwriting had turned a corner; the good songs were coming fast and furious. We cut an exciting demo session in Memphis in the fall of 2013 with his tight, well-rehearsed band. Impressed by his vision and professionalism, I signed him.[4]

We released his Alligator debut, *Refuse to Lose*, in May 2014, a month before Selwyn's album. Coming back to back, they made a public statement about Alligator's commitment to the new generation of blues and announced our belief that these two young men were among the most important and promising of the up-and-coming blues artists.

---

4. Exhilarated by the success of the Memphis sessions and inspired by what Jarekus had taught me about rap songwriting, I tried writing a song for him, and he loved it. I had written songs with Kenny Neal, Lil' Ed, Katie Webster, and Michael Burks, but I consider the lyrics I wrote for Jarekus among my best. Using the metaphor of police procedural TV shows, I titled the song "Crime Scene." Jarekus also insisted that I be credited on the album as coauthor of the other songs to which I had contributed lyrics. I decided to use my songwriter pen name, Harrison Sumner. It's a tribute to my mother, Harriett Iglauer (I'm "Harriett's son"), and the outspoken abolitionist senator Charles Sumner. My paternal grandfather was named Charles Sumner Iglauer in tribute to the senator.

Unlike Selwyn, Jarekus had no touring experience. He needed my help finding a booking agent and establishing himself on the national and international scene. We talked almost daily as I taught him how to budget road trips, set pay rates for the band, find the best routes from show to show, and deal with settlement payments from the booking agency. We shared our excitement about every successful gig and our disappointment when audience turnout was smaller than we hoped. I liked being needed and depended on. Jarekus shared that he felt closer to me than he ever had to his father. Having grown up without a father, I was very moved.

Jarekus was delivering killer live performances and gaining a reputation as one of the most energized and original new faces in blues. But as the months passed, he became more and more concerned that he was not reaching a younger and blacker audience. He urged me to send his album to some hip-hop radio stations and shows. I tried to explain to him that without songs that sounded more like what those stations were playing and concerted, expensive independent promotion, his music had no hope with those programmers. It wasn't what he wanted to hear.

As the time for planning the second album approached, he began asking to write and record it completely on his own. Like most of Alligator's artist agreements, his contract called for mutual approval of all songs, producer, studio, recorded performances, and mixes. He had grown as an artist, but I didn't think he was ready to write and produce his own record. I felt that he was still finding his way musically.

He sent some demo recordings of his new songs. When the Alligator staff and I heard them, we thought that the songs contained good ideas but were far from finished, and far from the blues. The lyrics weren't as compelling as those he had written for *Refuse to Lose*, and it seemed like he was moving from funky, hard-edged blues into mellow soul. I didn't think that the devoted blues audience he had won over would respond to this new material. I asked him to keep working on these songs, knowing that the rewrites I had asked for had improved the songs on *Refuse to Lose*. Instead, he dug in and declared that the songs were finished.

I was heartbroken; I felt like one of my sons had renounced the family heritage and spurned his father. Jarekus had come to Alligator proudly declaring his desire to be a bluesman. Now it seemed he wanted to be something else. In 2017, he asked me for a release from his contract, and I gave it to him.

By the end of the 1990s, I wasn't hearing many new Chicago artists who excited me. Not a lot of significant new talent had arisen in the city. One reason was that in the North Side clubs, blues had become, to a great extent, tourist music. Clubs like Buddy Guy's Legends catered to busloads of tourists who wanted to visit a "real Chicago blues club" for an hour or two and call requests for the few blues songs they knew. One club insisted that every band include a female vocalist and that the all-too-familiar warhorses be performed each night. The musicians, who had to make a living, generally bent to the pressure and began performing what they called "the set list from hell"—songs like "Stormy Monday," "Got My Mojo Working," "Hoochie Coochie Man," "Mustang Sally," and the dreaded "Sweet Home Chicago." Artists who had their own albums could at least mix their originals in with standards, but for the unrecorded, there was little reward in trying to perform original or fresh material. I got tired of hearing local musicians perform the same songs and started going to the clubs less frequently, usually only if an Alligator artist was performing or if one of the city's exceptional talents, like Jimmy Johnson or Lurrie Bell, had a gig.

One local bluesman I had seen, both as a sideman and occasionally performing with his own band, was left-handed guitarist Toronzo Cannon. I had considered him a good Chicago blues journeyman, solid player, and singer who performed a lot of those same familiar blues songs and sometimes delivered a good version of a Jimi Hendrix tune. In 2013, Toronzo called and asked if he could take me to lunch. By then, he had a self-released album and had been signed to Delmark Records by producer Steve Wagner. Delmark had released two albums by Toronzo. Each one showed promise and musical growth, including some fresh, well-crafted original songs along with more mundane ones.

During our lunch, Toronzo asked me a lot of questions about the record business. I found him to be a smart, likable, self-effacing, and outgoing man with a quick wit. In addition to being a musician, he drove a bus for the Chicago Transit Authority. He had been brought up on the South Side by his grandparents, who were blues fans, and he had started playing guitar in his early twenties. First attracted to reggae, he starting attending blues jams and found his musical home. In his midforties, he had been playing the blues circuit for almost twenty years, and appeared regularly at Kingston Mines, B.L.U.E.S. on Halsted, and Harlem Avenue Lounge in Berwyn. After a series of enjoyable lunches, Toronzo asked me if I would listen to some of his new songs. I invited him to my house for an evening meeting.

His new songs excited me. He was singing about subjects few other blues musicians were dealing with, including life on the city streets. For months after that, we met weekly in my home for song-honing sessions.[5] I pushed him to move further away from standard blues structures and rhythms. A keen observer of human nature with a sense of humor, he created songs about ruthless divorce lawyers, male midlife crises, and the joys of mature women. His years of living and working in Chicago's toughest neighborhoods had developed his social conscience, which he compressed into a song called "The Pain around Me." Whenever his vocals showed off his vibrato and

---

5. Writing effective blues songs is a challenge. Most blues is performed in clubs and noisy environments, where a song with a simple chorus, like "Hoochie Coochie Man," will get a good response. But for home listeners or radio programmers, blues anthems with repeated choruses or hook lines that may work well in bars can seem overly simple as compared to songs created by contemporary singer-songwriters. When I'm coaching blues songwriters, I often point to three very well-written songs that I feel have just the right amount of wordiness to work both in a blues bar and on record: "Gypsy Woman," by Muddy Waters; "It's Raining," written by Allen Toussaint (under the pen name Naomi Neville) and performed by Irma Thomas; and "Black Nights," by Lowell Fulson. All three are like short movies, with memorable visual images, well-crafted rhymes, and hook lines.

pitch bending, I complimented him. He quickly figured out what I liked and explained it by saying, "You want me to put more church in my singing." When we weren't working on his songs, we discussed politics, current events, racial issues, and the state of the world.

I still hadn't signed Toronzo. Since the virtual disappearance of record stores, the game plan of Alligator has been to create as much publicity, radio, and other media attention for every Alligator artist's live shows. Most of our artists were performing between 75 and 125 shows a year, playing mostly in clubs during the colder months and at festivals and outdoor events during the summers. Toronzo was driving a bus four days a week on ten-hour shifts. With a wife and daughter to support, he couldn't give up a day job that provided not only a steady paycheck but also health insurance. With astounding stamina, he would often play the Chicago clubs from 9 p.m. to 1 a.m., go home and sleep for three hours, and then head to the bus barn for a day of driving. We needed our musicians to tour nationally and internationally. His schedule seemed to make that impossible.

But the quality of his new songs, his growth as a singer, and his magnetic stage personality (as well as my personal liking and respect for him) overcame my business considerations and I brought Toronzo into the Alligator family. After much rehearsal, we cut his album in a few days, sticking with the tight recording budgets that are the new normal for Alligator. Toronzo is proud to be an inheritor of the Chicago blues tradition, so at his suggestion, we called the album *The Chicago Way*. Released in February 2016, it was named the number one blues album of the year by England's *Mojo* magazine and album of the year by *Living Blues* magazine's readers' poll, and it garnered four Blues Music Award nominations.

Toronzo is now being represented by a well-established booking agent, and I'm helping him with tour planning, just as I helped Jarekus Singleton. Toronzo won an audience in Europe, traveling there seven times in the year after the album's release. Because of his bus-driving schedule, he sometimes flies overseas on a Thursday, plays Friday and Saturday, returns Sunday, and is back driving the bus on Monday morning. For gigs in the United States, it isn't unusual for him to get up at 3 a.m. on a Friday, drive five hundred miles, play, drive another four or five hundred miles, play again, and then drive home on Sunday. In the first year after the release of *The Chicago Way*, his indefatigable work ethic resulted in eighty-four live performances. To see him go from playing weeknights at the Harlem Avenue Lounge to playing for tens of thousands of cheering fans at the Chicago Blues Festival and headlining the Great British Rock & Blues Festival has been a huge source of satisfaction for me.

As I had dreamed for Michael Burks, Toronzo Cannon is becoming one of the blues icons of his generation. His most creative and successful years are still ahead of him, and I'm confident that he will soon be recognized as one of the blues world's stars. I take special pride in the fact that Toronzo's talent was honed on the ultra-competitive Chicago club scene. He reaffirmed my belief in my adopted hometown's ability to nurture fresh and original blues talent. I hope that more local artists will arise to make their own statements—artists like Toronzo who are proud to carry forward the Chicago blues tradition without repeating what's already been done.

EPILOGUE

In the summer of 2018, Alligator's roster included established artists like Marcia Ball, Tommy Castro, Elvin Bishop, Coco Montoya, Shemekia Copeland, Lil' Ed & The Blues Imperials, Roomful of Blues, Curtis Salgado, Corky Siegel, Rick Estrin & The Nightcats, and Eric Lindell, along with rising artists like Selwyn Birchwood, Toronzo Cannon, and the recently signed Cash Box Kings, Nick Moss Band Featuring Dennis Gruenling, and singer/drummer Lindsay Beaver.

Many of the artists who were crucial to the Alligator story—Hound Dog Taylor & The HouseRockers, Big Walter Horton, Carey Bell, Son Seals, Fenton Robinson, Koko Taylor, Lonnie Brooks, Albert Collins, Professor Longhair, Johnny Otis, Johnny Winter, James Cotton, Roy Buchanan, Lonnie Mack, Big Twist, Katie Webster, Luther Allison, and more—have died. Alligator has created a great legacy, but my focus is always on the future.

I continue to seek out blues artists who have the vision, energy, and professionalism to be part of the Alligator family. Recognizing that the blues must remain relevant to younger audiences, I'm also looking for more blues-inspired roots artists with depth and musical integrity, like JJ Grey & Mofro and Anders Osborne.

I had assumed that by this point, the future of the label, with its three hundred releases and forty-six-year history, would have been secure. Instead Alligator is struggling. We are very aware that our customer demographic has aged, and much of our artists' audiences are in their fifties and sixties. They are resistant to new technologies for experiencing music, even as the old technologies are fading away. When we polled about one thousand members of our email fan list in 2017, we learned that their preferred method of listening to music was still CDs, followed by vinyl, then digital downloads, and, lastly, streaming services.

Declining CD sales have forced Alligator to take certain titles out of print because of the high cost of manufacturing them in smaller quantities to meet shrinking demand. The much-publicized vinyl boom has not resulted in a dramatic increase in sales; the dozen titles Alligator has released on vinyl have each sold from seven hundred to two thousand copies worldwide. Music industry professionals predict that iTunes and other download stores will eventually shut down as listeners increasingly turn to streaming services like Spotify and Apple Music. If our audience doesn't adapt to the new technology for accessing music and simply stays at home listening to their current music collections, Alligator won't make enough money to release new albums. We must either inspire a new, younger generation of fans or face becoming a catalog of existing recordings that generate small amounts of income as new listeners discover our old music.

Many of our former indie label competitors have given up on the blues. Rounder Records, sold to the huge Concord label group, is no longer releasing blues titles. Blind Pig, the independent label that released some of the finest blues recordings of the past thirty-five years, was sold in 2015 and is now only a catalog of existing recordings. Likewise, Arhoolie Records, founded by my hero Chris Strachwitz, has been sold to the Smithsonian Institution, and although its catalog will be preserved and the label operated by the staff of Smithsonian Folkways Records, I doubt there will be future Arhoolie releases. Delta Groove is struggling after the death of its founder, Randy Chortkoff. Ruf Records, the European label that brought us our wonderful Luther Allison releases, has moved more and more in a rock direction. Delmark continues to release blues records, primarily by local Chicago artists. Bob Koester, now in his eighties, sold Delmark in 2018. I'm glad that the Canadian label Stony Plain, run by my friend Holger Peterson, is still releasing top-quality blues records. However, as one artist has said, Alligator could end up as the "last man standing" in blues recording.

Because of this, I feel that it falls on me, perhaps more than on anyone else, to discover and develop the artists who will carry the blues into the future. Of course, it's always been my mission to find, expose, and nurture new artists. Watching the growth of the talent and popularity of Selwyn Birchwood, Toronzo Cannon, and Shemekia Copeland has been a source of great satisfaction and hope for me. Now, as I get older and the blues moves further from the mainstream of popular music, my mission of bringing forward the key artists of the next generation of blues seems ever more vital. I have to find artists who are committed to the blues, but blues that can speak to an audience in their teens and twenties, just like Mississippi Fred McDowell spoke to me when I was nineteen. My greatest fear is that, without the infusion of new and visionary artists creating contemporary blues to speak to contemporary audiences, the blues will become like traditional New Orleans jazz, a museum piece, like a prehistoric insect preserved in amber.

I hope that more visionary artists will spring from the Chicago blues clubs. Chicago still boasts more active blues clubs than any other city in the world, as well as the world's largest blues festival. Up-and-coming artists compete for gigs with established veterans here, and there are still jams and other opportunities for young artists to be seen and heard. The success of Alligator is intrinsically tied to Chicago. The label would never have been born without the inspiration of the groundbreaking recordings released by Bob Koester of Delmark Records. And I never would have discovered the joy of the city's wonderful South and West Side blues clubs without Bob as my guide and mentor. The huge talent pool of the Chicago blues scene inspired my vision of the role Alligator could play in bringing world-class bluesmen and blueswomen to a new audience. And it was in the Chicago ghetto clubs that I learned what the blues was supposed to sound like and how the blues should make us feel.

Koko Taylor always said, "Bless the bridge that carried you across." I've tried to make Alligator that bridge—a bridge between the artists and their potential fans. The artists and Alligator, working together, have often succeeded in creating lifelong performing and recording careers for musicians who might otherwise be working day jobs. Although the majority of Alligator's current roster hails from outside Chicago, the spirit of the Chicago blues clubs still infuses the label. Any of these artists would be warmly received by the crowd at Florence's Lounge.

I usually receive almost all the credit for the accomplishments of Alligator, but the success of the label has absolutely been dependent not only on my vision and energy, but also on the immense contributions of the loyal staffers who have committed themselves to our mission, working countless hours on behalf of our artists and records. These days, the Alligator crew is fifteen dedicated people, many of whom have been part of the staff for more than twenty-five years. These people give their all every day behind the scenes, doing marketing, publicity, radio promotion, advertising, national and international sales management, graphic design, finance, royalties, TV and film licensing, new media, mail order, shipping, and overseeing CD manufacturing, while I get almost all the credit. Few people are blessed to live out their dreams. I'm one of the blessed. And as a result of my work and the work of the Alligator staff, dozens of talented musicians have been able to live out their dreams too.

Although the disheartening business climate and our struggle to reach a younger audience make me uncertain about the future of Alligator, I am certain that the body of work released under the Alligator logo since 1971 will stand the test of time. I've always told artists, "I don't want you recording for Alligator unless you want to make an album that you can play for your grandchildren and say, 'That's my best music.'" The artists have very often created just those albums. One of the positive results of the digital revolution is that our music is now available virtually worldwide and will never go out of print because no physical copies are needed. All the music we've released over the years will continue to be available for new fans to discover and old fans to enjoy again. I know that the life-changing healing feeling that I felt hearing Hound Dog Taylor at Florence's Lounge will reach future generations just like it reached me—Genuine Houserockin' Music that will rock both their bodies *and* their souls.

THE ALLIGATOR
RECORDS CATALOG

1971

| Hound Dog Taylor | *Hound Dog Taylor and the HouseRockers* | AL 4701 |

1972

| Big Walter Horton | *Big Walter Horton with Carey Bell* | AL 4702 |

1973

| Son Seals | *The Son Seals Blues Band* | AL 4703 |

1974

| Hound Dog Taylor | *Natural Boogie* | AL 4704 |
| Fenton Robinson | *Somebody Loan Me a Dime* | AL 4705 |

1975

| *Koko Taylor | *I Got What It Takes* | AL 4706 |

1976

| *Hound Dog Taylor | *Beware of the Dog!* | AL 4707 |
| Son Seals | *Midnight Son* | AL 4708 |

1977

| Blind John Davis | *Stomping on a Saturday Night* | AL 4709 |

* Grammy Award Nomination   ** Grammy Award Winner   ▶ Blues Music Award Winner

1978

*Fenton Robinson	*I Hear Some Blues Downstairs*	AL 4710
Koko Taylor	*The Earthshaker*	AL 4711
Son Seals	*Live and Burning*	AL 4712
*Various Artists	*Living Chicago Blues—Vol. 1*	AL 7701
Various Artists	*Living Chicago Blues—Vol. 2*	AL 7702
*Various Artists	*Living Chicago Blues—Vol. 3*	AL 7703
*Albert Collins	*Ice Pickin'*	AL 4713

1979

Lonnie Brooks	*Bayou Lightning*	AL 4714
Phillip Walker	*Someday You'll Have These Blues*	AL 4715
Lonesome Sundown	*Been Gone Too Long*	AL 4716
Prince Dixon	*There Is No Excuse (For Not Serving the Lord)*	AL 1201
Johnny Jones	*Johnny Jones with Billy Boy Arnold*	AL 4717

1980

▶Professor Longhair	*Crawfish Fiesta*	AL 4718
▶Albert Collins	*Frostbite*	AL 4719
Son Seals	*Chicago Fire*	AL 4720
*Various Artists	*Living Chicago Blues—Vol. 4*	AL 7704
Various Artists	*Living Chicago Blues—Vol. 5*	AL 7705
Various Artists	*Living Chicago Blues—Vol. 6*	AL 7706
Black Slate	*Black Slate*	AL 8301
*Various Artists	*Blues Deluxe*	XRT 9301

1981

Lonnie Brooks	*Turn on the Night*	AL 4721
Tony Mathews	*Condition Blue*	AL 4722
Buddy Guy	*Stone Crazy!*	AL 4723
*▶Koko Taylor	*From the Heart of a Woman*	AL 4724
*▶Albert Collins	*Frozen Alive!*	AL 4725
*Johnny Otis	*The New Johnny Otis Show with Shuggie Otis*	AL 4726
Black Slate	*Rasta Festival*	AL 8302

1982

*Hound Dog Taylor	Genuine Houserocking Music	AL 4727
Magic Slim	Raw Magic	AL 4728
**Clifton Chenier	I'm Here!	AL 4729
Mighty Diamonds	Indestructible	AL 8303
Edi Fitzroy	Youthman Penitentiary	AL 8304
The Abyssinians	Forward	AL 8305

1983

▶Albert Collins	Don't Lose Your Cool	AL 4730
Lonnie Brooks	Hot Shot	AL 4731
Big Twist and the Mellow Fellows	Playing for Keeps	AL 4732
Mutabaruka	Check It!	AL 8306
Augustus Pablo	King David's Melody	AL 8307
Pablo Moses	In the Future	AL 8308
Mutabaruka	Johnny Drughead (EP)	AL 501

1984

Albert Collins	Live in Japan	AL 4733
Sonny Terry with Johnny Winter and Willie Dixon	Whoopin'	AL 4734
*Johnny Winter	Guitar Slinger	AL 4735
Fenton Robinson	Night Flight	AL 4736
James Cotton	High Compression	AL 4737
▶Son Seals	Bad Axe	AL 4738
The Skatalites	Scattered Lights	AL 8309
Various Artists	Rockers All-Star Explosion	AL 8310

1985

Lonnie Mack with Stevie Ray Vaughan	Strike Like Lightning	AL 4739
*▶Koko Taylor	Queen of the Blues	AL 4740
*Roy Buchanan	When a Guitar Plays the Blues	AL 4741
*Johnny Winter	Serious Business	AL 4742

**▶Albert Collins, Robert Cray, and Johnny Copeland	*Showdown!*	AL 4743
Jimmy Johnson	*Bar Room Preacher*	AL 4744
Pablo Moses	*Tension*	AL 8311
Various Artists	*High Times All-Star Explosion*	AL 8312
Joe Higgs	*Triumph!*	AL 8313

1986

*Clarence "Gatemouth" Brown	*Pressure Cooker*	AL 4745
*James Cotton	*Live from Chicago—Mr. Superharp Himself!*	AL 4746
Roy Buchanan	*Dancing on the Edge*	AL 4747
Johnny Winter	*3rd Degree*	AL 4748
Lil' Ed & The Blues Imperials	*Roughhousin'*	AL 4749
Lonnie Mack	*Second Sight*	AL 4750
Lonnie Brooks	*Wound Up Tight*	AL 4751
*▶Albert Collins	*Cold Snap*	AL 4752
Dr. John	*Gumbo*	AL 3901
Delbert McClinton	*Honky Tonkin'*	AL 3902
Various Artists	*Genuine Houserockin' Music*	AL 101

1987

Little Charlie & The Nightcats	*All the Way Crazy*	AL 4753
*▶Koko Taylor	*Live from Chicago—An Audience with the Queen*	AL 4754
Big Twist and the Mellow Fellows	*Live from Chicago!—Bigger Than Life!!*	AL 4755
Roy Buchanan	*Hot Wires*	AL 4756
A. C. Reed	*I'm in the Wrong Business!*	AL 4757
The Kinsey Report	*Edge of the City*	AL 4758
Lonnie Mack	*The Wham of That Memphis Man*	AL 3903
Dr. John	*Gris Gris*	AL 3904
Various Artists	*The New Bluebloods*	AL 7707
Various Artists	*Genuine Houserockin' Music II*	AL 102

1988

Lonnie Brooks	*Live from Chicago—Bayou Lightning Strikes*	AL 4759
Siegel-Schwall	*The Siegel-Schwall Reunion Concert*	AL 4760
Little Charlie & The Nightcats	*Disturbing the Peace*	AL 4761
The Paladins	*Years Since Yesterday*	AL 4762
Maurice John Vaughn	*Generic Blues Album*	AL 4763
Kenny Neal	*Big News from Baton Rouge!!*	AL 4764
Tinsley Ellis	*Georgia Blue*	AL 4765
▶Katie Webster	*The Swamp Boogie Queen*	AL 4766
Elvin Bishop	*Big Fun*	AL 4767
Lazy Lester	*Harp and Soul*	AL 4768
Rufus Thomas	*That Woman Is Poison!*	AL 4769
Various Artists	*Genuine Houserockin' Music III*	AL 103

1989

Lucky Peterson	*Lucky Strikes!*	AL 4770
Charles Brown	*One More for the Road*	AL 4771
Lil' Ed & The Blues Imperials	*Chicken, Gravy and Biscuits*	AL 4772
Delbert McClinton	*Live from Austin*	AL 4773
Kenny Neal	*Devil Child*	AL 4774
The Kinsey Report	*Midnight Drive*	AL 4775
Little Charlie & The Nightcats	*The Big Break!*	AL 4776
Katie Webster	*Two-Fisted Mama!*	AL 4777
Tinsley Ellis	*Fanning the Flames*	AL 4778
*Clarence "Gatemouth" Brown	*Standing My Ground*	AL 4779

1990

▶Saffire—The Uppity Blues Women	*Saffire—The Uppity Blues Women*	AL 4780
Charlie Musselwhite	*Ace of Harps*	AL 4781
The Paladins	*Let's Buzz!*	AL 4782
Raful Neal	*Louisiana Legend*	AL 4783
*▶Koko Taylor	*Jump for Joy*	AL 4784

Noble "Thin Man" Watts	Return of the Thin Man	AL 4785
Lonnie Mack	Live!—Attack of the Killer V	AL 4786
Sonny Boy Williamson	Keep It to Ourselves	AL 4787
▶William Clarke	Blowin' Like Hell	AL 4788
Lucky Peterson	Triple Play	AL 4789
▶James Cotton, Junior Wells, Carey Bell, and Billy Branch	Harp Attack!	AL 4790
Elvin Bishop	Don't Let the Bossman Get You Down!	AL 4791
Nappy Brown with the Heartfixers	Tore Up	AL 4792
The Mellow Fellows	Street Party	AL 4793
Various Artists	Genuine Houserockin' Music IV	AL 104

1991

Little Charlie & The Nightcats	Captured Live	AL 4794
Kenny Neal	Walking on Fire	AL 4795
Saffire—The Uppity Blues Women	Hot Flash	AL 4796
Otis Rush	Lost in the Blues	AL 4797
Son Seals	Living in the Danger Zone	AL 4798
Tinsley Ellis and the Heartfixers	Cool On It	AL 3905
Lonnie Brooks	Satisfaction Guaranteed	AL 4799
Johnny Heartsman	The Touch	AL 4800
*▶Charlie Musselwhite	Signature	AL 4801
Buddy Guy and Junior Wells	Alone and Acoustic	AL 4802
▶Katie Webster	No Foolin'	AL 4803
Various Artists	The Alligator Records 20th Anniversary Collection	AL 105/6

1992

Clarence "Gatemouth" Brown	No Lookin' Back	AL 4804
Tinsley Ellis	Trouble Time	AL 4805
William Clarke	Serious Intentions	AL 4806
Dave Hole	Short Fuse Blues	AL 4807

Lil' Ed & The Blues Imperials	*What You See Is What You Get*	AL 4808
Kenny Neal	*Bayou Blood*	AL 4809
Sippie Wallace	*Woman Be Wise*	AL 4810
Various Artists	*The Alligator Records Christmas Collection*	AL 9201
Saffire—The Uppity Blues Women	*Broadcasting*	AL 4811

1993

▶Little Charlie & The Nightcats	*Night Vision*	AL 4812
*Various Artists	*The Alligator Records 20th Anniversary Tour*	AL 107/8
Maurice John Vaughn	*In the Shadow of the City*	AL 4813
Sonny Boy Williamson and Willie Love	*Clownin' with the World*	AL 2700
Jerry McCain, Clayton Love, and Tiny Kennedy	*Strange Kind of Feeling*	AL 2701
Big Joe Williams, Willie Love, and Luther Huff	*Delta Blues—1951*	AL 2702
The Southern Sons	*Deep South Gospel*	AL 2802
Dave Hole	*Working Overtime*	AL 4814
Billy Boy Arnold	*Back Where I Belong*	AL 4815
Bob Margolin	*Down in the Alley*	AL 4816
Various Artists	*Genuine Houserockin' Music V*	AL 109
*▶Koko Taylor	*Force of Nature*	AL 4817

1994

*▶Charlie Musselwhite	*In My Time*	AL 4818
Sugar Blue	*Blue Blazes*	AL 4819
Luther Allison	*Soul Fixin' Man*	AL 4820
Michael Hill's Blues Mob	*Bloodlines*	AL 4821
Various Artists	*Shout, Brother, Shout*	AL 2800
Various Artists	*In the Spirit*	AL 2801
Sonny Boy Williamson	*Goin' in Your Direction*	AL 2803
Son Seals	*Nothing but the Truth*	AL 4822
Tinsley Ellis	*Storm Warning*	AL 4823

Corky Siegel	*Corky Siegel's Chamber Blues*	AL 4824
Kenny Neal	*Hoodoo Moon*	AL 4825
Saffire—The Uppity Blues Women	*Old, New, Borrowed and Blue*	AL 4826
William Clarke	*Groove Time*	AL 4827
Carey Bell	*Deep Down*	AL 4828

1995

Little Charlie & The Nightcats	*Straight Up!*	AL 4829
C. J. Chenier & The Red Hot Louisiana Band	*Too Much Fun*	AL 4830
Sugar Blue	*In Your Eyes*	AL 4831
Dave Hole	*Steel on Steel*	AL 4832
Elvin Bishop	*Ace in the Hole*	AL 4833
▶Luther Allison	*Blue Streak*	AL 4834
Bob Margolin	*My Blues and My Guitar*	AL 4835
Billy Boy Arnold	*Eldorado Cadillac*	AL 4836
Corey Harris	*Between Midnight and Day*	AL 4837
Cephas and Wiggins	*Cool Down*	AL 4838

1996

Long John Hunter	*Border Town Legend*	AL 4839
Various Artists	*The Alligator Records 25th Anniversary Collection*	AL 110/11
Saffire—The Uppity Blues Women	*Cleaning House*	AL 4840
▶Floyd Dixon	*Wake Up and Live*	AL 4841
▶William Clarke	*The Hard Way*	AL 4842
Lonnie Brooks	*Roadhouse Rules*	AL 4843
C. J. Chenier & The Red Hot Louisiana Band	*The Big Squeeze*	AL 4844
Michael Hill's Blues Mob	*Have Mercy*	AL 4845
Son Seals	*Spontaneous Combustion*	AL 4846

1997

Dave Hole	*Ticket to Chicago*	AL 4847
Ann Rabson	*Music Makin' Mama*	AL 4848
*▶Luther Allison	*Reckless*	AL 4849
▶Corey Harris	*Fish Ain't Bitin'*	AL 4850
Bob Margolin	*Up and In*	AL 4851
Tinsley Ellis	*Fire It Up*	AL 4852
Long John Hunter	*Swinging from the Rafters*	AL 4853
Albert Collins	*Deluxe Edition*	AL 5601
Lonnie Brooks	*Deluxe Edition*	AL 5602
Little Charlie & The Nightcats	*Deluxe Edition*	AL 5603
Kenny Neal	*Deluxe Edition*	AL 5604
▶Carey Bell	*Good Luck Man*	AL 4854

1998

Hound Dog Taylor	*A Tribute*	AL 4855
Saffire—The Uppity Blues Women	*Live and Uppity*	AL 4856
Shemekia Copeland	*Turn the Heat Up*	AL 4857
Michael Hill's Blues Mob	*New York State of Blues*	AL 4858
Elvin Bishop	*The Skin I'm In*	AL 4859
The Kinsey Report	*Smoke and Steel*	AL 4860
Long John Hunter	*Ride with Me (reissue)*	AL 4861
Little Charlie & The Nightcats	*Shadow of the Blues*	AL 4862

1999

Cephas and Wiggins	*Homemade*	AL 4863
▶Hound Dog Taylor	*Deluxe Edition*	AL 5605
Katie Webster	*Deluxe Edition*	AL 5606
William Clarke	*Deluxe Edition*	AL 5607
Corey Harris	*Greens from the Garden*	AL 4864
Dave Hole	*Under the Spell*	AL 4865
Lonnie Brooks, Long John Hunter, Phillip Walker	*Lone Star Shootout*	AL 4866

John Jackson	*Front Porch Blues*	AL 4867
Lil' Ed & The Blues Imperials	*Get Wild!*	AL 4868
*Luther Allison	*Live in Chicago*	AL 4869
Gaye Adegbalola	*Bittersweet Blues*	AL 4870

2000

Coco Montoya	*Suspicion*	AL 4871
Corey Harris and Henry Butler	*Vu-Du Menz*	AL 4872
*▶ Koko Taylor	*Royal Blue*	AL 4873
Elvin Bishop and Little Smokey Smothers	*That's My Partner!*	AL 4874
*▶ Shemekia Copeland	*Wicked*	AL 4875
Rusty Zinn	*The Chill*	AL 4876

2001

The Holmes Brothers	*Speaking in Tongues*	AL 4877
Roy Buchanan	*Deluxe Edition*	AL 5608
Johnny Winter	*Deluxe Edition*	AL 5609
Michael Burks	*Make It Rain*	AL 4878
▶ Marcia Ball	*Presumed Innocent*	AL 4879
Saffire—The Uppity Blues Women	*Ain't Gonna Hush*	AL 4880
Dave Hole	*Outside Looking In*	AL 4881
C. J. Chenier & The Red Hot Louisiana Band	*Step It Up!*	AL 4882
Various Artists	*The Alligator Records 30th Anniversary Collection*	AL 112/13

2002

▶ Koko Taylor	*Deluxe Edition*	AL 5610
Son Seals	*Deluxe Edition*	AL 5611
Little Charlie & The Nightcats	*That's Big!*	AL 4883
W. C. Clark	*From Austin with Soul*	AL 4884
Coco Montoya	*Can't Look Back*	AL 4885

Lil' Ed & The Blues Imperials	*Heads Up!*	AL 4886
►Shemekia Copeland	*Talking to Strangers*	AL 4887
Cephas and Wiggins	*Somebody Told the Truth*	AL 4888

2003

Various Artists	*Crucial Guitar Blues*	AL 114
Various Artists	*Crucial Harmonica Blues*	AL 115
Various Artists	*Crucial Chicago Blues*	AL 116
*Roomful of Blues	*That's Right!*	AL 4889
Dave Hole	*The Live One*	AL 4890
*►Marcia Ball	*So Many Rivers*	AL 4891
Michael Burks	*I Smell Smoke*	AL 4892
Various Artists	*Genuine Houserockin' Christmas*	AL 9202

2004

►The Holmes Brothers	*Simple Truths*	AL 4893
Kenny Neal and Billy Branch	*Double Take*	AL 4894
Various Artists	*Crucial Slide Guitar Blues*	AL 117
Various Artists	*Crucial Texas Blues*	AL 118
Various Artists	*Crucial Live Blues*	AL 119
Guitar Shorty	*Watch Your Back*	AL 4895
►Hound Dog Taylor	*Release the Hound*	AL 4896
W. C. Clark	*Deep in the Heart*	AL 4897
Carey and Lurrie Bell	*Second Nature*	AL 4898
►Mavis Staples	*Have a Little Faith*	AL 4899

2005

Charlie Musselwhite	*Deluxe Edition*	AL 5612
►Roomful of Blues	*Standing Room Only*	AL 4900
Corky Siegel	*Corky Siegel's Traveling Chamber Blues Show*	AL 4901
Little Charlie & The Nightcats	*Nine Lives*	AL 4902
*►Marcia Ball	*Live! Down the Road*	AL 4903
Tinsley Ellis	*Live Highwayman*	AL 4904

| ▶Shemekia Copeland | *The Soul Truth* | AL 4905 |
| Siegel-Schwall Band | *Flash Forward* | AL 4906 |

2006

Lee Rocker	*Racin' the Devil*	AL 4907
Saffire—The Uppity Blues Women	*Deluxe Edition*	AL 5613
Eric Lindell	*Change in the Weather*	AL 4908
Various Artists	*Alligator Records 35x35*	AL 120/21
▶Lil' Ed & The Blues Imperials	*Rattleshake*	AL 4909
Cephas and Wiggins	*Shoulder to Shoulder*	AL 4910
▶Guitar Shorty	*We the People*	AL 4911

2007

▶The Holmes Brothers	*State of Grace*	AL 4912
Coco Montoya	*Dirty Deal*	AL 4913
JJ Grey & Mofro	*Country Ghetto*	AL 4914
*▶Koko Taylor	*Old School*	AL 4915
Various Artists	*Crucial Rocking Blues*	AL 122
Various Artists	*More Crucial Guitar Blues*	AL 123
Various Artists	*Crucial Acoustic Blues*	AL 124
Tinsley Ellis	*Moment of Truth*	AL 4916
Lee Rocker	*Black Cat Bone*	AL 4917
Mofro	*Blackwater*	AL 3906
Mofro	*Lochloosa*	AL 3907

2008

Eric Lindell	*Low on Cash, Rich in Love*	AL 4918
Roomful of Blues	*Raisin' a Ruckus*	AL 4919
Smokin' Joe Kubek and Bnois King	*Blood Brothers*	AL 4920
Eddy Clearwater	*West Side Strut*	AL 4921
*Marcia Ball	*Peace, Love and BBQ*	AL 4922
Michael Burks	*Iron Man*	AL 4923
▶Janiva Magness	*What Love Will Do*	AL 4924
JJ Grey & Mofro	*Orange Blossoms*	AL 4925

▶Lil' Ed & The Blues Imperials	*Full Tilt*	AL 4926

2009

Saffire—The Uppity Blues Women	*Havin' the Last Word*	AL 4927
Eric Lindell	*Gulf Coast Highway*	AL 4928
**▶Buckwheat Zydeco	*Lay Your Burden Down*	AL 4929
Rick Estrin & The Nightcats	*Twisted*	AL 4930
▶Tommy Castro	*Hard Believer*	AL 4931
Tinsley Ellis	*Speak No Evil*	AL 4932
JJ Grey & Mofro	*The Choice Cuts*	AL 3908

2010

The Holmes Brothers	*Feed My Soul*	AL 4933
Guitar Shorty	*Bare Knuckle*	AL 4934
Janiva Magness	*The Devil Is an Angel Too*	AL 4935
Anders Osborne	*American Patchwork*	AL 4936
Smokin' Joe Kubek and Bnois King	*Have Blues Will Travel*	AL 4937
JJ Grey & Mofro	*Georgia Warhorse*	AL 4938
*Charlie Musselwhite	*The Well*	AL 4939
*James Cotton	*Giant*	AL 4940

2011

Roomful of Blues	*Hook, Line and Sinker*	AL 4941
Shemekia Copeland	*Deluxe Edition*	AL 5614
Various Artists	*The Alligator Records 40th Anniversary Collection*	AL 125/26
*Marcia Ball	*Roadside Attractions*	AL 4942
Tommy Castro	*Tommy Castro Presents The Legendary Rhythm and Blues Revue— Live*	AL 4943
JJ Grey & Mofro	*Brighter Days—Live* (CD/DVD)	AL 4944

2012

Joe Louis Walker	*Hellfire*	AL 4945
Janiva Magnus	*Stronger for It*	AL 4946
▶ Curtis Salgado	*Soul Shot*	AL 4947
Anders Osborne	*Black Eye Galaxy*	AL 4948
Lil' Ed & The Blues Imperials	*Jump Start*	AL 4949
Rick Estrin & The Nightcats	*One Wrong Turn*	AL 4950
▶ Michael Burks	*Show of Strength*	AL 4951

2013

Anders Osborne	*Three Free Amigos* (EP)	AL 1230
Jesse Dee	*On My Mind/In My Heart*	AL 4952
JJ Grey & Mofro	*This River*	AL 4953
*James Cotton	*Cotton Mouth Man*	AL 4954
Roomful of Blues	*45 Live*	AL 4955
Anders Osborne	*Peace*	AL 4956

2014

Holmes Brothers	*Brotherhood*	AL 4957
Tommy Castro & The Painkillers	*The Devil You Know*	AL 4958
Joe Louis Walker	*Hornet's Nest*	AL 4959
Jarekus Singleton	*Refuse to Lose*	AL 4960
▶ Selwyn Birchwood	*Don't Call No Ambulance*	AL 4961
Rick Estrin & The Nightcats	*You Asked for It . . . Live!*	AL 4962
* ▶ Elvin Bishop	*Can't Even Do Wrong Right*	AL 4963
Marcia Ball	*The Tattooed Lady and the Alligator Man*	AL 4964

2015

The Kentucky Headhunters with Johnnie Johnson	*Meet Me in Bluesland*	AL 4965
*Shemekia Copeland	*Outskirts of Love*	AL 4966

Tommy Castro & The Painkillers	*Method to My Madness*	AL 4967

2016

*Various Artists	*God Don't Never Change: The Songs of Blind Willie Johnson*	AL 4968
Toronzo Cannon	*The Chicago Way*	AL 4969
▶Curtis Salgado	*The Beautiful Lowdown*	AL 4970
Moreland and Arbuckle	*Promised Land or Bust*	AL 4971
Various Artists	*The Alligator Records 45th Anniversary Collection*	AL 127/28
Lil' Ed & The Blues Imperials	*The Big Sound of Lil' Ed & The Blues Imperials*	AL 4972

2017

*Elvin Bishop	*Elvin Bishop's Big Fun Trio*	AL 4973
Coco Montoya	*Hard Truth*	AL 4974
Selwyn Birchwood	*Pick Your Poison*	AL 4975
The Cash Box Kings	*Royal Mint*	AL 4976
Rick Estrin & The Nightcats	*Groovin' in Greaseland*	AL 4977
Tommy Castro & The Painkillers	*Stompin' Ground*	AL 4978

2018

Tinsley Ellis	*Winning Hand*	AL 4979
Curtis Salgado and Alan Hager	*Rough Cut*	AL 4980
The Nick Moss Band Featuring Dennis Gruenling	*The High Cost of Low Living*	AL 4981
Marcia Ball	*Shine Bright*	AL 4982
Elvin Bishop's Big Fun Trio	*Something Smells Funky 'round Here*	AL 4983
Shemekia Copeland	*America's Child*	AL 4984
Eric Lindell	*Revolution in Your Heart*	AL 4985
Lindsay Beaver	*Tough as Love*	AL 4986

INDEX

Page numbers in *italics* indicate photographs.